Wisdom in the World

Princeton Theological Monograph Series
K. C. Hanson, Charles M. Collier,
and Robin A. Parry, Series Editors

Recent volumes in the series:

Robert A. Hand
Theological Epistemology in Immanuel Kant's Transcendental Idealism and Karl Barth's Theology

Scott P. Rice
Trinity and History: The God-World Relation in the Theology of Dorner, Barth, Pannenberg, and Jenson

Hakbong Kim
Person, Personhood, and the Humanity of Christ: Christocentric Anthropology and Ethics in Thomas F. Torrance

Lisanne Winslow
A Trinitarian Theology of Nature

Matthew T. Prior
Confronting Technology: The Theology of Jacques Ellul

Edmund Fong
Obedience from First to Last: The Obedience of Jesus Christ in Karl Barth's Doctrine of Reconciliation

Chad Michael Rimmer
Greening the Children of God: Thomas Traherne and Nature's Role in the Ecological Formation of Children

Steven Schafer
Marriage, Sex, and Procreation: Contemporary Revisions to Augustine's Theology of Marriage

Matthew Hutton Hartline
Crowned with Immortal Glory: Eschatological Hope in the Spirituality of William Perkins

Wisdom in the World
Toward a Renewed Christian Reading of Proverbs 8

BRIAN C. HUGHES

FOREWORD BY Walter Moberly

☙PICKWICK *Publications* · Eugene, Oregon

WISDOM IN THE WORLD
Toward a Renewed Christian Reading of Proverbs 8

Princeton Theological Monographs Series

Copyright © 2024 Brian C. Hughes. All rights reserved. Except for brief quotations in critical publications or reviews, no part of this book may be reproduced in any manner without prior written permission from the publisher. Write: Permissions, Wipf and Stock Publishers, 199 W. 8th Ave., Suite 3, Eugene, OR 97401.

Pickwick Publications
An Imprint of Wipf and Stock Publishers
199 W. 8th Ave., Suite 3
Eugene, OR 97401

www.wipfandstock.com

PAPERBACK ISBN: 979-8-3852-1596-6
HARDCOVER ISBN: 979-8-3852-1597-3
EBOOK ISBN: 979-8-3852-1598-0

Cataloguing-in-Publication data:

Names: Hughes, Brian C. [author]. | Moberly, R. W. L. [foreword writer].

Title: Wisdom in the world : toward a renewed christian reading of Proverbs 8 / Brian C. Hughes.

Description: Eugene, OR: Pickwick Publications, 2024 | Series: Princeton Theological Monograph Series | Includes bibliographical references and index.

Identifiers: ISBN 979-8-3852-1596-6 (paperback) | ISBN 979-8-3852-1597-3 (hardcover) | ISBN 979-8-3852-1598-0 (ebook)

Subjects: LCSH: Bible. O.T. Proverbs I–IX—Criticism, interpretation, etc. | Wisdom (Biblical personification). | Wisdom—Biblical teaching. | Bible—Criticism, interpretation, etc.—History. | Bible—Theology. | Bible—Hermeneutics.

Classification: BS1465.2 H84 2024 (print) | BS1465.2 (ebook)

Unless otherwise indicated, all translations from of ancients text are my own.

*To Mandy, who faithfully encouraged me
and loved me through this process.*

"Brian Hughes' book offers an informed and renewed Christian reading of Proverbs 8, a key text in the history of interpretation of the Bible. He insightfully characterizes wisdom as 'embodied know-how' relating to individual and communal interactions. He looks insightfully at the text with a thorough philological and interpretative analysis. He also then moves beyond it, charting ever changing and dynamic interpretations, and stands in front of it with modern readings that confront the text today. This is a lively study and a refreshing approach for contemporary Christian readers."

—Katharine Dell, professor of Old Testament literature and theology, University of Cambridge

"When I was a college student, I learned to read the Bible with an open heart and mind, expecting to learn something that would apply personally to my life. Then when I went to seminary, I learned to read the Bible with the historical and critical skills of modern scholarship. Fr. Hughes' book helps me put together these two approaches in a new way that will benefit both my devotional life and my instruction of others."

—David Montzingo, assistant professor of Anglican studies, spiritual formation, ministry leadership, Pacific Theological Seminary

"Brian Hughes offers a perceptive analysis of the issues surrounding the interpretation of Proverbs 8 and its reception history. He provides a close reading of the text in conversation with a range of historical critical and traditional interpreters, then draws upon the hermeneutical insights of Hans-Georg Gadamer, Paul Ricoeur, and Charles Taylor to advance a case for the text's ability to lay claim upon future readers who inhabit the world 'in front of the text.' His book is a useful resource for those who are interested in recovering the theological wisdom of Proverbs 8 for the contemporary church."

—Don Collett, professor of Old Testament, Trinity Anglican Seminary

"As recent centuries of biblical study have opened new insights into the history and literature of Proverbs 8, the theological meaning 'in front of the text' has been regarded as unnecessary. Drawing skillfully on Hans Gadamer and Paul Ricoeur, Brian Hughes demonstrates that theological reading is not simply something some of us add to our 'factual' interpretation, but the only appropriate end to our encounter with divinely revealed Scripture. Here, in the reading of Woman Wisdom's longest speech, Hughes demonstrates clearly how ethics and faith meet; the know-how wisdom of right living in God's world comes together with the wisdom of the only begotten Son through whom and for whom the world was made."

    —Ryan O'Dowd, academic director and senior chaplain,
      Chesterton House

Contents

Foreword—Walter Moberly | *xi*

Acknowledgements | *xiii*

Introduction | xv

SECTION 1: ORIENTING TO PROVERBS 8 AS CHRISTIAN SCRIPTURE

1 Orienting to the Old Testament as Christian Scripture | 3

2 Reading Proverbs 8 in Its Literary Context | 19

SECTION 2: READING THE HISTORY OF INTERPRETATION TO DEEPEN ENGAGEMENT WITH PROVERBS 8

3 The Historically Effected Consciousness | 49

4 Pre-Modern Readings of Proverbs 8 | 59

5 Modern Historically Oriented Scholars | 86

6 Modern Historically Oriented Christian Scholars | 111

Summary of Section 2 | 135

Contents

SECTION 3: TOWARD A RENEWED CHRISTIAN READING OF PROVERBS 8

7 Engaging Significant Thinkers for a Renewed Christian Reading | 139

8 A Contemporary Conception of Wisdom | 155

9 Three First Attempts at a Renewed Christian Reading of Proverbs 8 | 176

Conclusion | 226

Bibliography | 229

Scripture Index | 237

Name/Subject Index | 242

Foreword

READING THE BIBLE WELL is a challenge. And the challenge is made the greater by the gulf, as it often appears, between the use of the Bible in church and Christian life and its handling in the scholarly world of the academy. Perhaps paradoxically, however, the well-known stand-offs between "conservative" and "liberal" approaches to the Bible are usually marked by a set of shared assumptions about what biblical interpretation should involve: a focus on the supposed original meaning of the text alongside questions of how best to transfer or translate that original meaning into something meaningful for the world of today.

Of course, there has been considerable diversification of approaches in recent years, with feminist and postcolonial perspectives having particular weight at the present time. Nonetheless, approaches primarily oriented towards the text as exemplifying ancient thought together with possible, though increasingly optional, concern for its relation to present thought still seem to constitute the default mode of biblical scholarship.

Illustrative of this is the recent major work by the most eminent living British Old Testament scholar, John Barton: *A History of the Bible: The Story of the World's Most Influential Book*. Alongside a history of the formation of the Bible and an account of its interpretation down the ages, Barton also makes an argument about what is necessary for good biblical interpretation. This involves making a sharp distinction between the meaning of the biblical text, i.e., its sense as an ancient text, and its possible theological or philosophical truth, i.e., what the church has made of it down the centuries and may make of it today. This approach was first formulated by Baruch Spinoza, a formative early Enlightenment thinker, in the seventeenth century. Barton gives more space to Spinoza than to any other biblical interpreter of the last four hundred years, for the apparent reason that the ground rules set out by Spinoza ought still to obtain for serious biblical interpretation today.

Foreword

Yet the move to the "postmodern" in recent years has been marked by a change of mood and perspective and interest (and it is that change of mood, rather than whether we call it "postmodern," that is important). There has been a growing realization that important dimensions of life and language and thought had got lost in the formative early modern period. Hence movements that can be called "the literary turn" and "the hermeneutical turn," with formative thinkers setting out fresh possibilities. It is not always clear yet how these possibilities should be best understood and implemented. Nonetheless, the context is changing and with it come fresh ways of understanding the Bible and its relationship to thought and life today.

This is the context for Brian Hughes' work. His study of Proverbs 8, one of the most famous and historically influential passages of the Old Testament, still does justice to the historical awareness and concern for philological precision that has characterized modern biblical study. But he also draws on the work of key recent thinkers, especially Paul Ricoeur and Charles Taylor, both of whom engage deeply with Christian understanding of the world, to utilize the conceptual resources they make available for creative handling of the language and subject matter of the Bible.

By way of contrast, Barton mentions Ricoeur only in passing and Taylor not at all. And he comments on Proverbs 8:22 that "a modern biblical scholar would tend to say that it is about wisdom as personified in the thought of the ancient Israelite wisdom tradition, and has nothing to do with Jesus."[1] To be sure, the writer of Proverbs 8 was not thinking of Jesus. But the hastily dismissive "nothing to do with Jesus" entirely elides important questions about how the subject matter of the Proverbs passage may relate to the subject matter of Christian faith in Jesus as the Wisdom of God. These are the questions that Brian Hughes discusses. His work contributes well to constructive rethinking of what constitutes good and wise biblical interpretation.

Walter Moberly

---

1. Barton, *History*, 353.

Acknowledgements

I AM THANKFUL FOR the practice of writing acknowledgments in projects such as this, and particularly for including them in the opening pages of the work. Their placement alerts the reader right from the start that, despite their being only one name on the title page, this is in some ways the achievement of a community, each playing distinct but important roles. I am grateful for the opportunity to delineate them here.

First, I want to thank my doctoral supervisor, Professor Walter Moberly. Before contacting him, I heard glowing reviews of Professor Moberly both professionally and personally. Now, on the other side of my doctoral program, I am happy to join the chorus of positive reviewers. Walter has shepherded me through this process in many ways. Academically, his awareness of the nuances of hermeneutics and the Christian study of the Bible have shaped my own approach. His many suggestions for rewriting or editing wording were always aimed at clarity as to the issues at stake, balancing significant engagement with an irenic tone. Personally, Walter consistently reminded me that my commitments to family and parish ministry were not to be denigrated in favor my academic ones. I consider myself blessed to be one of his students.

My journey toward academic study of the Bible was initially kindled in seminary, and I want to thank the many people at Trinity School for Ministry who encouraged me toward this path. Erika Moore gave me a first academic opportunity through the invitation to be her teaching assistant in my second year at Trinity School for Ministry. She has continued to support me in the years since graduation. Don Collett patiently coached me and taught me about canonical interpretation through many conversations over the years. I am grateful for their investment in me, and the opportunities that they gave me to teach and learn with them.

I also want to thank three friends who have been of particular help in this process. The first is Paul Gibbons, who has supported me in ministry,

Acknowledgements

scholarship, and personal endeavors in life for so long. I am so grateful for his exemplary friendship. Second, I want to thank Nathan Chambers. I had the chance to meet Nathan at my first SBL. He was finishing up his program under Moberly and I was just starting. When I felt particularly lost, hopeless, or isolated, Nathan was there to buoy me up. Being a distance PhD student was a particular challenge, but I could not have kept going without his friendship and wisdom. I also would like to thank Dustin Saunders for his enthusiasm about my research. He particularly helped me with my studies on Puritans and Matthew Henry. However, our conversations in the office hallways are also a source of joy that has kept the light on, so to speak, for the past few years.

Throughout my time of researching a writing this book, I have been the rector of Holy Spirit Anglican Church, a congregation in the Anglican Church in North America, located in San Diego, CA. Even though the demands of ministry are high, these good people have always been supportive of my studies. The support of my mentor, the Rev. Cn. Dr. David Montzingo, and many members of the church staff and leadership has been invaluable.

Finally, I need to thank my parents, Nelson and Maribeth, and in-laws, Gary and Stephanie, for their support of this process. My children, Caroline, Evelyn, and Theodore have been excited for me and put up with some time away for the sake of this project. Most especially I am honored to thank my wife, Mandy, for her unwavering encouragement and patience. While it may seem odd for these to be last on the list, I am comforted that they will be the names which have most recently been read by the reader prior to starting the first pages, and so, it is my hope, they will be honored most as integral parts of its contents (errors and mistakes excluded). Home life, like a tree's root system, is often hidden from view, and yet for any to reach any heights of accomplishment it is absolutely necessary. Thank you for the sacrifice of time, money, and energy that you have made to enable the completion of the book.

Introduction

IN THE ANGLICAN TRADITION, of which I am part, each Sunday service features multiple readings of the Bible. After a reading is finished, the reader commonly declares that what has been read is the Word of the Lord. This book represents an attempt to unpack what that acclamation of the Bible as the Word of the Lord might mean. In particular, I attempt to read Proverbs 8 in such a way that the text shapes Christian life today. In this endeavor, I seek to maintain an awareness of the insights of modern biblical scholarship, which have brought to light the complexity of the Bible in ways distinct from the pre-modern period. The Bible comprises many ancient documents, each arising from various socio-historical moments, each with its own norms and literary standards. These documents have been collected over time into various corpora and then ultimately bound and recognized as Scripture in various religious communities. In turn, these communities have generated traditions of interaction with these texts, and these traditions have ongoing impact on readers today. Each of these facets of the Bible and its history offers its own challenges. And yet, within a Christian frame of reference, the task remains to read the text in such a way that it generates an encounter with the Triune God whom Christians worship.

The book is divided into three sections, each emphasizing a particular methodological approach to the text. The first section lays the foundation for reading the Old Testament as Christian Scripture (chapter 1) and then deploys standard philological tools in a first reading of Proverbs 8 (chapter 2). The goal of this section is to ground subsequent readings in the received form of the text available to a modern scholar. Chapter 2 in particular offers safeguards for later readings by offering a necessary critical pole for dialectical conversation between the text and its history of reception (section 2) and the text and Christian theology (section 3).

The second section approaches the history of interpretation of Proverbs 8. Chapter 3 lays out an orientation to this history via an interpretation

INTRODUCTION

of Hans-Georg Gadamer's concept of *wirkungsgeschichtliches Bewußtsein*. Following this, chapter 4 summarizes and analyzes the readings of two representatives of pre-modern Christian interaction with Proverbs 8: Athanasius of Alexandria and Matthew Henry. Even though these two are separated by centuries and use distinct methods, both seek to read the passage within a Christian framework, and do so prior to the advent of modern biblical scholarship. Chapters 5 and 6 move into this modern milieu. Chapter 5 summarizes and analyzes the approaches of four contemporary scholars who read the text in an historically-oriented frame, apart from any explicit goal for engagement for the sake of faith. Chapter 6 then summarizes four scholars who read the passage as Christians, and ostensibly for the sake of Christian faith, and yet do so within the environment of modern academic study of the Bible. The aim of this section is to enrich a reading of Proverbs 8 by illustrating a range of the passage's possible meanings.

The third section of the book returns to Proverbs 8 for a renewed Christian reading of the text. The work of sections 1 and 2 are not set aside, but taken up in a way which is constructive for Christian faith. Chapter 7 engages in a dialog with two significant contemporary thinkers on the nature of language and texts, Paul Ricoeur and Charles Taylor. These two, as important voices, offer a chance to revisit the text in a way more fully engaged with contemporary discussions. Both scholars emphasize the dialogical nature of the task of reading a text, but they are not the only source of this kind of approach. Reading the text as Christian Scripture, I will argue, also invites the Christian reader to relate to the reality of God through the text. Having acknowledged the reader's context as an aspect of dialogical reading, chapter 8 explicates an understanding of wisdom drawn from contemporary reflection. Doing so offers a heuristic for engaging the biblical text, using a thicker account of the subject matter. Chapter 9 then offers three first attempts at a renewed Christian reading of Proverbs 8: one that reads the text existentially, one that focuses on Proverbs 8:22 and its potential for Trinitarian theology, and a third that seeks a two-testament witness to the ultimate subject matter of the Christian Bible.

The shape of this study is a manifestation of two commitments on my part for the reading of the Bible as Scripture. The first is that the Bible is intended to be a means of encountering God. This undergirds the drive of the book to generate readings which assist such an encounter. Alongside this first commitment is a second, which is that this God is at work in the world, even the world of biblical scholarship. As such, I seek to honor both the

INTRODUCTION

history of interpretation and the modern enterprise of biblical scholarship. Together with my hope to offer readings of one particular passage which would aid Christian faith today, I also hope to model a way of engaging the text of the Bible which beneficially uses the tools offered by the historical-critical disciplines.

SECTION 1

Orienting to Proverbs 8 as Christian Scripture

Orienting to the Old Testament as Christian Scripture

THE STUDY THAT FOLLOWS aims to read Proverbs 8 as Christian Scripture, that is, as an ancient document that is part of a larger canonical collection handed down through the church in order to shape Christian life today. Such an approach may strike some as antithetical to academically informed study of the Bible. On the contrary, my contention is that this approach can be grounded appropriately in philosophical reflection on the nature of interpretation. The goal of this chapter is to explicate this foundation that will then be applied and further nuanced in the remainder of the work. Sandra Schneiders' book, *The Revelatory Text: Interpreting the New Testament as Sacred Scripture*,[1] offers helpful scaffolding for these concerns. Schneiders adroitly applies the hermeneutical and linguistic insights of Hans-Georg Gadamer and Paul Ricoeur to the latter portion of the Christian canon and does so in an accessible and well-organized fashion. She lays an ideal foundation on which to build an approach to understanding and interpreting the Christian Old Testament.[2] The subtitle of Schneiders' work makes

---

1. Sandra Schneiders, *The Revelatory Text*. For the remainder of this and the next section, citations for this work will be given parenthetically in the text.

2. Throughout this work I will use this phrase to refer to those thirty-nine books of the Christian Old Testament, rather than identifying them as the Hebrew Bible. I prefer Christian Old Testament because it at least implicitly carries with it a relationship with the New Testament, whereas "Hebrew Bible," as a term, tends to address these books as they stand on their own.

plain her concern is for the New Testament, so it is necessary to extend her discussion to the first portion of the Christian canon.

At the outset, it is good to acknowledge those factors present in handling the Old Testament that are unique to the first portion of the Christian canon. Schneiders is not unaware of such difficulties (11). Here I want to raise for the reader some initial facets that necessitate careful application rather than wholesale adoption of Schneiders' work. First, the New Testament is a collection of texts explicitly written in reflection on the life of Jesus of Nazareth, written to foster the life of the community founded on faith that he was and is the Christ, the Son of God, and one in being with the LORD of Israel.[3] The same cannot be said, at least not in the same way,[4] of the Christian Old Testament. The books of the Christian Old Testament lack the situational immediacy to the people and events of the life of Jesus and the early church. And yet the Christian church, from its earliest days, read these books in the context of their worship services and claimed that they do reveal Christ.[5] Navigating this claim while respecting the historical distance, as well as other differences between the testaments, requires attention. A corollary to this initial factor is that the Christian church is not the only faith tradition that holds the books under question to be revelatory. Judaism comes to these same books as the foundation for its faith, practices, and doctrines as well. This further complicates Schneiders' already nuanced discussion of the New Testament as the church's book.[6] Distinct questions need to be asked and answered in order to understand how one could say that the Old Testament is the church's book.

The Christian Old Testament as Symbol

As an initial step toward a methodology for reading the Bible, it is important to explicate an orientation to this book of books; what is this that we take up and read? A common expression for a Christian orientation to the Bible is that it is the Word of God. Through interaction with scholars such as Paul Ricoeur, Hans-Georg Gadamer, Martin Heidegger, Schneiders' second

---

3. One can see this made explicit in places such as John 20:30–31.

4. As we will see in the summary of Athanasius' work in chapter 4, there are many examples throughout the centuries of Christian interaction with the Old Testament of approaches to the Old Testament as a distinct witness to the reality of Christ.

5. See Luke 24:44 for one NT instance of this conviction.

6. See Schneiders' chapter 3, which will be discussed further below.

chapter offers an explanation of what this appellation might be taken to mean. In her take, the expression is best understood as a metaphor holding in tension, on the one hand, the Bible's human authors and, on the other hand, its role as a locus of symbolic revelation of God's self-gift.

The orientation toward the Bible as a symbol offers several helpful ways to understand how to take up and read. As a symbol, the Bible participates in, but is not exhaustive of, God's revelation or reality. Not only do symbols participate non-exhaustively in the reality to which they point, but they are also are ambiguous, and so require interpretation. Ascribing ambiguity to Scripture fits God's desire for divine-human relationship; Scripture as symbol invites readers into a dialogical process. As a way of making transparent the symbolic and dialogical nature of Scripture, it is appropriate to speak of the Bible as *potentially* revelatory.[7] This potential is activated through the right approach of the reader.

What the Bible potentially reveals is not information, according to Schneiders. Rather, the content is personal and transformative; a shared life with God brought about by the inspiring influence of the Holy Spirit in the reading event.[8] In keeping with the emphasis on relationship, Scripture's authority is disclosive, in the form of an appeal, rather than evidential or coercive. The reader is invited into life with God rather than commanded or solely informed of that life. The disclosive nature of the Bible does not rob it of any sort of authority. The Bible still functions as the norm of the church's life, as the foundational dialogue partner for theology, the church's mission, and the individual Christian. As the church (corporate and individual) inhabits its particular times and places, the text of the Bible is the "first, last, and constant" focus in the task of understanding and rendering the saving effect of the gospel.[9]

Schneiders acknowledges, along with many others, that one's orientation to the text impacts what one finds therein. To properly interpret the Bible *as a text* requires an openness to the kind of transcendental claims the Bible makes. One may still read and find the truth claims of the Bible to be unpersuasive. However, to close oneself off to these truth claims is to improperly project possibilities (or impossibilities) on the text from one's own horizon.[10] To interpret the Bible *as Scripture* calls for more than openness

---

7. As opposed to the Bible as revelation in an absolute sense.
8. One can discern here Gadamer's influence. See *Truth and Method*, 320.
9. Gadamer, *Truth and Method*, 279, 319.
10. It is to ward off precisely this kind of misunderstanding that Gadamer argues

to the transcendent; the title of Scripture requires some form of acceptance of the New Testament's claims regarding Jesus Christ.[11] This "higher" requirement is a reflection on the difference it makes to approach the Bible as Scripture. To read the Bible as Scripture recognizes the collection of books "as a privileged place that is potentially generative of a transformative encounter with God."[12] In Schneiders' formulation, a commitment to read the Bible as Scripture is to read it seeking to hear, and open to respond to, the divine offer of self-gift in the text.

This book seeks to read a passage from the Old Testament in a way that is fruitful for Christian life today; Schneiders' orientation to the text as symbol of divine self-gift is one way to approach the text for this purpose. Even though her comments focus on the New Testament, the Old Testament can also be taken up as a symbol of divine self-gift, which requires interpretation and calls for relationship. The majority tradition[13] of the church has received the books of the Old Testament as the first portion of its two-testament canon. Christopher Seitz points beyond the inclusion of these texts to their acceptance *as a testament*, a word once spoken, completed, and having placed alongside it a second witness (the New Testament).[14] Surveying early Christian writings supports the contention that these books norm the Christian faith, as the Old Testament was appealed to in

---

for a rehabilitation of our historical consciousness. Gadamer, *Truth and Method*, 316. Gadamer's understanding of history will be explored in more depth in chapter 3, "The Historically Effected Consciousness."

11. How one understands the necessity of these claims vis-à-vis the Old Testament will be discussed below. I will return to the difference made by the ascribing "Scripture" to a set of books in the final section of chapter 7.

12. Moberly, *The God of the Old Testament*, 6.

13. I use this phrase to indicate my awareness of movements to expel the Old Testament from the Christian canon, as well as those wishing to relegate it to a lesser status. My position here stems less from explicit doctrinal statements affirming the Old Testament as Christian Scripture (although those exist) and more from the practice of the church to read and study the books of the Old Testament, publicly and privately, as an act of Christian faith so that they can be shaped to live that faith.

14. Seitz, *The Character of Christian Scripture*, 19–20. Such a move of acceptance as completion can be understood over against other possibilities such as simply tacking what became the New Testament documents on at the end of the OT to form a single testament Bible, or "Christianizing" the Old Testament through insertions or additions. Seitz's argument does not depend on the outcome of the debate regarding the OT as a closed canon in the first century. Even as the canon exhibits fluctuation through the first millennium of the church, there is a unified witness to the acceptance of an Old Testament as such. Ibid., 70–76.

Christian doctrinal debates as well as funded reflection on how to live a life of faithfulness to the Triune God.[15] The books of the canonical Old Testament can be understood as symbolic and necessitating interpretation in order to receive the divine self-gift offered therein. As will be explored in this chapter below, such a belief enjoins rather than abrogates the need to seriously engage with the text in its historical and literary contexts in order to navigate the difference(s) between the originating and contemporary frames of reference (98).

Admittedly, the history of understanding the Old Testament's normative role is diverse and fraught with controversy.[16] Any claim to the Christian Old Testament's normativity will need to be explicated to situate one's position within the constellation of alternative understandings. That a view of the Old Testament was once held by some does not guarantee that it is the best perspective for all time. Earlier interpreters interacted with the Bible within a different frame of reference from today. While a contemporary Christian shares creedal agreement with these forebears in the faith,[17] there are numerous differences between the assumed interpretive background of the periods (early church vs. modern). These differences are many and significant, none of the least of which is the rise of a characteristically modern historical consciousness, aware of differences and distance between the social conditions of the past and the present.[18] All this is to say that a case must be made for receiving and reading the Old Testament as Christian Scripture which is in dialogue with contemporary conversations regarding the Bible.

---

15. Perhaps the most famous example of this is the debates surrounding the Council of Nicaea and the doctrine of the Son of God. Proverbs 8:22 was a major text in this debate. This will be addressed at various points in the book, but most directly in chapter 4.

16. The controversy regarding the Old Testament's role as Christian Scripture is not contained to the past. Even where there is a wide range of agreement in other matters of faith, exactly *how* the OT is Christian Scripture is variously understood. Edward Klink and Darian Lockett survey five schemes for understanding biblical theology, and within them the Old Testament is understood as: (1) not properly related to the NT, (2) related by way of historically progressive revelation, (3) related as an unfolding drama of salvation, (4) related through being a discrete witness to the triune God, or (5) related as books from which the church may draw on for theological reflection. There is overlap between these five approaches, yet each has its own distinctions. See *Understanding Biblical Theology*.

17. This is the case even though the spoken language and specific wording of the Nicene Creed has changed over the centuries. See Lash, *Easter in Ordinary*, 261.

18. Section 2 of the book explores and illustrates the differences in approach to Proverbs 8 through the history of interpretation through a select group of interpreters.

The recently developed canonical approach to the Old Testament, associated especially with the pioneering work of Brevard Childs, offers an avenue for receiving and reading these texts as Christian Scripture. In this approach, rather than limiting the scope of meaning to the text's originating context,[19] the transmission of the text through the community of faith, its inclusion in the canonical collection, and its use over time by the community of faith is incorporated for reflection.[20] A canonical approach broadly understands the community that passed on these texts as a community of *faith*. As such, what mediates and governs the historical transmission process is a theological standard (whatever else it may be). This theological standard, or rule of faith, is taken as the primary definition of "canon" in the canonical approach, taking priority over canon as list of books.[21] The ordering of verses, passages, books, and collections, is interpreted for its theological witness to the being of God. The two testaments of the Christian Bible are both understood to bear witness to the triune life of God, as revealed in Jesus Christ, by the Spirit.[22] Within this view, both testaments have this function and are therefore potential channels for the mediation of God's life to the reader.

The Christian Old Testament as the Church's Book

The above section grounded this book's approach to Proverbs 8 in a view of the text of both testaments as symbolic revelation. However, one challenge particular to the Christian Old Testament is that the church is not the only community of faith that claims this book as Scripture. Schneiders' third chapter explores the claim that the New Testament is the church's book, and her views can be helpful in navigating how a Christian can similarly take the Old Testament in relation to the church. The basis for Schneider's take is "the integral and living relationship between the Bible and tradition as constituting, together, the locus of Gospel revelation" (65). All interpretation is done within a tradition of some sort, by the experiences through which

---

19. Jon Levenson remarks that the classic, historical-critical interpretation of a text only against the background of its originating context evinces a lack of interest in the texts of the Bible precisely at that point when they become biblical. *The Hebrew Bible, the Old Testament, and Historical Criticism*, 107.

20. In this way, the canonical approach is not anti-history; its interest in history is simply not confined to the originating context of a passage.

21. Seitz, *The Character of Christian Scripture*, 41.

22. I owe the form of this articulation to Don Collett. It is, of course, contestable.

Orienting to the Old Testament as Christian Scripture

we have lived and the language with which we describe those experiences.[23] The historical consciousness of the church is founded on the experience of Jesus Christ in the flesh and the church's ongoing understanding of itself as, in some sense, the presence of Christ in the world. The content of the church's tradition is the interaction between the indwelling Spirit and the situations in which the church finds itself.

Schneiders addresses the Reformation controversy between Scripture and tradition by asserting that both are tradition: Scripture is the written witness to the founding experience of the church and tradition (as the term is normally used) is its continuing reflection and interaction with this experience. Scripture, as written, "is a touchstone of fidelity to the meaning of the original event that spoken tradition cannot, in the very nature of the case, assure" (77). Tradition is also the mode of church life, as it receives the experience of the past, draws deeper meaning from some portion of it, perhaps leaves some behind, and so forth. In this process, "the relationship between tradition and scripture is that of a hermeneutical dialectic. Scripture is produced as part of and witness to tradition; it functions as the norm of that tradition; but it can only function as norm if it is interpreted from within and in terms of that tradition" (83). The canon itself is an artifact of the church's tradition, as the early church came to realize its need for the apostolic experience to be written down and placed alongside the Jewish Scriptures to form the two-testament Christian Bible.

The Old Testament can also be understood as an ongoing reflection on the people of God's experience of God. To adopt this in coherence with the New Testament and its witness to Jesus Christ requires that the broader claims of the New Testament vis-à-vis Jesus Christ be taken seriously. These claims include that Jesus is one-in-being with the God of Israel.[24] This is, of course, the central claim of the church as worked out in the Nicene Creed. New Testament passages such as Philippians 2:5–11 and John 8:48–59 bear witness to this claim. These New Testament passages bear witness to the early church's understanding of its faith as standing in continuity with what is witnessed to in the Old Testament.[25] Indeed, reading within the church's tradition opens up this possibility for the reader. Correspondingly, some familiarity with the Christian tradition is required to interpret the

---

23. To use Gadamer's term, humans are shaped by "historically effected consciousness" (*wirkungsgeschichtliches Bewußtsein*). See *Truth and Method*, 312.

24. Seitz, *Word without End*, 5.

25. Yaego, "The New Testament and Nicene Dogma," 152–64.

text produced by the tradition; openness to the text's invitation would also be necessary to hear the meaning of the text beyond its original historical sense; and "the optimal position from which to engage the meaning of the New Testament is that of full participation in the tradition that produced the book," that is, such participation is not a hindrance but an advantage to interpretation (90). It is in this way that Schneiders advocates the claim of the New Testament as the church's book.

It is perhaps obvious that the relationship between the tradition of the community and written documents is complicated when one applies the above argument to the Christian Old Testament. For a Christian, one receives these books from the Christian tradition; it is only because of the historic treasuring and concomitant passing on of these books that they are read as Scripture. However, as noted at the outset of this discussion, in relation to the Old Testament the Christian encounters another reading tradition in the Jewish community. To claim these books as "the church's book" could be misconstrued as supersessionist if applied without consideration and comment. Even as it may at first appear uncharitable to claim these books as Christian Scripture, it is at least an honest recognition of the role tradition plays in the reading process. One is always reading from within a tradition, whose influence can be discerned in the fore-understandings we bring to a text throughout the reading event.[26] As this project seeks to read Proverbs 8 as Christian Scripture, it must therefore be honestly read within a frame that acknowledges the role of the church's tradition which has accepted the Old Testament as the first of the two testaments which make up the Christian Bible.[27]

---

26. I say "throughout the reading event" because fore-understandings do not cease to be a factor once we begin reading. Readers must always have some sense of the whole to make sense of the particular. With texts, our projected understandings of the text's whole meaning are re-evaluated as we read, but they are still present. See Gadamer, *Truth and Method*, 278–84.

27. A position which acknowledges the importance of tradition may raise concerns about a reader being overly involved in the text such that the meaning of the passage is, in some way, pre-determined. As I hope to illustrate in the last section of the book, my aim is not to pre-determine the meaning of any particular passage. Rather, it is to acknowledge at least one set of factors at work in taking up Proverbs 8 in order to read it fruitfully. What this text is, how it makes sense, and what counts as a good or fruitful reading all depends upon the tradition in which one is reading. In this way, even an academically oriented reading takes place within a tradition. More will be said about the role of tradition in chapter 3 on "The Historically Effected Consciousness."

Even though I have set out to read Proverbs 8 as Christian Scripture, interacting with sources in other traditions can still be fruitful. Reading, for example, historical and contemporary Jewish interpretation of these books offers a chance to make the books strange to the reader by exposing the reader to other possibilities of meaning in the text. The role of reading sources outside of one's position in history and tradition ideally sends the reader back to the text. The text is that "first, last, and constant"[28] object of our interaction, of which we seek to make sense.[29] Even so, this sense-making is *always* done within a tradition. The Christian tradition operates with a two testament canon. As Jon Levenson, a Jewish scholar, articulates, "I have argued that though a certain sense of scripture requires this limitation [to study the Hebrew Bible as a discrete unit], Christians must ultimately aim for another sense as well, one that upholds the idea that their two-volume Bible is a meaningful whole, lest their scripture decompose before their very eyes."[30]

My aim here has been to establish an orientation to reading the Old Testament as the locus of potential revelation through which God offers to share the divine-life with the reader. This facet of the Old Testament is both a function of the text as symbolic medium and arises from reading the Old Testament from within the Christian tradition.

The Three Worlds of the Text

Above, I have outlined an approach to Proverbs 8, as a passage in the canonical Christian Old Testament, which understands it as symbolically revelatory when read within the Christian tradition. Earlier I noted that part of the nature of symbol is that it is ambiguous and therefore calls for interpretation. Within the Christian tradition, this is understood as a function of God's desire for relationship with the Christian. In this next section, a methodology which can be taken to support this orientation toward the text is explicated. Again drawing on Schneiders, we can understand the text

---

28. Gadamer, *Truth and Method*, 279.

29. As such, this book engages with historical and contemporary readings in the second section and then returns to the text of Proverbs 8 in the third section.

30. Levenson, *The Hebrew Bible, the Old Testament, and Historical Criticism*, 103. The entirety of Levenson's essay "Jews and Christians in Biblical Studies" offers a nuanced evaluation of the advantages and disadvantages of historical study of the Bible, along with a trenchant critique of incipient anti-Semitism in much classical usage of historical-critical tools.

as having three "worlds": the world *behind* the text, the world *of* the text, and the world *in front of* the text. While the concept of these worlds may be common knowledge in the academy, Schneiders offers a way of taking them up that is attentive to a particularly Christian approach. Below I will summarize her approach to each and then apply it to the present study of Proverbs 8 as Christian Scripture.

Beginning with the world behind the text, there is no doubt that the texts of the Bible are historical; they refer to historical events using historical genres, although these genres are governed by ancient standards and expectations, not modern. A maxim of modern historiography is that no history is value-free, but every work of history contains perspective and agenda. This is certainly true of the New Testament, whose aim is to form faith in the reader, particularly faith in Jesus Christ. Schneiders differentiates between three forms of Jesus to which the text relates: the actual Jesus (the person in his "facticity" on earth and now as the glorified Savior), the historical Jesus (the literary construct that mediates the historical dimensions of his career), and the proclaimed Jesus (the construct of Christian faith). If historical is defined as that which can be investigated using historical methods, then certain elements of the proclaimed Jesus are historical, i.e. his birth and death, but others are not, i.e. his incarnation and resurrection. "The subject matter of the text is not exclusively or exhaustively the historical Jesus. Rather, the historical Jesus is the symbolic medium for the presentation of the proclaimed Jesus . . . a construction of the Christian theological/spiritual imagination" (102). Schneiders is careful to state that this does not make the Christ of faith a fantasy. The proclaimed Jesus in the text is a result of the church's reflection on their experience with Jesus grounded in the paschal imagination. The Gospel accounts are a work of this paschal imagination, which does not preclude historical methods from uncovering the historical elements of Jesus' career. These are helpful, but they cannot be exhaustive, because of the imaginative nature of this work and its subject matter as trans-historical. The notion by which these texts are accurate is that they are truth-bearing, which is not to say that it is historically vacuous nor that the reader should ignore the historical Jesus. Rather, "the historical Jesus, precisely because of its rootedness in and relationship to the actual Jesus, creates a critical tension in the proclamation itself that grounds the endless efforts of scholars to interpret the text and of believers to understand it" (109). Historically critical methods engage the reader in discovering their own blind spots so that the proclaimed Jesus can better come forth for the church.

The content of this chapter by Schneiders is methodologically and hermeneutically helpful. The concerns regarding application to the Old Testament again have to do with the question of scope. The tripartite division of actual, historical, and proclaimed Jesus works because of the relatively narrow focus of the New Testament. Not so with the Christian Old Testament. Even though the chronological span of the events of the Old Testament is a matter of debate, all agree that it is much longer and more varied than the sixty to eighty years that are the concern of the New Testament. Be that as it may, the resultant challenges for a similar approach to the Christian Old Testament are not insurmountable, especially if one contents oneself with particular passages rather than the whole corpus. Any understanding of the proclaimed God of the whole testament would be built on the work of its constituting passages, books, and divisions. Nevertheless, Schneiders' approach vis-à-vis the historical and proclaimed can be adapted to the Old Testament is a way that involves one in a dialectic rather than an either/or approach to the historical nature of the Old Testament. The books of the Old Testament are read *as Scripture*, mediating events behind the text to the reader in order to bring about the fear of the LORD.[31] In this book, especially in section 3, I will bring the text of Proverbs 8 into such a dialectical relation with the proclaimed faith of the church, understood in various ways.

The second of the text's three worlds relates to the text as literary. Schneider's approach to this is to understand the shaping of these texts as a sort of witness testimony. Witness testimony is always perspectival and incomplete, as it naturally involves selection of material to a particular end, and this is true of the New Testament. The apostolic generation selected and shaped material so that others might know the significance of Jesus of Nazareth as the church understood his significance. The shaping of the witness includes presenting it within the confines of literary genres. Literary methods of interpretation focus on these facets of presentation that the reader might confront "the personal challenge to Christian faith that arises not from the nature of the historical events recounted but from the character of the text as witness to Jesus as the Christ, the definitive revelation of God" (138). In these endeavors, scholars have expended much effort

---

31. Walter Moberly writes that "'Fear of God / the LORD' in the OT is the prime term for right human responsiveness to God and is not a matter of emotional fear or fright." *The God of the Old Testament*, 17n13, 108–9.

to ground the text's meaning in the author's intentions. However, this is limited at best, as contemporary hermeneutical and linguistic philosophy has labored to show. Language always stands against a background of what is not said, it is symbolic and metaphoric. These facets collude to suggest that one always says less than and more than they intend to say. Therefore, interpretation is not taken up with the task of nailing down authorial intention, even though it can remain a contributing factor to understanding.[32] Rather interpretation is an engagement with the subject matter of the text *through* the text, brought about by a dynamic process of questioning and answering. The process is not inert but moves forward on the basis of the questions asked by the interpreter. Those questions shape the "responses" of the text, what one sees in the text. The aim is to arrive at the question which the text is asking so that one can then better see its answer (142). The result of this work is an understanding of the text's ideal meaning, which is "a mental structure that governs the interaction between the subject matter of the text and the interpreter" (146). It is the ideal meaning which, like the rules of a game, governs subsequent attempts to appropriate the reality of the text, which relates to the world in front of the text.

Characterizing Scripture as witness helpfully highlights its inherent perspectival and purposive nature, that is, its role in forming the faith of future generations. In considering the Christian Old Testament, one needs to answer "witness to what?" Throughout the history of study since at least the eighteenth century, these books have been taken to be a witness to salvation history, history of religious thought, traditions behind the text, ideological power struggles, and more. One needs clarity on par with the New Testament's focus as witness to Jesus Christ. From a position which reads the Old Testament as Christian Scripture, the text is taken to witness to the Triune God of Christian faith.[33] As a witness, the text has been shaped in accordance with particular genres. As such, attention is called for to the way the

---

32. Schneiders draws on Paul Ricoeur to assert that the nature of the text as written discourse distances it from authorial intention. The act of inscribing the text endows it with a certain semantic autonomy; the author is no longer present to adjudicate its meaning. I interact more fully with Ricoeur's perspective in chapter 7, "Engaging Significant Thinkers for a Renewed Christian Reading."

33. As one of two testaments in the Christian Bible, the witness of the Old Testament is coordinated with the witness of the New Testament such that there is two-way traffic between them, building up a robust view of God and leading into reflection on one's life lived before God in the world. In chapter 9 I offer an attempt to coordinate the witness of Proverbs 8 with the theme of light in John's Gospel, as an illustration of a two-testament reading.

text has been structured in order to properly understand its witness. In this book, chapter 2 attends to the particularities of the text of Proverbs 8, thereby providing a foundation for further interaction with the text.

The third of the text's three worlds is the world in front of the text. Schneiders' penultimate chapter addresses in more depth the nature of the reader's interaction with the text through the aspect of the world in front of the text. The reader is involved with the text throughout the process of interpretation, beginning with preunderstanding, which provides the initial and necessary framework in which to understand the text's meaning. This initial framework of expectation also sets in motion the process of interpretation. Reader involvement continues throughout the dialectical interaction between what is discovered and what is known until one achieves understanding epistemologically and ontologically. These two senses of understanding are interrelated, as what is "known, if it is really understood and not simply added to a collection of facts, is always known in and through the experienced historical consciousness of the knower and in relation to everything else that is known, never 'by itself'" (161). The meaning of the text that moves one toward understanding is the textual meaning, which includes the ideal meaning of the text (the sense-reference of the text) and the meaning of the work (the way the text challenges and renews the world of the reader). Again, this is posited as a dialectic, two poles between which one traverses in the process of reading.

As Schneiders' perspective is markedly different from one in which the text is a static object and the reader/knower a possibly little-interested observer, one may worry about criteria for valid interpretation. Schneiders notes in multiple locations in her book that, while there are a potentially unlimited number of valid interpretations, there are still criteria. Two global criteria she offers are that methodology fit the text and that the meaning of the interpretation is fruitful. The former relates to the process of interpretation and calls for the appropriate methods to be used while excluding those inappropriate to it on the basis of genre. The latter global criterion of fruitfulness relates to interpretation as a result. If the interpretation results in the text becoming banal, contrary to its history of significance, it is suspect. However, if the interpretation illuminates the believing community, and is in the bounds of methodological fit, it can be deemed valid. She goes on to offer other possible criteria, but then notes that these "are actually discovered in their application more easily than they can be elaborated in the abstract" (166).

The goal of valid interpretations of Scripture is not only epistemological understanding, but also the transformation of the reader by engagement with the world in front of the text. The world behind the text is concerned with everything that coincides to produce the text. The world of the text is concerned with the text's character as linguistic witness. The world in front of the text addresses the alternate reality into which the text invites the reader such that the reader "returns" from reading changed. This change is, as Schneiders expresses it, "existential augmentation" (167). The goal of augmentation or transformation is achieved through the participation of the reader in the world in front of the text. Schneiders offers the helpful analogy of attending a play, during which audience members experience a world other than that of their "mundane existence" and through which "One has lived a different life, in a different world, and returns to the reality of everyday life changed in some way" (167). Even though certain genres may more readily align with the analogy of a play (such as gospels or historical books), all texts can be taken to project a world into which the reader is called.

The world in front of the text is the reality toward which the text, in its historical and literary context, gestures. It is the constructed space created by the truth claims of the text. Texts, as works of art, are meant to create such spaces.[34] Applying this to the narratives of the Gospels, Schneiders writes, "the text, through its use of plot, character, dialogue, irony, and so on, creates a world within which, and according to whose dynamics, the reader operates for the duration of the aesthetic experience."[35] As stated above, the world in front of the text is not confined to narrative. Paul Ricoeur, from whom Schneiders draws, includes all written works as having this capacity to project a world.[36] He further describes it as "the totality of references opened up by texts." Where discourse works with ostensive reference, literary texts lack this reference. In the place of ostensive reference is the world of the text. Ricoeur asserts that this

> implies that the meaning of a text lies not behind the text but in front of it. The meaning is not something hidden but something disclosed. What gives rise to understanding is that which points towards a possible world, by means of the non-ostensive references

---

34. Paul Ricoeur, "Hermeneutical Functions of Distanciation," 98–101.
35. Schneiders, *The Revelatory Text*, 173.
36. Paul Ricoeur, "Metaphor and the Problem of Hermeneutics," 138.

of the text. Texts speak of possible worlds and of possible ways of orientating oneself in these worlds.[37]

Another essay of Ricoeur's expands on this last point: "the abolition of first order reference . . . is the condition of possibility for the freeing of a second order of reference, which reaches the world not only at the level of manipulable objects, but at the level that Husserl designated by the expression *Lebenswelt* [life-world] and Heidegger by the expression 'being-in-the-world.'"[38] The world in front of the text opens up a different way of living in the world at the deepest level.

Transformation occurs through appropriating the text, which is itself a process of distancing and drawing near. Schneiders evokes Ricoeur's description of the journey from the first naïveté through critical distancing to the second naïveté. The first naïveté is one's initial reading, which may assume immediacy with the text and its subject matter. However, in order to protect the reader from the text and the text from the reader, critical distancing must take place through the use of critical methods (historical, literary, ideological, theological, etc.). Distancing functions to prevent a premature appropriation of the text by the reader by raising the awareness that the text is an historical object.[39] Only once this distancing has taken place can the reader arrive at the second naïveté through aesthetic surrender and critical existential interpretation. Aesthetic surrender relates to the reader conceding to the text's world "at least long enough to be caught up in its existential horizon" (174). Once this is done, the latter step of critical existential interpretation can take place, in which the reader opens themselves to the text's truth claims at the level of ultimate personal significance. Schneiders again sees this as a dialogue between the text and its subject matter of divine self-gift. The dialogue can occur because of the nature of written text: it is open to successive interpretations and it can come to mean something other than it was originally intended (175). The dialogue can only take place in the context of aesthetic surrender as this is the way to fully engage the world the text projects as reality. Appropriation continues as a dialogue as one seeks to receive the gift of the divine being offered through the text in a way that transforms the reader and the

---

37. Ricoeur, "Metaphor and the Problem of Hermeneutics," 139.

38. Ricoeur, "Hermeneutical Functions of Distanciation," 103–4.

39. However, this statement must not be understood as advocating a view of history as accessible through objective readings. See the introduction to section 2 below for further discussion.

believing community. Chapter 9 offers one attempt to explicate the world in front of Proverbs 8 as well as how a twenty-first-century Western Christian might appropriate this world.

The approach outlined in this chapter of *The Revelatory Text* is refreshing, as it offers a responsible consideration of the role of the reader in interpretation that navigates between the Scylla of absolute relativism and the Charybdis of wholesale elimination of the reader from consideration. With regard to general interpretation of the Christian Old Testament, the interaction between Christian faith and these (historically) pre-Christian documents would need to be carefully handled so as not to violate the foundational claim that these books are held to be revelatory by their inclusion in the canon. There is a dialectic between the text's familiarity as being received and read within the Christian tradition and the nature of these texts as "other" than the reader. The explanation phase of reading (literary analysis, historical readings, etc.) does not replace appropriation of the text. Instead, this step deepens the transformative potential of a text, pushing beyond the surface level reading of the passage in order to articulate a meaning of the text which can then be appropriated.[40]

The subjectivity of this approach no doubt presented a challenge to Schneiders in writing it. While one might want more guidance on appropriation, it is by nature related to the background with which one enters the process of interpretation. Therefore, no exhaustive account or manual could be written. Rather, what can be provided are examples of work with discrete passages which are explicit about conflicts between the world of the text and the world of the reader, and how those might be resolved, leading to transformation.

The interpretation of Proverbs 8 that follows is intended as an application of the approach outlined above. In the following pages, Proverbs 8 will be read as an ancient text, set within the context of the Scriptures of Israel, taken up into the Christian Old Testament, set alongside the New Testament, and handed down through the ages of the church in order that those who share the Rule of Faith might take up and read to the edification of their faithfulness to the presence of God. To do this well, I will read the passage in its literary context. To deepen the reading, I will then attend to various interpreters throughout the centuries who have reflected upon Proverbs 8. I will then return to the text in order to explicate the world in front of the text and set out the mode-of-being which this passage offers to a Christian living in twenty-first-century Western culture.

---

40. Paul Ricoeur, "What Is a Text? Explanation and Understanding," 120–26.

2

Reading Proverbs 8 in Its Literary Context

MY GOAL IS TO read Proverbs 8 as Christian Scripture, that is, as a text received by the Christian tradition in order to shape a mode of life faithful to the reality of God's presence in the world. In some ways, this was the classical mode of reading for centuries in the church. However, speaking very simply, such a reading has become complicated in the last few centuries. This complexity arises from the increasing awareness of the difference between the past and the present along with a sense of the dangers inherent in uncritically imposing the present on the past. These are salutary developments which have sought to produce a more honest reading of the text, even as we can acknowledge that the tools of historical criticism have frequently been put toward aims other than strengthening the readings of the faithful.

As a first step toward reading Proverbs 8 as Christian Scripture, the text can be placed within its literary context. Not only is this an expected mode of reading for much academic study of the Bible; it also serves to support a reading of the text as Scripture. This is because the tools of criticism can open the text up as an ancient and/or literary document which then highlights possible meanings of the text otherwise unavailable to a contemporary reader; "some of the insights into the text that historical criticism generates will be appropriated by the Jews or the church themselves, and they can thereby convert history into tradition and add vitality to an exegetical practice that easily becomes stale and repetitive."[1] One reason for the stalling of exegesis is the danger of a too-hasty appropriation of the passage by the reader's expectations. Responsible interpretation, especially

---

1. Levenson, *The Hebrew Bible, the Old Testament, and Historical Criticism*, 105.

one within a frame recognizing the effects of history and tradition, calls for allowing the text of the Bible to have its own integrity.[2] That is, to allow the text to speak in its own way, as can best be ascertained by a modern reader. While interpreters can never fully remove themselves from the interpretive process, saying so does not commit one to relativism. The tools of textual criticism and literary analysis reveal *something* as they allow the text to have its own integrity by opening space between the world of the interpreter and that of the text.

On the Way to Proverbs 8: The Book of Proverbs in Context

The Historical Context of Proverbs 1–9

In this section, I will locate Proverbs 8 in its historical and canonical setting of the book of Proverbs within the so-called prologue chapters of Proverbs 1–9. This will ground the meanings we read in Proverbs 8 in those of the book as a whole.

As laid out in the foundational orientation of chapter 1, the texts of the Bible are historical.[3] As such, some comments regarding the historical setting of this section of the book are appropriate. The background of Proverbs 1–9 as a species of literature from the ancient Near East is debated. In an earlier period of research into the world behind the text of the book, comparisons have been made between Proverbs, in its constituent parts, and similar material of the ancient world. So, for example, Whybray compares the book with the instructional material of Egypt and Babylon, and finds there to be considerable similarity in form and content.[4] The ten discourses he traces to "the tradition of international wisdom" but considers that they "are not derived from . . . the Yahwistic tradition."[5] The passages in which wisdom is the central figure he considers to be later additions, the function

---

2. Schneiders makes a similar point when she writes that one of the goals of criticism is to "protect the text from a premature appropriation by the reader." *The Revelatory Text*, 171.

3. In the preceding chapter, the concept of the text as historical was nuanced. The role of history in studying Proverbs 8 will again be addressed in chapter 3.

4. Whybray, *Wisdom in Proverbs*, 35.

5. Whybray, *Wisdom in Proverbs*, 37. To make his case, Whybray deems certain passages in the discourses as later additions. This facet of his argument will be taken up in a moment in relation to Weeks' evaluation of Whybray's work.

of which was to bring the instructions more in line with the mainstream theology of Israel.[6] Michael Fox advocates a similar position: for him, the father-son dialogues (similar to Whybray's instructional material) came first, to which were added the interludes (mainly those passages in which wisdom is personified).[7]

Over against both Whybray and Fox, Stuart Weeks' study finds wanting both the contention that Proverbs 1–9 is dependent upon a fixed form of international wisdom literature and the developmental schemes of Whybray and Fox.[8] In a careful study of the extant representative literature, Weeks finds no "strong convention of form or content: what made an instruction was principally its depiction of material as advice passed from one generation to the next, usually father to son."[9] Aside from this broad device of passing on teaching, the diversity in the material defies a fixed formula.[10] As for the question of Proverbs 1–9's composition, while not denying the presence of later additions, Weeks considers these chapters to be largely a unity. Again based upon a study of comparative material, Weeks finds no evidence of an anthology of instructions. He suggests that the different parental introductions be understood as a device that unifies the work, rather than indicators of different sources.[11] With regard to personified Wisdom, Weeks finds a great deal of overlap between these and other images used throughout these chapters, in particular the imagery of the path.[12] Weeks helpfully presses beyond a catalog of terms to how these terms actually work in Proverbs 1–9.

As Proverbs 8 features the longest speech of personified Wisdom, it is of central concern to the present reading of the chapter. As with the instructional material of Proverbs 1–9, so with the figure of Wisdom, parallels have been sought in the literature of the ancient Near East. Albright advances the thesis that personified was based upon a Canaanite goddess

---

6. Whybray, *Wisdom in Proverbs*, 72–76.

7. Fox, *Proverbs 1–9*, 322–30.

8. Weeks, *Instruction and Imagery in Proverbs 1–9*.

9. Weeks, *Instruction and Imagery in Proverbs 1–9*, 30.

10. Weeks objects to Whybray's "radical divisions and excisions" he performs "in an attempt to align the text with some 'model' instruction." *Instruction and Imagery in Proverbs 1–9*, 53.

11. Weeks, *Instruction and Imagery in Proverbs 1–9*, 53–54.

12. Weeks, *Instruction and Imagery in Proverbs 1–9*, 78–79.

of wisdom.¹³ Gustav Boström proposes the goddess Astarte as a source for this figure.¹⁴ According to Boström, "Selbst wenn man nicht so weit geht, dass man die Weisheit durch Astarte personifiziert oder hypostatisiert sein lässt, muss man doch feststellen, dass bei der Ausgestaltung und Färbung der Weisheit gewisse Züge einer fremden (oder verlorengegangenen einheimischen) Göttin entliehen worden sind."¹⁵ Bauer-Kayatz argues that the personification of Maat in Egyptian literature provides a major source for this figure.¹⁶ In one place, in relation to the presentation of Wisdom in Proverbs 8, Bauer-Kayatz writes, "Hier die Maat als Kind, als Kleines vor Atum, da die Weisheit als spielendes Kind, als Liebling vor Jahwe: Der Schluß liegt nahe, daß die ägyptischen Vorstellungen von der Maat als einem geliebten Götterkind der israelitischen Konzeption der Weisheit als einem vor Jahwe spielenden Liebling als Modell gedient haben."¹⁷

These proposals for possible sources of personified Wisdom face a number of difficulties in relation to how the text actually deploys this figure.¹⁸ In the last chapter, I stated that interaction with the history of interpretation and other traditions is helpful for making the text strange, and thereby raising questions with which to return to the text. This applies to proposals for the origins of the text. Recurring to Weeks' analysis, these proposals for the origin of personified Wisdom "constitute at most a footnote to the portrayal of Wisdom, if they cannot answer such questions as why she invites the uneducated to turn to her, why finding her will earn the favour of YHWH, and how she is the antithesis of both robbers and the foreign woman."¹⁹ Our goal is to read the received form of the text in order to receive the divine self-gift offered through the Bible, read as Scripture. Weeks' evaluation is helpful because it comes out of careful reading of comparative material while also reminding us of the purpose of the enterprise

---

13. Albright, "The Goddess of Life and Wisdom," 258–94. Albright's comments pertaining to Wisdom in Proverbs can be found on pages 285–86.

14. G. Boström, *Proverbiastudien*, esp. 156–74. Boström's argument is that a foreign sexual cult is lurking in the background of the book, and provides the motivation for the construction of personified Wisdom.

15. G. Boström, *Proverbiastudien*, 174.

16. Bauer-Kayatz, *Studien zu Proverbian*, 93–119; Bauer-Kayatz, *Einführung in die alttestamentliche Weisheit*.

17. Bauer-Kayatz, *Einführung in die alttestamentliche Weisheit*, 90.

18. Fox features a concise summary and evaluation of many of the prominent proposals in his commentary. See *Proverbs 1–9*, 333–41.

19. Weeks, *Instruction and Imagery in Proverbs 1–9*, 89–90.

of reading Proverbs 1–9. Later on in the book some of the above outlined proposals will be revisited in order to raise questions of how they impact our reading of the text.

Placing Proverbs 8 in the Literary Context of Proverbs 1–9

The book of Proverbs opens with a statement of its purpose. Chapter 1, verses 1–7 are as follows:

> **1** The proverbs of Solomon, son of David, king of Israel;
> **2** to know wisdom and discipline,
>   to understand sayings of understanding;
> **3** to take up the discipline of insight,
>   righteousness, justice, and equity;
> **4** to give to the callow shrewdness,
>   to the youth knowledge and foresight.
> **5** Let wise ones listen and enhance instruction,
>   and let understanding ones acquire guidance;
> **6** to understand a proverb and figure,
>   words of wisdom and riddles.
> **7** The fear of the LORD is the beginning of knowledge,
>   fools despise wisdom and discipline.[20]

This introduction outlines the goals and purposes of the book. It promises that with its teachings a student will grow in their ability to live life successfully. These verses feature numerous significant terms for the definition of that success. Some of the terms come from the common ethical vocabulary of the Old Testament, others do not. That they are included here together invites us to see them mutually informing and expanding on one another. Thus, verse 3b offers to the student "righteousness, justice, and equity." These values are held throughout the Old Testament (cf. Gen 18:19; Pss 9:9 [Heb.]; 58:2; 90:9; Isa 11:4; 33:15; 45:19).[21] Surrounding these familiar terms are those related to one's intellect (v. 2, 3a), morals (v. 4), hermeneutical skill (vv. 5–6), and existential orientation (v. 7). Proverbs 1:1–7 outlines the goals for the book in this holistic manifesto for successful

---

20. Unless otherwise indicated, all translations are my own. I found Michael Fox's explanation of the various words for wisdom and folly particularly helpful and instructive in the translation. See Fox, *Proverbs 1–9*, 28–43.

21. O'Dowd, *Proverbs*, 53. Waltke characterizes these as "that which serves and heals the community." Waltke, *The Book of Proverbs*, 177. Proverbs 8 also includes a communal benefit of wisdom. See below.

living. The kind of life in view is not simplistic but complex, featuring these many facets.

The introduction dazzles the reader with the scope of its promise. To those who would take up and read, Proverbs offers the way to successful living. However, it is noteworthy that such success is not here defined in terms of health or wealth. Rather, the introduction focuses on the formation of virtuous character, which will enable the reader to discern and remain within the prescribed boundaries God has set for the good life.[22] Raymond van Leeuwen argues that this understanding of life aligns with the wider witness of the Old Testament: "Like other symbol systems in Old Testament thought, Proverbs depicts the world as segmented by boundaries, by limits that apply to every person, thing, and function (cf. Genesis 1)."[23] With regards to the introduction, faithfulness to live within the limits of the created order is offered to the young and the callow. If we accept van Leeuwen's view of life within limits, of which we will have more to say later, then we can surmise that the characteristics listed in Proverbs 1:1–7 are those which enable the young to discern the limits and stay within them.

The introduction presents the book as not only for the beginner but also as a manual of profitable reading for those who have already achieved those introductory purposes. The introduction includes not only the neophyte; the wise (חכם) and understanding (נבון) are also addressed (vv. 5–6). Those mentioned in verse 5 have attained the goal established by verse 2, in that they evidently "know wisdom and discipline" and "understand sayings of understanding" (v. 2). This advanced group is invited to increase in "interpretive skills."[24] They will learn to understand, presumably with more depth, the proverbs, figures, riddles, and other wisdom sayings of the book.

That this group is invited to increase in learning suggests to some that a hermeneutical aspect is included in the formation process envisioned by the introduction. Fox notes that the introduction conceives of Proverbs as a book, rather than oral teaching, in which case, verses 5 and 6 invite the advanced reader to contemplate the words of the book with greater depth and insight.[25] However, when we consider the rest of the structure and content of Proverbs 1–9, this invitation could be understood as applying to more than the book itself. The book's concern is not only for its right

---

22. Van Leeuwen, "Liminality and Worldview in Proverbs 1–9," 111–44.
23. Van Leeuwen, "Liminality and Worldview in Proverbs 1–9," 117.
24. Fox, *Proverbs 1–9*, 63.
25. Fox, *Proverbs 1–9*, 63.

interpretation, but for the formation of learners for life lived outside of the confines of the book. We could understand this hermeneutic to be a way of life, a *know-how* rather than a *know-what*, in which one is ever learning, never finished.[26]

The introduction to the book ends with Proverbs 1:7, which functions as the key-note of Proverbs.[27] It grounds the formation offered by Proverbs in a stance towards God. To say that the fear of the Lord is the beginning (ראשית) of knowledge could mean either that it is the first in principle or that it is the first temporal step.[28] It is best to understand this as a statement of the temporal sequence of student's path in wisdom: fearing the Lord is the starting place for growing in wisdom. "The fear of the Lord is the *musar* of wisdom—its propaedeutic, the discipline that prepares the way to it."[29] As such, it is indispensable for the subsequent acquisition of wisdom; the fear of the Lord is not left behind as one "progresses" in wisdom.[30] The verse contrasts this with fools who despise wisdom and discipline. Fox, again, provides helpful insight: "Deep seated attitudes, rather than lack of raw intelligence, prevent them from gaining wisdom."[31] Both of the lines speak to the learner's attitude, their stance toward God and the instruction offered by the book. Proverbs does not offer a mechanistic approach to formation in which the book works on the student *ex opere operato*. On the contrary, the student must participate in their formation in a particular way for it to be efficacious. Primacy is placed on how the student approaches the Lord God of Israel. Their reverence for the Lord will be seen in how they approach the instruction offered by the book. Verse 7 links these attitudes together such that one is seen in the other.

Proverbs 1:1–7 sets out the purpose of the book as enabling both the amateur and the advanced to grow in the capacity to live a successful life, expressed in ethical-intellectual capacities and grounded in one's virtuous stance toward God and wisdom. The introduction ushers the reader into the rest of the book. Scholars have divided the book into two broad

---

26. I say more about this possible understanding of wisdom as *know-how* in the chapter, "A Contemporary Conception of Wisdom."

27. Fox, *Proverbs 1–9*, 67.

28. Waltke, *The Book of Proverbs*, 181.

29. Fox, *Proverbs 1–9*, 68.

30. Waltke, *The Book of Proverbs*, 181.

31. Fox, *Proverbs 1–9*, 68.

sections: chapters 1–9 and chapters 10–31.[32] As our concern is more specifically with Proverbs 8, we will primarily attend to its location in chapters 1–9. An intriguing proposal for understanding these chapters comes from Raymond van Leeuwen, with whom I have already interacted in this chapter. Some scholars divide the chapters in the prologue of Proverbs based on their themes, metaphors, and speculated date of origin.[33] Van Leeuwen's focus is primarily on the world of the text to associate these chapters into a holistic scheme. This does not negate the more detailed work of others; van Leeuwen's essay is a short piece aimed at goals different from those of a historical-critical commentary writer.

Van Leeuwen notes that the "subunits of Proverbs 1–9 are particularly rich in intertextual cross referencing, repetitions, coordinated contrasts and juxtapositions."[34] His proposal is to attend to this richness without attempting to resolve inherent tensions. Others have focused on the metaphor of the road or way, and still others on the contrast of the two women. Van Leeuwen offers an approach that allows both of these, along with the remaining metaphors in these chapters, to continue to operate. "The mutual significance of the roads, the young men, and the two Women cannot be explained by one 'root metaphor' or 'nuclear symbol.' . . . Rather, both the 'roads' and 'women' in these chapters are root metaphors which *together* embody different, though related aspects of one underlying worldview."[35] This underlying view of the world is one in which God has set limits, and it is within those limits that one finds life. Limits are expressed through Wisdom's teaching and are grounded in the created order. "Thus, far from being an isolated theological curiosity within Proverbs 1–9, the famous passage on Wisdom's role in creation (8:22–31; cf. 3:19–20) serves as the cosmological warrant for the paraenesis of the entire collection."[36] The various metaphorical offerings in the prologue of Proverbs 1–9 attempt

---

32. Fox, *Proverbs 1–9*, 322–30.

33. Michael Fox treats the chapters containing father-son dialogue separately from those of personified wisdom. Supporting this move is his conclusion that these comes from different authors at different times (the former from a single author, the latter from multiple authors responding to one another). He does offer some harmonizing of these voices in the last paragraph of his excursus "Wisdom in the Interludes." Fox, *Proverbs 1–9*, 359.

34. Van Leeuwen, "Liminality and Worldview in Proverbs 1–9," 112.

35. Van Leeuwen, "Liminality and Worldview in Proverbs 1–9," 113. Emphasis original.

36. Van Leeuwen, "Liminality and Worldview in Proverbs 1–9," 117.

to convert the neophyte and affirm the convinced to walk the path of life outlined by God.

Van Leeuwen's proposal is attractive in that it allows for variety in the text by resisting the urge to elevate one metaphor above the others. His proposal gives detail to the more general understanding that Proverbs 1–9 provides the theological frame for the rest of the book. The idea of exploring boundaries set by God in the social order, which require the various characteristics set out in Proverbs 1:1–7, paints these chapters in their own distinct hue. They define what one might mean by stating that Proverbs 1–9 provide a theological frame for the remainder of the book. The boundaries of God's order are ethical and moral, and they find their basis in the divinely created order witnessed to by the Old Testament, both here and elsewhere.

Van Leeuwen does not specifically address the world behind the text. As I read it, his proposal operates on the received text, if we can take that term rather broadly.[37] Alongside van Leeuwen, we can attend to Michael Fox's proposal regarding the formation of the two types of chapters in Proverbs 1–9: the father-son lectures and the personified wisdom passages (which he labels as interludes). Fox understands this formation as "a process of growth, in which later authors read, learned from, and elaborated the themes of the earlier text."[38] On the basis of the homogeny of structure and language in the lectures, he considers these units to come from a single hand. Fox does not detect the same level of homogeneity in the interludes: language varies more between these interludes, and the concept of wisdom changes between the lectures and the interludes. In contrast with the lectures, with the interludes "we can pictures the process of growth as a series of insertions by scribes learning from and building on the lectures rather than as a compilation and reorganization of unrelated texts by a redactor."[39] James Loader agrees with this proposal of Fox, concluding that what Fox terms interludes "seem to serve the purpose of constructing the architectonic symmetry that the lessons alone do not impart" to these early chapters of Proverbs.[40] Thus later scribes sought to offer further reflections on

---

37. The "received text" is an easy to write but hard to define term, as the questions of "which text?" and "received by whom?" can be answered differently. Moberly, *The God of the Old Testament*, 5–6.

38. Fox, *Proverbs 1–9*, 323.

39. Fox, *Proverbs 1–9*, 328.

40. Loader, *Proverbs 1–9*, 10.

the nature of wisdom and attempted to mold these new words in the style of the lectures and contributing to the structure of the book in the process.[41]

The above scheme for the formation of the book of Proverbs helps to account for both the continuity between certain sections and the distinct features of others. Regardless of whether one accepts Fox's proposal wholeheartedly, it does open up further exploration. Specifically, it raises the question as to the unique contribution of the interludes, the passages in which wisdom is personified. In Fox's scheme, scribes studying in the tradition of Proverbs were led to add these passages, presumably to aid in the accomplishment of the goals of the book. In other words, without these passages it was perceived that something was missing, or that adding these interludes added an element which that further the reader on the goal of formation in wisdom.

In summary, the introduction to the book of Proverbs set a framework of moral and ethical formation oriented by the boundaries set by God in creation. The origination of the various passages within the prologue come together to support this purpose. Having seen the purpose, we can understand the stages of the prologue's development as oriented toward it. A passage like Proverbs 8, with its strikingly developed personification of Wisdom, is to be understood as somehow contributing to the formation of the reader to live life within the limits set by the God of Israel.

Proverbs 8

In the above paragraphs, we explored how, in the history of the text, the passages which personify wisdom are likely an addition responding to the lecture passages. If this is the case, then a canonical reading that seeks to incorporate diachronic and synchronic readings reads the personification passages as having something distinct to offer in achieving the aims of the book. We now turn to Proverbs 8 itself.

The chapter is the longest sustained personification of Lady Wisdom in the book of Proverbs. It is preceded by the longest chapter on Lady Wisdom's counterpart, Dame Folly, in Proverbs 7. Chapter 8 begins with three verses in third-person with "eine kurze Einführung der Rednerin durch

---

41. Fox, *Proverbs 1–9*, 329.

den Weisen."⁴² These are the only verses in the chapter not spoken by Lady Wisdom.⁴³

> ¹ Does not wisdom call?
>   And understanding raise her voice?
> ² On top of high places, along the path,
>   at crossroads she takes her stand.
> ³ Beside gates, before towns,
>   in entrances to portals, she gives a ringing cry.

These verses describe Lady Wisdom in her accessibility. She is not silent, but calls and raises her voice.⁴⁴ "Whereas the Strange Woman [of chapter 7] speaks in hushed tones in dark corners (a paradox, because she is rowdy), Wisdom proclaims her message in a bold voice in the most public of venues."⁴⁵ The last phrase of Proverbs 8:1 (תִּתֵּן קוֹלָהּ) is identical to Proverbs 1:20b, which forms a tie (in addition to the conceptual link of personified wisdom) between the presentation of Wisdom in chapter 8 and the earlier passage.⁴⁶ Wisdom desires to be heard by her audience. Indeed, the rhetorical nature of the opening questions assumes that the readers do hear her voice.⁴⁷ Loader links this hearing with the words of the teacher in the book;⁴⁸ however, the poem does not explicitly makes this connection,

---

42. Meinhold, *Die Sprüche*, 134.

43. Loader incorporates these three verses with verses 4–11 to make one section which he labels "First Admonition" (*Proverbs*, 321). He then delineates four subunits: where Wisdom calls (vv. 1–3); what she calls out (vv. 4–6); why she calls out (vv. 7–9); and the value of what she calls for (vv. 10–11). This arrangement does not see the shift in speaker (third person vv. 1–3, first person vv. 4–11) as determinative. Even though I do not ultimately find Loader's outline persuasive, it does illustrate the connectedness of these early verses.

44. Reflecting on the distinction between saying and crying out, David Ford writes, "For the crier the act expresses a profound relationship to what is said. The speaker and the message are powerfully identified with each other. As for the content that is cried out, rather than just spoken, it is highlighted, amplified. It is a sign of the limits of speech, a gesture towards the inadequacy of any words to this content, an indication of the superlative, of breaking the bounds of terms and categories, of transcendence." Ford, *Christian Wisdom*, 19.

45. Fox, *Proverbs 1–9*, 265.

46. The first verb in Proverbs 1:20 (תָּרֹנָּה) is used to end 8:3. Additionally, the locations are very similar lexically and conceptually: שְׁעָרִים (1:21 / 8:3), פִּתְחֵי (1:21) / פְּתָחִים (8:3).

47. Waltke, *The Book of Proverbs*, 394.

48. Loader, *Proverbs*, 325.

which invites the reader to consider how they might be hearing Wisdom in other experiences of life.

The locations of her calling also suggest her accessibility. Her chosen locations are significant when read in light of the preceding chapter. "The localities are chosen to contrast with the adulteress of Chap. 7 who skulks around corners at night. Wisdom, on the other hand, calls from locations where she could be publicly seen."[49] Wisdom communicates accessibility by calling out in public spaces. Meinhold argues that the various designations of places in verses 2 and 3 "meinen offenbar ein und dieselbe Stelle."[50] However, his arguments are hesitant: "Der Bezeichnung 'Mund der Stadt' läßt auf die Außenseite des Stadttores schließen . . . Die Bezeichnung 'Haus der Steige' meint vermutlich den Knotenpunkt von Straßen am Stadttor."[51] Another suggestion comes from Fox, who interprets verses 2 and 3 as identifying two distinct locations for Wisdom's call. The first is the convergence of main roads in the center of the town whereas the second is the city gates, where business transactions would often take place. "This means that the chapter is describing not a unique incident or sequence of events but an ongoing, typical occurrence."[52] Additionally, the event is somewhat of an "everyplace," not confined to one specific town or even those within Israel. Fox's reading is coherent with the broader audience Wisdom names in verses 4–5; "Wisdom plunges into the midst of this hustle and bustle to reach people where *they* are."[53] Wisdom is construed to be accessibly present in the world of the readers. Similar to the word of God as stated in Deuteronomy 30:11–14, Wisdom is not far off but Wisdom is "very near" the reader.[54]

A frequent feature of the description of Lady Wisdom in Proverbs 8 is similarity and overlap with descriptions of the LORD God of Israel. The immanence of Wisdom offers one example of this. Like the word of God, which is near to Israel (cf. Deut 30:14), Wisdom is present to Israel in public spaces. These parallels between Wisdom and the LORD remain suggestive throughout the poem: an overt identification is never made and there are plenty of moves throughout the chapter to maintain a separate

49. Loader, *Proverbs*, 325.
50. Meinhold, *Die Sprüche*, 136.
51. Meinhold, *Die Sprüche*, 136.
52. Fox, *Proverbs 1–9*, 267.
53. Fox, *Proverbs 1–9*, 267. Emphasis original.
54. Fox, *Proverbs 1–9*, 267.

identity for Wisdom vis-à-vis the LORD. This topic will be directly engaged in a later chapter.

The accessibility of Wisdom continues to be a theme at the opening of Wisdom's words in verse 4, in a section that continues through verse 11.

> 4 To you, O men, I call,
> and my voice is for the sons of Adam.
> 5 Gullible one, learn foresight!
> and mockers, learn sense![55]
> 6 Listen! For forthright things[56] I speak,
> and the utterances of my lips are upright words.
> 7 For my mouth ponders truth;
> evil is an abomination to my lips.
> 8 All the words of my mouth are in righteousness,
> there is nothing in them that is torturous or twisted.
> 9 All of them are straightforward to the understanding ones,
> and upright to those finding knowledge.
> 10 Take my discipline and not silver
> and my knowledge is a better choice than gold
> 11 For wisdom is better than corals
> and everything desired is not comparable to her.

In these verses, Wisdom appeals to her audience. While both this section and the next (vv. 12–21) speak of Wisdom's benefits, Meinhold's observation that, apart from verses 1–3, "Die restlichen Abschnitte werden jeweils durch ein inhaltlich aussagekräftiges Wort eingeleitet" helps to differentiate them.[57] The section containing verses 4–11 begins with אֲלֵיכֶם, drawing our attention to those addressed by Wisdom. As at the outset of the chapter, in verse 4 we find Wisdom calling, casting a wide net in doing so. The verse marks the beginning of her first-person speech, initiating an "'I-thou'

---

55. This half of the verse commands the mockers to learn לֵב. In Fox's survey of words for wisdom and folly, he writes on the phrase חסר־לב that "In this phrase, *leb* always refers to faculties we would consider specifically cognitive, namely, the ability (and willingness) to make a prudent, sensible decision." Fox, *Proverbs 1–9*, 39.

56. The word here נְגִידִים appears only three other times in the OT (2 Chr 11:11; Job 29:10; Ps 76:13). All four are translated as relating to nobility or princes based upon a root of *nagid*, "prince." This certainly fits the context of Chronicles and the psalm (I have some hesitation on the Job reference). However, the word could also be rooted in *neged*, "opposite" or "in front of." My translation takes this latter option, offering what I consider an adjectival form of this prepositional idea. I am gesturing toward things placed out in the open and therefore morally upright, which would stand in nice parallel to "upright" (מֵישָׁרִים) in the second half of the verse. Fox, *Proverbs 1–9*, 269.

57. Meinhold, *Die Sprüche*, 135.

encounter."⁵⁸ Her desired audience is the ethnically and socially undifferentiated⁵⁹ "men" (אישים) and "sons of Adam" (בני אדם).⁶⁰ She even speaks to some unexpected hearers, the gullible (פתאים) and the mockers (כסילים). The mockers are particularly surprising, for these are the complacent (Prov 1:32) who hate what wisdom has to offer (Prov 1:22). One way to resolve this tension between these two speeches of Wisdom is that, through this address in Proverbs 8, "wird die erzieherische Absicht der harten Warn- und Drohrede . . . offengelegt."⁶¹ Wisdom narrows her focus from a general address to humanity to speak directly to the gullible and the mocker: "Die Weisheit appelliert an die Einfältigen, die zur Lebensklugheit (עָרְמָה), schon in 1,4 in das Erziehungsprogramm der Weisheit aufgenommen, notwendigen intellektuellen Kräfte zu schulen, um das zu hören und aufnehmen zu können, was die Weisheit an kostbaren Gaben zu bieten hat."⁶² Wisdom's call is for her audience to gain in her what they lack; namely shrewdness (ערמה) and sense (לב). That the mockers are included communicates the possibility of all kinds of people growing in wisdom.⁶³

Having named her desired audience, Wisdom moves on to speak of the value of her words. She begins by naming their virtues and ends comparing her words to precious materials such as gold and corals. Her speech is forthright, upright, and righteous. These latter two virtues directly connect with the introduction to Proverbs (1:3), thereby claiming that listening to this voice in chapter 8 will move one along the path of formation set out by the book. The description of Wisdom's words as forthright is not a lexical reference to the introduction, but it does reflect the implication of the introduction, namely that the way of wisdom will be plainly set forth

---

58. Waltke, *The Book of Proverbs*, 395.

59. L. Boström suggests that the universal scope of wisdom's audience may have come from the acknowledgement, in the world of ancient Israel, of the international nature of wisdom discourse. L. Boström, *The God of the Sages*, 88.

60. Having noted the lack of differentiation, the context of the book is not so undifferentiated. Proverbs is a product of ancient Israel and its readers would certainly have been largely confined that to community. As to social status, the *Sitz im Leben* of Proverbs is debated; some see it as a court manual for nobility, others as a text for the formation of sages, among other proposals. See Fox, *Proverbs 1–9*, 6–12 for a survey of some of these options. The point to make here is that Wisdom's broad call does not necessarily tell us of her actual reading audience. Rather, it is a rhetorical move for the *reader/hearer* to know something of how Wisdom calls and whom she wishes to reach.

61. Meinhold, *Die Sprüche*, 137.

62. Plöger, *Sprüche Salomos*, 88.

63. Loader, *Proverbs*, 328.

Reading Proverbs 8 in Its Literary Context

for the reader/hearer. This idea is picked up in Proverbs 8:9; for those seeking knowledge and understanding, Wisdom's words are "straightforward" (נחכים).

The valuation of Wisdom's authority in terms of her ethical purity is reminiscent of the Lord, providing another point of connection between these two. Deuteronomy 32:4–5 shares much of the vocabulary of Proverbs 8:7–9: "speaking אמת as opposed to speaking רשע (Prov 8:7), speaking with צדק as opposed to עקש and what is נפתל (root פתל) (Prov 8:8), God of אמונה as opposed to עול (Deut 32:4), God as צדיק as opposed to people called עקש and פתלתל (root פתל) (Deut 32:4, 5)."[64] It could be, as Loader advocates, that this connection is meant to undergird Wisdom's authority.[65]

Verses 10 and 11 end this section with a comparison[66] of Wisdom with precious materials: silver (כסף), choice gold (מחרוץ נבחר), and corals (מפנינים). This is not the first time in Proverbs that these comparisons have been made (cf. Prov 3:14–15)[67] and they will be echoed again in Proverbs 8:19. What is better than these precious things is "my discipline" (מוסרי), knowledge (דעת), and wisdom (חכמה). These words are common through Proverbs, and are particularly prominent in the introductory verses.

With the various allusions and echoes between Proverbs 8:4–11 and other portions of Proverbs 1–9, it seems that little is added by these verses. We get no new data in this section.[68] The main contribution is to be put these words into the mouth of Lady Wisdom. She is speaking them, rather than the father or narrator. Whybray offers one possible explanation related to the development of wisdom in Israel. He asserts that Proverbs 8:4–11 belongs to the first of two stages of this development: the first sought to identify wisdom with the words of the father; the second connects this wisdom with the Lord God of Israel.[69] Plöger offers a similar conclusion, with less focus on the world behind the text: "Gewiß könnte so auch der Weisheitslehrer geredet haben, und die Verse 10 und 11 nehmen modifiziert auf,

---

64. Loader, *Proverbs*, 329.

65. Loader, *Proverbs*, 330.

66. Syntactically speaking only verse 11 is a comparative statement.

67. Proverbs 8:10–11 are almost identical to Proverbs 3:14–15, particularly if we read the qere rather than the ketiv in 3:15.

68. Whybray offers a catalog of the overlapping descriptions of wisdom and the rewards offered by the father/teacher figure in the other portions of Proverbs 1–9. He deploys this list in his arguments regarding the development of wisdom, which as a figure was built off of the father-son discourses. *Wisdom in Proverbs*, 76–77.

69. Whybray, *Wisdom in Proverbs*, 73–75.

was er in 3,14 und 15 selbst gesagt hat. Aber im Munde der personifizierten Weisheit, die wie Jahwe zu reden vermag, gewinnen diese Worte an Hoheit und Würde."[70] For both Whybray and Plöger, the phenomenon of personification as a metaphor adds to what is communicated. Whybray's focus is how the metaphor's nature as a supplement attests to the history of the book's material. Plöger is more concerned with the world within the text and the internal dynamics presented there. The metaphor's contribution to the book's goal of formation and the path within the limits set out by Proverbs 1–9 are addressed later in this work.

Having described the value of her words, Lady Wisdom moves on to speak of her benefits to individuals and society in verses 12–21.

> **12** I, Wisdom, I inhabit shrewdness,
>   and knowledge of hidden things I find.
> **13** The fear of the LORD means to hate evil,[71]
>   pride and exaltation and the way of evil and the mouth of perverse things I hate.
> **14** I have counsel and efficient wisdom,
>   I am understanding, I have might.
> **15** By me rulers rule,
>   and princes decree righteous things.
> **16** By me leaders lead,
>   and nobles, all judges of the earth.[72]
> **17** I love those loving me,
>   and the one who looks for me diligently will find me.
> **18** Riches and glory are with me,
>   valuable wealth and righteousness.
> **19** Better is my fruit than gold, even pure gold,
>   and my produce than choice silver.

---

70. Plöger, *Sprüche Salomos*, 89.

71. Fox and many others read this as an insertion. The line does serve to connect Wisdom, her virtues, and her benefits to the goals of Proverbs and with the broader OT canon. While it is likely a later addition we need not eliminate it (contra Toy, Meinhold). The line's presence speaks to the redactional process by which the Israelite community of faith perceived Wisdom's connection to the LORD God of Israel. Thus it is helpful for a present-day transformational reading of the text.

72. MT has "righteousness" (צדק). However, multiple manuscripts, the *Mikraot Gedolot*, and the Septuagint all have "earth" (ארץ / γης). In addition to the manuscript evidence, the expansive definition of judges "of the earth" fits the passage. Judges "of righteousness" reads as a limiting statement (only those who judge righteously; perhaps only Israelite judges. See Fox, *Proverbs 1–9*, 274) whereas the rest of this section lacks such restrictions. See also Whybray, *Proverbs*, 126.

> 20 In the way of righteousness I walk,
>   among pathways of justice,
> 21 To grant an inheritance[73] to those loving me,
>   and their storehouses I will fill.

The way in which Wisdom leads is one of great benefit to society and individuals. Her teaching is valuable in that it leads to these blessings. The section begins with a statement of her qualifications in verses 12 and 13.[74] In declaring her proximity to shrewdness (ערמה), Wisdom proclaims her ability to use whatever tactics necessary to meet her goals.[75] The dwelling of Wisdom in ערמה teaches that "finding Wisdom would automatically mean finding the acumen inherent in shrewdness."[76] Aiding her in attaining her goals is her knowledge of hidden things (דעת מזמות).[77] These self-declarations support her earlier exhortation in verse 5 for the gullible to learn shrewdness and the mockers to learn sense. She is able to lead into what they need because she herself has these capacities. Verse 13 then grounds her abilities in the ethical world of the Old Testament through their affirmation of Wisdom's moral purity. If the fear of the LORD means hating evil, Wisdom has this in spades; the four items she hates serve to fill out the general aversion to evil.

Once again, we note a connection to the introduction to the book of Proverbs. The book seeks to equip with shrewdness (ערמה), knowledge (דעת), and foresight (מזמה) (Prov 1:4). In chapter 8, Wisdom has issued her invitation to those needing these (cf. v. 5) and now asserts her possession of them. In the world of the text, Lady Wisdom is a means of attaining what the book promises. Loader helpfully notes a difference between these two passages: in the introduction "the speaking teacher more or less promises to 'give'" these qualities, whereas in chapter 8 "this is intensified, for the qualities yet to be striven for by humans are qualities already at the

---

73. The Hebrew of this half verse is להנחיל אהבי יש. Fox notes that it is only here and in Sir 42:3 that יש is found as a noun meaning possessions. "The pairing of *yēš* with *nḥlh* in Sir 42:3 suggests that *yēš* is enduring, stable property, and not just any valuables." Fox, *Proverbs 1–9*, 278.

74. This section is marked off from the preceding by its introductory first person pronoun אני.

75. Fox, *Proverbs 1–9*, 35.

76. Loader, *Proverbs*, 334.

77. Fox, *Proverbs 1–9*, 34.

disposal of wisdom."[78] That Wisdom already has these qualities accounts for the boldness of her self-recommendation and exhortation. However, Loader points out that this is another place at which personification does not operate as mere ornamentation, but opens up something new vis-à-vis the aims of the book.

Verses 14 through 16 boast of Wisdom's benefits to statecraft and, by extension, the good of society. Syntactically, each of these verses begins with a preposition marked by a possessive first person pronoun. Verse 14 states that Wisdom (here also personified as Understanding) exhibits all of the requisite characteristics for wise rule: she has counsel (עצה), efficient wisdom (תושיה), and might (גבורה). To paraphrase, Wisdom has the ability to discern the right path forward, plan its implementation, and execute that plan to great effect. Fox notes that these "are not inherently ethical attributes, though they may and should be employed justly."[79] Be that as it may, in the context of Proverbs 8 the company these attributes keep is certainly ethical (cf. vv. 4–13). Establishing these ethically neutral traits within a setting aimed at righteousness, justice, and equity (cf. Prov 1:3) is part of Proverbs' program to set its students on a path within the limits of God's created framework.

Verses 15 and 16 each begin with a paranomastic phrase: by Wisdom rulers rule (מלכים ימלכו) and leaders lead (שרים ישרו). It is only with Wisdom that kings and chiefs are able to do that which constitutes their office. When verse 15b claims that by Wisdom princes decree[80] righteousness, the point here is not about the qualities of just rule and/or rulers in and of themselves. Rather, these lines continue to exalt Wisdom and thereby garner her the attention of the reader: readers are to learn (8:5) and listen (8:6) because Wisdom is she by whom effective rule takes place.[81] She benefits society through enabling righteous leadership and this serves as a powerful illustration of the kind of benefit Wisdom offers to any who follow

---

78. Loader, *Proverbs*, 335.

79. Fox, *Proverbs 1–9*, 273.

80. It is perhaps the case that Wisdom enables this activity in that she was present with the LORD inscribed the circle on the of the deep (8:27) and limited the waters (8:29); in all three cases the verb used is חקק. I will explore this more later on.

81. I have added the qualifier "effective" here, which is not present in the text. Still, as Fox points out, "Verses 15–16 are not claiming that all kings and princes actually rule wisely or mandate righteous laws—no one would suppose that—but rather that wisdom is the principle of rulership, and effective governance depends on it." Fox, *Proverbs 1–9*, 274.

her. "Was den Fürsten, insofern sie Liebhaber der Weisheit sind, gelingt in ihrem guten Regiment, verheißt die Weisheit mutatis mutandis allen ihren Liebhabern."[82] Loader similarly points out "the *function* of the [royalty] motif is to explain to non-kings, that is, the young pupils who identify with the general public at the city gate (v. 3), how important it is to acquire wisdom."[83] Successful rulers offer a common reference point toward which Wisdom can point for evidence of her fruit.

Wisdom's self-promotion continues in verses 17 through 21 with her benefits to individuals. She is not confined to those few who rule, but loves all those who love her (v. 17). Kayatz[84] finds the background for this formula of reciprocal love in Egyptian "wisdom literature."[85] Within the biblical canon, the formula itself is not prominent. With that said, the concept is most often tied to loving the LORD God of Israel (cf. Deut 6:5; 7:8; 10:15; Hos 2:4ff.; 3:1).[86] Within the narrow confines of verses 17 to 21, Wisdom's love appears to mean she will accrue her benefits to the ones who love her. These benefits include riches and glory (or perhaps glorious riches), valuable wealth, and righteousness (v. 18). Verse 20 works in tandem with verse 17 to nuance what it means to love and seek wisdom; it means to meet her on her path of righteousness and justice. Once again, a reward is promised: to those who meet her on her way she gives an inheritance and fills their storehouses (vv. 20–21).[87] Between these two couplets (vv. 17–18 / 20–21) stands verse 19 which relativizes material gain. Wisdom's produce (פריי, "my fruit"; תבואתי, "my produce") are better than any treasure which may capture the desires of her learners. Although wealth follows in her wake, her real benefit is righteousness and justice. This does not necessarily denigrate material wealth; the material is used positively to evaluate her worth.[88]

---

82. Plöger, *Sprüche Salomos*, 90.

83. Loader, *Proverbs*, 338.

84. Noted in Fox, *Proverbs 1–9*, 276.

85. I put this term in scare quotes following Will Kynes work, *An Obituary for "Wisdom Literature,"* esp. 26–27. Kynes notes that the designation "wisdom literature" originated in the field of biblical studies and was adopted later by Egyptologists, not the other way around. As the term itself obscures as much as it reveals, Kynes advocates its "death" in the guild of biblical studies.

86. Loader, *Proverbs*, 340.

87. That she walks "among (בתוך) paths of justice" fits van Leeuwen's concept of liminality; wisdom herself does not stray to the left or right, but remains within the limits set forth by God. See Loader, *Proverbs*, 342–43.

88. Loader, *Proverbs*, 342.

Still, her benefits of righteousness and justice surpass the worth of precious minerals. With this higher purpose, Wisdom again claims that following her is the means by which to attain the goals of Proverbs as a whole (cf. Prov 1:3).

The next section of Proverbs 8 is probably the most famous and controversial passage of the book. Verses 22 through 31 speak of Wisdom's relationship with the Lord and the created order.

> 22 The Lord brought me forth[89] at the beginning of His way,
>   the first of His works from of old.
> 23 From eternity I was woven,[90] from the beginning,
>   from the first of the earth.
> 24 Before the depths, I was given birth,
>   before springs were heavy with water,
> 25 before the mountains were sunk,
>   before the hills, I was given birth;
> 26 when He had not yet made the earth and wild lands,[91]
>   nor the first clods of the dry earth of the world.
> 27 I was there when He established the heavens,[92]
>   when He inscribed a circle on the face of the deep,
> 28 when He made firm the clouds above,
>   when He strengthened the springs of the deep,
> 29 when He put into place His decree for the waters,
>   that they should not transgress His command,
>   when he inscribed the foundations of the earth.

---

89. The verb קנה can mean "acquire" or "possess" (the Vulgate adopts this latter option). Many Greek translations use the word εκτισεν, "he created," which caused much controversy in the fourth-century debates on the nature of Christ. It can also mean "acquire by birth" (cf. Gen 4:1). I discuss my translation choice in comments below.

90. I follow Fox's suggested change to the vocalization, away from the MT's "I was poured out" to mean "woven, formed" which is used of gestation in Ps 139:13b.

91. Hebrew חוצות. This word usually means "outside" and refers to city streets, but this meaning does not fit the context of primeval creation. Fox, *Proverbs 1–9*, 283. Following the LXX's αοικητους ("uninhabited place") I have glossed the word as "wild lands" to communicate the far-off places "outside" the comforts of cultivated land, attempting to capture a sense of the world in its early moments.

92. In my translation here I move שָׁם אָנִי to the front of the clause in order to better represent that the following prepositional phrases, all beginning with the ב preposition, are tied to this statement of Wisdom's presence for these creative acts of the Lord. See Weeks, "The Context and Meaning of Proverbs 8:30a," 437.

Reading Proverbs 8 in Its Literary Context

30 I am[93] faithfully[94] by His side, I am daily His delight,[95]
   laughing before Him at all times;
31 laughing in the world, His earth,
   and my delight is in the sons of Adam.

These verses continue Wisdom's explication of her qualifications by associating her intimately with the LORD and involving her to the present day in His creation. Verses 22 through 25 speak of Wisdom's presence with the LORD before all else was created. Her relationship with Him is intimate: she was woven by Him (נסכתי, v 23a), given birth by Him (חוללתי, vv 24a, 25b), brought forth by Him (קנני, v 22a; I discuss my understanding of this verb in the next paragraph). The overall message of these verbs is that the LORD was deeply involved in the bringing forth of Wisdom, which further recommends her to the readers' attention. The commendation is in contrast to the path of the adulteress: the way of Wisdom is intimately connected with the way (דרך) of the LORD; the way of the adulteress leads to Sheol and death (cf. Prov 7:25–27). Verses 24 and 25 assert Wisdom's temporal priority over the depths (תהמות), springs (מעינות), mountains (הרים), and hills (גבעות). If we read this passage in conjunction with Genesis 1, Wisdom is stating her presence with the LORD prior to the beginning of all things.[96] In the setting of the ancient Near East,[97] as well as the Greco-Roman milieu,[98]

---

93. In translating verse 30 as present tense, I am following Weeks' analysis of this passage as before creation (vv. 22–25), during creation (vv. 26–29), and after creation (vv. 30–31). "The Context and Meaning of Proverbs 8:30a," 438.

94. The word אמון is a *hapax legomenon* within the OT. Three translational options are prevalent: (1) "architect/master worker"; (2) "nursling child"; or (3) "faithfully." To a greater or lesser extent, all three can be read to support the passage's goal of exalting Wisdom in the eyes of the reader. The first two options find support in the manuscripts and interpretive traditions. The third option, I would argue, allows one to garner an intended sense of either 1 or 2 without overly identifying with either. The master worker needs to be faithful to the creator, and the nursling child to his/her caretaker. Both ideas are present in other passages as well: for Wisdom's involvement in creation see 3:19–20; for her as a child of the LORD, see 8:22–25. As such, we lose little and gain much by adopting the third sense of the word. See also Moberly, *The God of the Old Testament*, 24–25.

95. In this I adopt the LXX ᾗ προσέχαιρεν, as opposed to the MT משחקים, "rejoicing."

96. Along these lines, *Bereshit Rabba* begins its reflection on Genesis 1:1 with a quotation of Proverbs 8:30 and goes on to postulate that Torah was the *reshit* through which God created the world. This interpretation is representative of the trend in Jewish interpretation of this passage. See Loader, *Proverbs*, 367–71.

97. Cf. Job 15:7–9.

98. Young, *Biblical Exegesis and the Formation of Christian Culture*, 51–52. Young writes, in the Greco-Roman world "Nothing could be both new and true." Young, *Biblical*

Wisdom's antiquity bestows great status on her. However, more than her longevity, she is "the sole eyewitness to creation available to man. Through wisdom, man had the key to the correct understanding of the world."[99]

While being intimate with the LORD, verses 22 through 25 present Wisdom as distinct from the LORD. The various statements regarding the LORD's intimate involvement in bringing her forth only work if she is not the LORD. Yet, she is present with Him from of old, prior to all created[100] things. The nature of her priority is debated and centers around the proper understanding of קנה. My translation choice is influenced by C. F. Burney's article, "Christ as the APXH of Creation,"[101] in which Burney surveys the eighty-four instances of קנה in the Old Testament, as well as its use in cognate languages, to advocate an understanding of "begat" in Proverbs 8:22. Within the text, two usages of חלל in verses 24 and 25 suggests a semantic field of birth may be most appropriate for verse 22. Even so, there are detriments to translating the term "begat," not the least of which is the question of "the normal sexual component of procreative activity."[102] For this reason, the gloss "brought forth" seems to me to fit the purpose of this section to establish Wisdom's presence with God from the very beginning, without overly identifying this process of her origin as internal or external to God. She could have been brought forth from nothing or brought forth in terms of a new revelation of God's own being to the yet-to-be-created world. Loader, who favors an understanding as the verb as "create," orients the debate back to the purpose of the section in his comments: "the uniqueness of this first act of creation justifies a concept that expresses her privileged status."[103] Wisdom's high position vis-à-vis creation is reinforced by a special verb of intimate relation to the LORD, which sets her apart from the rest of creation.

Verses 26 through 29 describe Wisdom in relation to God's creative acts. The central statement of this section is "I was there" (שם אני, v. 27).[104] When God laid out the created world, Wisdom was already on the scene

---

Exegesis and the Formation of Christian Culture, 52.

99. L. Boström, *The God of the Sages*, 54.

100. The acts of God toward Wisdom in this section are distinct from those toward the rest of creation. The significance of this can at least be said to be Wisdom's unique place and therefore high status.

101. *JTS* 27 (1926): 160–77.

102. Loader, *Proverbs*, 348.

103. Loader, *Proverbs*, 348.

104. Weeks, "The Context and Meaning of Proverbs 8:30a," 437.

and able to discern the order of God's work. As such, she is preeminently qualified to lead her students on the right paths, for she has seen God's paths. This works to buttress her appeal to readers who are simultaneously tempted by the adulteress of chapter 7. The righteousness and fruitfulness of Wisdom's paths is certified by her intimate connection with the Lord God and her presence during his creative work.[105] The passage particularly focuses on the Lord's restraint of water. Verse 26 tells us that what Wisdom saw was prior to the appearance of the dry land. Verses 27a describes Wisdom's presence at the creation of the heavens (שמים) which, according to Genesis 1, are made to hold back the "waters above" (cf. Gen 1:7–8). Wisdom was also present when the Lord "inscribed" (בחוקו) a circle on the deep (תהום), another reference to water. This focus continues in verse 28b and 29a. The passage does not proceed along the same sequence as Genesis 1, nor contain all of the elements with which that passage deals: "so übergeht sie z.B. die Erschaffung der Vegetation, der Tiere und der Menschen, obwohl in V.31 die Menschen vorausgesetzt werden."[106] This could be explained as an accident of textual history (i.e., that Genesis 1 was not available and/or known to the author). Raymond van Leeuwen offers another route: the focus on waters is a culturally appropriate one for teaching Wisdom's knowledge of the limits of creation.

> The appearance of this phrase [לא עברו־פיו, "so as not to transgress my mouth"] in reference to the waters of the chaotic sea in Prov 8:29 establishes the congruity of Wisdom's order with the divine word of command. We might say that to disobey or transgress ('br) the limits set by God via his agent Wisdom is both to act contrary to the nature of reality and to disobey the "word" of God.[107]

In van Leeuwen's interpretation, the focus on water is due its role as a symbol of death and chaos. Various passages throughout the Old Testament attest to the Lord's conquest of these forces of chaos (cf. Job 26:12; Pss 74:12–17; 77:16; 89:10). However, here the purpose is not to glorify God's

---

105. The nature of these contesting appeals is not one of piling up evidence and counter-evidence on rational scales. Rather, it appeals to the desires of the reader and their sense of what kind of person they want to be. This kind of dynamic is explored by Charles Taylor under the heading of "Strong Evaluation" in his article "What is Human Agency?" and then deployed in his magisterial *A Secular Age*.

106. Plöger, *Sprüche Salomos*, 94.

107. Van Leeuwen, "Liminality and Worldview in Proverbs 1–9," 124.

conquest, but to raise the profile of Wisdom as a worthwhile guide to a successful life.[108]

Wisdom then, in verses 25–29, asserts her qualifications to teach her students of the right way because she was present when the LORD put the waters in their place. "Wisdom's presence not only at the abyss [of waters], but even at the void before its origin, impressively establishes her claim to authority."[109] At the abyss the decrees of the Lord restrain or bound chaos: the LORD decreed/inscribed (בחוקו) a circle on the face of the deep (v. 27b); He decreed (חקן) the boundaries of the sea (v. 29a) and the foundations of the earth (בחוקו מוסדי ארץ) (v. 29b). Lexically, this connects with the previous assertion that by Wisdom "princes decree righteous things" (8:15b). Wisdom enables this effective rule because she knows of God's foundational decrees, which hold back primordial chaos. The selection of only certain features of the creation account focuses on this capacity for right relationship in creation. "Es geht ihr darum, die beiden wesentlichen Schöpfungswerke, Himmel und Erde, Himmelsgewölbe und Erde in Form einer Scheibe über der Tiefe, in die rechte Beziehung zum wässerigen Element zu bringen."[110] Within the realm of governance, Wisdom facilitates the restraint of societal chaos such as injustice and unrighteousness. Conceptually one can then discern a link with the rest of Proverbs 8. Wisdom calls for attention to her words because they offer one that which is needed to live within the God-ordained limits of the created order (her words functioning similarly to the decrees of the LORD). Her paths are paths of righteousness and justice (v. 20), qualities which maintain the human character and behavior within morally appropriate limits. Thus, the description of the acts of creation in verses 25–29 function to exalt Wisdom in the eyes of the reader.[111]

The final two verses of this section of Proverbs 8 speak of Wisdom's ongoing relationship with the LORD God of Israel. Wisdom is still present with the LORD, faithfully (אָמוֹן) by His side as a recipient of His delight. The proper translation of אָמוֹן has been a *crux interpretum* for many centuries. Not only is the word a *hapax legomenon*, but there are other theological considerations which come into play, most notably the idea that Wisdom was an active agent in the creation of the world. Some are ambivalent about this idea even being present in the text. For example, Bernd Schipper, who

---

108. Cf. Loader, *Proverbs*, 351.
109. Loader, *Proverbs*, 353.
110. Plöger, *Sprüche Salomos*, 94.
111. L. Boström, *The God of the Sages*, 72–73.

favors an adverbial translation ("continually"), asserts that "the role of Wisdom [in the creative acts of the LORD] remains unstated in this understanding of אָמוֹן."[112] On the other hand, Fox argues that the text disallows the idea of Wisdom as an active agent: "the emphasis on play and delight makes the stanza seem an almost deliberate repudiation of the idea that Wisdom served as a craftsman or architect in creation.... In Prov 8, during creation Wisdom only frolicked about and gave pleasure to her divine guardian."[113] In something of a middle position stands R. W. L. Moberly, who translates the word adverbially ("faithfully") yet, through an intertextual connection to Proverbs 3:19–20, reasons "Thus, the Wisdom who is present when God creates should be seen as in some way God's agent in that act of creating: God creates in/by/with/through Wisdom."[114] In this issue the wider context of reading shapes what options one views as available and reasonable. It is not apparent that Wisdom's role in creation is a central concern of this section of the poem.[115] However, when read alongside Genesis 1,[116] the intertextual relationships suggests that Wisdom corresponds with God, the Spirit, and/or the spoken word of God and therefore was actively involved. Reading these passages together depends on other factors, such as one's view of potential meanings of the text other than an original, historical meaning.

Wisdom's reception of the LORD's delight is reciprocated by her own joy, which she then also shares with His created world. Her own delight is bestowed upon humanity.[117] Indeed, her joy is being *with* them (את־בני אדם), analogous to God's delight in her as she is alongside (אצלו) the LORD. Wisdom is thus pictured as standing both in the presence of God and of

112. Schipper, *Proverbs 1–15*, 313. This view is shared by Plöger, *Sprüche Salomos*, 95–96.

113. Fox, *Proverbs 1–9*, 288.

114. Moberly, *The God of the Old Testament*, 27.

115. Of course, this argument may be circular. If a translation of אָמוֹן as artisan was taken, then it would pressure one to view Wisdom's role as a main point of the poem. Which comes first, the translation or the sense of the passage?

116. Genesis Rabbah provides a non-Christian example of these two passages being brought together. The book came together sometime around A.D. 400. See *Genesis Rabbah: The Judaic Commentary to the Book of Genesis*, 1:1–2.

117. The phrase ending verse 31 is בני אדם, which is fitting for two reasons. First, it nicely rounds off this section which began with the divine Name. Thus, Wisdom's movement, as it were, is from the LORD toward humanity. Second, it echoes her call to all humanity (בני אדם) in verse 4, which reiterates her invitation to all to hear her and learn from her.

humanity within creation. Her presence is characterized by joy, laughing, and delight. The function of these verses vis-à-vis the aim of Proverbs 8 to exalt Wisdom is two-fold. First, Lady Wisdom remains faithful to the Lord and can therefore be a trustworthy guide to His paths and plans for those who would learn from her and fear the Lord. Second, she delights in sharing with the sons of Adam that which she has received from the Lord, once again underlining her trustworthiness as a guide to right living.[118]

The final verses of Proverbs 8 offer a final exhortation to the hearer/reader to heed Wisdom's call.

> 32 And now, O sons, listen to me,
>   for blessed are they keeping my ways.
> 33 Hear discipline and be wise;
>   Do not neglect it.
> 34 Blessed is the man who listens to me,
>   who watches at my doors daily,
>   who guards the doorposts of my doorways.
> 35 For the one who finds me finds life,
>   and obtains favor from the Lord.
> 36 But the one who offends against me harms his life,
>   and all those who hate me love death.

These closing words reiterate the call to attend to Wisdom. The previous thirty-one verses have related Wisdom's self-revelation of her worth. Now the purpose of that description is made clear: that the sons would listen and find blessing (אשרי), divine favor (רצון מיהוה), and life (חיים).

The way of Wisdom is characterized as discipline (מוסר), a term used in the introduction to the book (cf. Prov 1:2). The term designates "correction, whether by verbal rebuke or physical punishment."[119] The connotation is that Wisdom's path is difficult and requires constant vigilance, a feature also communicated by the need to keep watch "daily" (v. 34). This daily work of the student mirrors Wisdom's own daily habit of being in God's presence (cf. 8:30). To find her and love her diligently renders one in good standing with the Lord of Israel. Significantly, "Wisdom plays the primary role in relation to man, but the fact that favour from the Lord results from finding her is of theological importance."[120] To spurn this invitation and its

---

118. Loader approves of van Leeuwen's reading of the passage which grounds human order in the cosmic order. "That is why vv. 22–31 culminate in the incorporation of humankind in the celebration." Loader, *Proverbs*, 356.

119. Fox, *Proverbs 1–9*, 34.

120. L. Boström, *The God of the Sages*, 150. An understanding of the theological

requisite discipline is to love death. Such a stark statement strikes a similar note to the ending of Proverbs 7, which describes the way of the "forbidden woman" (זרה) as one leading to the chamber of death (Prov 7:27).

Proverbs 8 thus ends on the call for the reader to decide on one of two paths, and there are only two from which to choose in the presentation of the book. The way of Lady Wisdom offers life while the way of the forbidden woman offers death. The way of life requires daily, constant vigilance on the part of the student. One reason for this is the ubiquitous call of Wisdom: she can be heard in any location (Prov 8:1–3) and calling to all sorts of people (Prov 8:4). She knows the ways of God woven into all of creation (Prov 8:22–31) and, presumably, must be heard in all aspects of life. However, as people attend to her virtuous ways, they not only are promised material gain, but a reward even better than that: righteousness, justice, blessing, life, and divine favor.

---

importance of this relationship between Wisdom and the LORD will be explored particularly in the portion of chapter 9 entitled, "A Possible Trinitarian Reading of Proverbs 8."

SECTION 2

Reading the History of Interpretation to Deepen Our Engagement with Proverbs 8

IN THE LAST CHAPTER, Proverbs 8 was read within its literary context. Doing so provides a firm basis for understanding the text. My aim in this book is to read this passage as Christian Scripture, such that one's life can be more faithfully lived before the presence of God. This goal is concomitant with taking up Proverbs 8 as Scripture, rather than only as an historical document and/or a literary classic. To read Proverbs 8 as Christian Scripture is to read it as part of a tradition. But how should we understand the impact of tradition on reading an ancient document? What dangers does this pose for reading, and what benefits might be offered through a proper awareness of the tradition?

In this second section I take up these questions. First, Hans-Georg Gadamer provides a philosophical foundation for understanding the influence, danger, and benefit of tradition for reading. Then I embark on a representative survey of the history of interpretation of Proverbs 8 in order to deepen our awareness of the potential meaning of this text for Christian faith. I will then conclude with some reflection on what has been gained and lost through the ages.

3

The Historically Effected Consciousness

HANS-GEORG GADAMER ASSERTS THAT "historically effected consciousness (*wirkungsgeschichtliches Bewußtsein*) is an element in the act of understanding itself and, as we shall see, is already effectual in *finding the right questions to ask*."[1] In the scope of Gadamer's argument, the role of history in interpretation is different from a prominent understanding of it in biblical studies since at least the eighteenth century. Krister Stendahl's famous article on contemporary biblical theology offers a helpful foundation upon which to appreciate the role of history in some forms of biblical studies,[2] and from which to understand the difference that Gadamer's approach might make.[3] As such, my aim below is to offer an account of Stendahl's argument for a constructive, rather than argumentative, purpose. Then I will engage Gadamer's concept of *wirkungsgeschichtliches Bewußtsein* within the parameters set by Stendahl's approach.

Stendahl's article provides a dictionary statement of the approach of biblical theology in the mid-twentieth century. He credits the *religionsgeschichtliche Schule* with emphasizing a "distance between biblical times and modern times."[4] Three effects of this new emphasis were: a loosening of assumptions regarding progression or regression in different stages to which

1. Gadamer, *Truth and Method*, 312. Emphasis original.

2. Stendahl, "Biblical Theology, Contemporary," 418–32.

3. Gadamer's arguments have generated a vast amount of scholarly material. My aim is to provide a clear articulation of the difference his approach makes for biblical studies vis-à-vis the somewhat paradigmatic statement of Stendahl's. I am not offering a history of Gadamer's reception nor an evaluation of said reception. Therefore, I am passing over this material.

4. Stendahl, "Biblical Theology, Contemporary," 418.

the Bible bears witness; the facticity of events was relativized to the import of the message of a text, as understood within its particular *Sitz im Leben*; and the "question about relevance for present-day religion and faith was waived, or consciously kept out of sight."[5] Various responses to this school of study have been advanced, to which Stendahl gives his attention. From the remainder of his article, two facets are worth noting for the present study: the possibility of descriptive theology and the question of the meaning of the Bible for the present.

As for this first concern, Stendahl advocates a strong distinction between what a text meant within its own historical setting and what it can mean today. The former is the descriptive task of biblical theology and the latter offers a translation of this description into the life-world of the present. In maintaining this distinction, Stendahl is not unaware of the historians' position within their own particular moment. "Every historian is subjective in the selection of his material, and it is often said that he does more harm when he thinks himself to be objective—i.e., when he does not recognize, not to say openly state, what his presuppositions and preconceived ideas are."[6] Human objectivity is, for Stendahl, a relative objectivity, and preconceptions can be corrected through attention to the material itself.[7] Within this slightly chastened objectivity, "our only concern is to find out what these words meant when uttered or written by the prophet, the priest, the evangelist, or the apostle—and regardless of their meaning in later stages of religious history, our own included."[8] Stendahl's model suggests two static components of the interpretive event: one being the interpreter and the other the text under study. The interpreter is as a miner coming with tools to the text: he or she must remove the rust (preconceptions) in order to uncover the raw ore (the historical meaning of the text).

---

5. Stendahl, "Biblical Theology, Contemporary," 419.

6. Stendahl, "Biblical Theology, Contemporary," 422.

7. As such, these preconceptions only function negatively. This is not a position unique to Stendahl. Robert Elliot detects this same overly negative conception of one's "horizon" in the work of Jean-Luc Marion. "Marion . . . argues that the horizon constrains phenomena and prohibits them from giving themselves in the fullest degree of what they are in themselves, for the horizon delimits in advance the way in which these phenomena can appear. The horizon, on his account, has an inherently violent and alienating function, for all phenomena are required to derive from it." Elliot, "Givenness and Hermeneutics," 667–68.

8. Stendahl, "Biblical Theology, Contemporary," 422.

The static nature of both the reader's presuppositions and the text is illustrated by Stendahl's statement that the "descriptive task can be carried out by the believer and agnostic alike."[9] Both are capable of a proper description of the meaning of the text in its historical setting. The believer must be mindful that their faith "constantly threatens" to contemporize[10] the text; the agnostic "has the advantage of feeling no such temptation, but his power of empathy must be considerable if he is to identify himself sufficiently with the believer of the first century."[11] In this illustration, the interpreters are marked as different from one another on the basis of the presence of faith commitments that may or may not threaten the enterprise. The presence of a strong faith commitment is seen as a threat; whereas the lack of faith is an advantage in the task at hand. Both can come to a common conclusion because they are both looking at a fixed object using the same method.[12]

How then would these texts be read for what they mean today? Stendahl's answer to this question stands in continuity with his attention to the difference between what a text meant and what it means. The question of application, as we might call this, comes once "we go beyond the descriptive approach."[13] The text of the Bible is applicable when understood within the concept of canon. "It is as canon, and only as canon, that there is a Bible, an OT and a NT as well as the whole Bible of the church as a unity."[14] By reading these texts as canonical Scripture, a contemporary believer finds meanings in them for today. This meaning is found in reading the biblical texts historically and interpreting the present through that historical description. "Such a theology would conceive of the Christian existence as a life by the fruits of God's acts in Jesus Christ, rather than as a faith

---

9. Stendahl, "Biblical Theology, Contemporary," 422.

10. Stendahl uses the term "modernize." However, it seems to me that this word takes on a particular hue in present discussions regarding modernity vs. pre- and post-modernity. "Contemporize" captures more of his sense.

11. Stendahl, "Biblical Theology, Contemporary," 422.

12. Stendahl subsequently wrote about the context of his article as the debate over women's ordination in the Church of Sweden. His professors and colleagues "declared ordination of women to the priesthood to be contrary to the Bible—with no if, and, or but! . . . I had to give reasons for not signing on, and when you are in a minority of one, you have to think harder. Hence the urgent need to take the hermeneutical gap more seriously." "Dethroning Biblical Imperialism in Theology," 62–63.

13. Stendahl, "Biblical Theology, Contemporary," 428.

14. Stendahl, "Biblical Theology, Contemporary," 429.

according to concepts deduced from the teaching of the prophets, Jesus, and Paul regarding God's acts."[15] This approach of having a high regard of the text's otherness, through a sharp distinction between what it meant and what it means, nullifies one's presuppositions, and opens them up to understand, in the present, the historical utterance of the prophet, priest, evangelist, or apostle. Stendahl later came to understand that this description task involved imaginative creativity. Even so, "other members of the theological team, not least creative systematic theologians" were necessary to bring the meaning of the past into the present frame of reference.[16]

In surveying Stendahl's position I am not asserting that he represents all biblical scholars today. There has been development in the discipline since Stendahl wrote his article in 1962. Rather, the aim is to understand Gadamer and introduce the difference his approach makes for the role of history in biblical studies. Gadamer was not a biblical scholar; Stendahl provides the perspective of a practitioner of biblical studies. His article introduces the issues of history, distance, and application within the conversation in biblical studies. Thus, he has opened areas into which we may draw Gadamer in this present project to understand a biblical text in the contemporary frame.

Before moving on, we should note certain weaknesses in Stendahl's interpretive model, aptly summarized in the distinction between what the text *meant* and what it *means*. Some of these will recur in the presentation of Gadamer's position. A chief weakness of his approach is the sequential conception of first studying the past and then moving to the present. Such a model ignores the reality that one must have some conception of what one is looking for in order to find it. This is especially the case when so much of the text under study (the Bible) relates to existential and theological questions: "is there not a sense in which it is a necessary condition for understanding, with any depth and sensitivity to what . . . the texts in question 'originally meant', that we have some articulated grasp of those fundamental features of the human predicament to which those texts are constructed as elements of a response?"[17] If this is the case, then it is possible for elements of the past to be out of reach for certain cultures or

---

15. Stendahl, "Biblical Theology, Contemporary," 428.

16. "Dethroning Biblical Imperialism in Theology," 63. In this later reflection, Stendahl writes that the descriptive task "unmasks those elements in the Scriptures that have caused and do cause harm, what I like to call the undesirable side effects of our holy medicine."

17. Lash, "What Might Martyrdom Mean?," 80.

"structures of feeling."[18] Understanding the past (as well as the present) is more complicated than Stendahl's excavation model, in which the past is an inert object to be mined. This static sequential model should arguably be replaced by a dialectical model of mutual interdependence between past and present.[19]

When taken up in a Christian frame of reference there is an additional problem with the approach outlined by Stendahl. This problem is not so much his conception of the role of faith; Christians are certainly tempted to read into the past what they hope to find, perhaps more so than others "because of their conviction that certain words spoken and deeds enacted in the past are of unique and enduring significance."[20] No, for the Christian the troubling feature of Stendahl's model is his treatment of the object of interpretation as meaning, rather than truth. The historical nature of academic biblical study can sometimes defer this distinction by falling back on its "historical" adjective. However, as was highlighted in the paragraph above, interpreter's experiences are drawn on in historical study and influence their understanding of the subject matter. As the Bible deals with topics of existential import, the historian is put on the spot. "It appears to be the case, therefore, that recognition of the fact that the interpretive process is concerned not only with 'meaning' but also with 'truth' obliges us to consider questions concerning the relationship between the practice of faith and the goal and function of academic reflection and inquiry as constitutive features of the hermeneutical problem."[21] For the Christian, the aim of biblical interpretation is "the faithful 'rendering' of those events, of those patterns of human action, decision and suffering, to which the texts bear original witness."[22] The interpretive process ends not in information so much as it ends in, and consists of, performance. A sharp distinction between the past and the present ignores the dialectical relationship between the two and puts the reader in the wrong attitude vis-à-vis the text for a Christian reading.

Having noted problems with Stendahl's approach, we can now proceed to Gadamer's. Three topics arise when reading Gadamer alongside Stendahl: a different understanding of the role of prejudice; the nature of

18. Lash, "What Might Martyrdom Mean?," 80.
19. Lash, "What Might Martyrdom Mean?," 81.
20. Lash, "What Might Martyrdom Mean?," 77.
21. Lash, "What Might Martyrdom Mean?," 89.
22. Lash, "What Might Martyrdom Mean?," 90.

temporal distance; and the relationship between understanding and application. Like Stendahl, Gadamer acknowledges the presence of prejudice and its capacity to distort one's reading of a text. However, for Gadamer prejudice represents a more positive and central element to the hermeneutical enterprise. Prejudice arises from one's particular horizon of life and "serves, not only as the limit of our understanding, but also as the condition of possibility for coming to understand anything unfamiliar."[23] Prejudice provides a fore-conception of the meaning of the whole of the text and its subject matter, without which one could not understand the constituent parts or details. According to Gadamer, "'prejudice' certainly does not necessarily mean a false judgment, but part of the idea is that it can have either a positive or a negative value."[24]

Prejudices arise from one's embeddedness in history; it is a facet of one's participation in traditions of reading.[25] However, people are not always aware of their participation in a tradition, and the incumbent presence of prejudice. Prejudices, which enable an initial understanding of the text, are brought to the fore when the text becomes confusing, and a reader can then submit the prejudice to questioning. A prejudice is negative if it does not accord with the text, and the only way to correct it would be through interaction with the text. Gadamer is here consistent with Stendahl, with one crucial difference: for Gadamer, these presuppositions are not set

---

23. Elliot, "Givenness and Hermeneutics," 668.

24. Gadamer, *Truth and Method*, 283.

25. Mark Gilks critiques Gadamer for "hypostasizing tradition as an extra-individual, ontological force which 'effects' consciousness." Gilks, "Aesthetic Experience and the Unfathomable," 195. His article is nuanced; however, his comments display reliance on an anthropology in which reality is confined to what goes on in one's head, with an attendant disengaged or disembodied epistemology. For example, he summarizes one set of his remarks as follows: "To put it crudely, if the artwork 'speaks' to me, then the voices are in my head. To the extent that what I have argued follows, the proper object of hermeneutical analysis should be this internal dialogue, and the focus should be on immanent fore-conceptions of temporality." Gilks, "Aesthetic Experience and the Unfathomable," 197. Within such a view, redolent of so much labelled "Cartesian," it is understandable why tradition as an external force would be unacceptable. If, however, we understand Gadamer as coming from an epistemology and anthropology in which one is embedded and engaged in the world, then knowledge comes about through interaction with the known. And these interactions take place within a habitus of practices which are required to make sense of them. As such, this is a more social and embodied view of humanity. A useful conversation partner here would be Charles Taylor, particularly his "Lichtung or Lebensform," 61–78.

aside in historical study.²⁶ Rather than being discarded, they are adjusted through the process of interpretation. This is the case because the rightness or otherwise of one's prejudices is only known through an interaction with the text; this cannot be determined beforehand. Consequently, some prejudices remain and some are sifted out, but they are always present as an enabling factor for reading. Because these prejudices are passed on to a reader as tradition, Gadamer can argue, "Understanding is to be thought of less as a subjective act than as participating in an event of tradition, a process of transmission in which past and present are constantly mediated."²⁷

In Stendahl's approach, present prejudice was to be set aside, which includes any faith commitments and concomitant awareness of a text's meaning in the present, in order to engage in a descriptive, historical reading of a text. Tradition, it seems, is a disadvantage for the study of the Bible. In contrast, for Gadamer, tradition is an essential part of understanding the Bible and becomes a feature for consideration in the interpretive process. This raises the question of whether there is any value in an historical mode of study; what significance is there in the temporal distance between a text's originating context and a reader?

Gadamer shares with Stendahl a value for respecting the otherness of the text. For Gadamer this value is not expressed and maintained through grounding the meaning of the text in its historical moment of origination (the "what it meant" phase). Texts do arise out of particular historical circumstances, but Gadamer's position leads him to maintain a high value for the historical particularity of the reader, such that if the reader understands at all, "we understand in a different way."²⁸ Following on from this, the aim of understanding a text is the truth of what is said rather than "a mere expression of life" by an individual.²⁹ Within this frame, temporal distance

---

26. These tradition-provided points of view cannot be set aside because "history does not belong to us; we belong to it." Gadamer, *Truth and Method*, 288–89.

27. Gadamer, *Truth and Method*, 302.

28. Gadamer, *Truth and Method*, 307. This position militates against two views: one, that history can be understood objectively, as a fixed object independent of the observer; and two, that we can adopt wholesale, and without alteration, positions held in the past. Sandra Schneiders writes, "there is a real difference, due to effective historical consciousness, between a naive precritical literalism in biblical interpretation and postcritical fundamentalism, even though they might both defend the historical facticity of the story of Jonah and the sea monster. Pre-Enlightenment naive literalists enjoyed an immediacy with the subject matter of the text that is no longer possible, no matter how committed to the historical inerrancy of the text one might be." Schneiders, *The Revelatory Text*, 68.

29. Gadamer, *Truth and Method*, 308.

plays a positive role, rather than presenting an obstacle to be overcome. Knowledge of temporal distance forms an historical consciousness, which opens the reader to the possibility of prejudices which lead to a misunderstanding of the text, alongside those which lead to understanding. Consequent reading of others' interpretations in the tradition helpfully raises questions about the contemporary reader's prejudices, and aid in the filtering process to bring about an understanding of the text's claims to truth.

Thus, to say that understanding takes place with a historically effected consciousness (*wirkungsgeschichtliches Bewußtsein*) is both a description and a challenge. It is a description because history, in the form of tradition, provides one with the prejudgments necessary to understand a text at all (and also to take the trouble to engage with the text in the first place). It is a challenge to be aware of this formation, aware of one's hermeneutical situation, and therefore open to the dialectic by which the text and the reader can "mutually inform, enable, correct and enlighten each other."[30]

With regards to reading in an historical mode, one might be tempted to think of two horizons: the present horizon of understanding of the reader and the past horizon of the original author or voice of tradition. To posit this would not be unlike a restatement of Stendahl's position, in which one's expectations and preconceptions are fixed, can be set aside, and a fixed object can be studied. However, this is not the case. Per Gadamer, horizons are not fixed, but always in motion, always changing based on the constant changes of one's life.

> When our historical consciousness transposes itself into historical horizons, this does not entail passing into alien worlds unconnected in any way with our own; instead, they together constitute the one great horizon that moves from within and that, beyond the frontiers of the present, embraces the historical depths of our self-consciousness.[31]

Reading a text historically is thus a deepening of our self-consciousness rather than a discovery of something "out there." This is not a philosophical form of narcissism, but a position that presents a consistent position on what it means to understand; "we must imagine the other situation. But into this other situation we must bring, precisely, ourselves."[32] In this dia-

---

30. Lash, "Interpretation and Imagination," 25.
31. Gadamer, *Truth and Method*, 315.
32. Gadamer, *Truth and Method*, 315.

The Historically Effected Consciousness

lectic, one must remain open to the text, as the "other," and seek out places in which our prejudices are provoked and challenged.

The impossibility of excluding ourselves in the hermeneutical process helpfully clarifies the aim of interpreting a text. Per Gadamer, it is a fusion of horizons, a new understanding of one's present situation in life. One can hear an echo with Stendahl's aim in his desire for the reality presented in the text to define one's contemporary life.[33] Both see that prejudice can mislead one in this quest. However, for Gadamer, tradition remains salutary; "Only then [when one guards against overhasty assimilation of the text to the present] can we listen to tradition in a way that permits it to make its own meaning heard."[34] The past is not reified but is a facet of present understanding by which one can gain a greater understanding of the truth of life vis-à-vis a conversation with the text in light of tradition.

These considerations lead us into a final area of reflection, which is the relationship between understanding the text and application. This question is addressed again in the third section of the book. As such, our discussion here can be brief. In Stendahl's approach, application follows on after the descriptive task of biblical theology. However, as we have seen, for Gadamer, "understanding always involves something like applying the text to be understood to the interpreter's present situation."[35] As there is no way of making the text a totally alien environment, the interpreter is always present and understanding the text within their own frame of reference. As such, understanding and application cannot be conceived of as successive steps in the interpretive enterprise. Within this frame, attention must be paid to the text's relation to the present, otherwise one is ignoring the fact that they understand with an historically effected consciousness, and one's tradition-provided prejudices remain hidden and unexamined.

In this second section, I approach the history of interpretation of Proverbs 8 in a mode informed by Gadamer. This survey functions to interact with the tradition which has valued the passage in various ways. At the outset of the present argument, I quoted Gadamer's assertion that "historically effected consciousness (*wirkungsgeschichtliches Bewußtsein*) is an element in the act of understanding itself and, as we shall see, is already effectual in *finding the right questions to ask*."[36] Following this perspective,

---

33. Stendahl, "Biblical Theology, Contemporary," 428.
34. Gadamer, *Truth and Method*, 316.
35. Gadamer, *Truth and Method*, 318–19.
36. Gadamer, *Truth and Method*, 312. Emphasis original.

then, I will engage with the history of interpretation in order to find questions to ask of the text, and the text of the reader.[37] My aim is to survey enough of the interpreters' work to gain an appreciation of the historical particularity of their approach which can correspondingly illuminate the historical particularity of the contemporary reader. As we then return to the text, the potential for a mutual encounter between the text and the contemporary world will be deepened.

---

37. Stephen Fowl also engages with Gadamer and the concept of *wirkungsgeschichtliches Bewußtsein*. "Effective History," 153–61. His aim is to provide a different account for engaging with the history of tradition, distinct from the theory and practice of reception history. His conclusion is focused on the general practices of theological interpretation, advocating patience for the discipline to develop over time.

4

Pre-Modern Christian Readings of Proverbs 8

Athanasius' Exegesis of Proverbs 8

MAURICE DOWLING OBSERVES, "In Patristic Christology, the concept of Wisdom became very prominent, and the portrayal of Wisdom in Proverbs 8—especially vv. 22–31—was one of the most popular OT passages applied to Christ."[1] Athanasius of Alexandria stands in this tradition of reading Proverbs 8 in relation to the doctrine of Christology. Although Athanasius of Alexandria drew on many texts of Scripture in his work defending Nicene Christology, Proverbs 8 was a crucial text for him and his opponents. The current project seeks to read Proverbs 8 within a Nicene framework. Because of the prominence of Athanasius' writings in the church's vigorous debates regarding the nature of Christ vis-à-vis God,[2] it behooves us to explicate his views and exegetical moves. Even so, it should be acknowledged that Athanasius followed something of an innovative interpretation of the passage, in relation to many who had preceded him. As will be explored below, Athanasius read the passage as, at least in part,

---

1. "Proverbs 8:22–31 in the Christology of the Early Fathers," 99. Dowling provides a helpful summary of some of the major interpreters who preceded Athanasius. Drawing the same conclusion, Christopher Seitz asserts that Proverbs 8 received so much attention from Athanasius because "it was the place where the battle was already being fought, and had been for some time." Seitz, *The Elder Testament*, 204. On the issue of referring to Arians in a unified way, Rowan Williams asserts that "there was no such thing in the fourth century as a single, coherent 'Arian' party." Williams, *Arius*, 233. It is possible that Athanasius' presentation of such a unified position is, in fact, a rhetorical and polemical strategy. See Lewis Ayres, *Nicaea and Its Legacy*, 106–7.

2. Pelikan, *The Christian Tradition*, 172.

referring to the incarnation of the Son of God. This strategy had previously been deployed by Marcellus of Ancyra, who faced resistance on the basis of its novelty, as well as its difficulty in maintaining consistency in relation to the whole of Proverbs 8:22–31.[3] Athanasius' interpretation changes that of Marcellus. However, even though he "avoids the strained exegesis which we find in Marcellus . . . Athanasius too is open to the charge of inconsistency in his handling of Proverbs 8:22–31."[4]

In what follows, I will survey Athanasius' argument in his *Second Oration Against the Arians*[5] because, of Athanasius' writings, this work interacts most with Proverbs 8, particularly verse 22.[6]

A Survey of Athanasius' Second Oration Against the Arians

Athanasius' interaction with Proverbs 8 begins in section 18b of his work (357). "Athanasius announces this text [Proverbs 8] three times only to defer treatment of it while dealing with other major texts (the first two times) or presenting a lengthy introductory essay on related themes (the third time)."[7] In the light of the work of Frances Young, these introductory comments (or essays, due to their length) are best understood as appropriate parts of the interpretive process derived from the Greco-Roman literary culture. Young includes terms such as *to methodikon* and *to historikon* as essential moves propounded by Quintilian in his rules for rhetoric, rules which influenced early Christian biblical interpretation.[8] The first of these, *to methodikon*, involved "analysing its sentences into parts of speech and its verses into metre, noting linguistic usage and style, discussing different meanings of words, elucidating figures of speech or ornamental devices."[9] Also included in this aspect of analyzing texts was resolving perceived problems in the text through recourse to other parts of the text.[10] As a reading of

---

3. Dowling, "Proverbs 8:22–31 in the Christology of the Early Fathers," 106. Dowling summarizes Eusebius' objections to Marcellus' interpretation.

4. Dowling, "Proverbs 8:22–31 in the Christology of the Early Fathers," 116.

5. Athanasius of Alexandria, *Contra Arianos II*, 348–93. Because this is the primary text for this section, I will note references using in-text parentheses.

6. Ernest, *The Bible in Athanasius of Alexandria*, 118–20.

7. Ernest, *The Bible in Athanasius of Alexandria*, 119–20.

8. Young, *Biblical Exegesis and the Formation of Christian Culture*, 78–81.

9. Young, *Biblical Exegesis and the Formation of Christian Culture*, 78.

10. In the Greco-Roman tradition, the texts which arguably received most attention were the Homeric epics. Young, *Biblical Exegesis and the Formation of Christian Culture*, 78.

Pre-Modern Christian Readings of Proverbs 8

Athanasius' comments illustrates, for him *the text* was not confined to the book of Proverbs, but was the entire Bible, Old and New Testaments.[11] He appeals regularly to passages in both testaments in his study of Proverbs 8. The second of Quintilian's modes of inquiry was *to historikon*, which sought to explain the story of the text. "The critical question about narrative was whether it was probable or persuasive, and the methods of assessment were *anaskeuē* (refutation) and *kataskeuē* (confirmation). . . . The methods of criticism were based in logic and comparison."[12] In this light, Athanasius' "deferrals," noted by Ernest, are understood as establishing important preliminary factors which guide the interaction with Proverbs 8.[13]

Athanasius devotes sections 18b–43 to this preliminary work, establishing what counts as appropriate speech of the Son vis-à-vis God the Father. Already in the history of reading this text, it had been established that Proverbs 8 had a Christological reference.[14] The debate into which Athanasius wades is in what way this text bears witness to Christ and what that means for the doctrine of the Son of God. In sections 18b–24, he begins by rebutting the Arian claim that the Word is a creature, albeit unlike other creatures. In congruence with Young's account, Athanasius refutes this argument through logic and comparison. First, he argues that no two creatures are alike, meaning this additional phrase "unlike other creatures" does nothing to elevate the Word above creation (II.19, 358). He rejoins, "Let the Word then be excepted from the works, and as Creator be restored to the Father, and be confessed to be Son by nature; or if simply He be a creature, then let Him be assigned the same condition as the rest one with another" (II.20, 359). Having thus established two clear options, Athanasius argues that the Word cannot be a creature because the Word created the world.[15] To establish this claim, Athanasius appeals to texts such as Proverbs 8:30

---

11. Kugel, *How to Read the Bible*, 14–17.

12. Young, *Biblical Exegesis and the Formation of Christian Culture*, 80.

13. Young writes, "Proper exegesis is achieved not simply by paying attention to words and syntax, but by attending to more overarching considerations about what is appropriate to the divine reality of which the text speaks" (*Biblical Exegesis and the Formation of Christian Culture*, 38).

14. Frances Young, "Proverbs 8 in Interpretation," 102–15. In her essay, Young cites examples from the Apologists, such as Athenagoras and Theophilus of Antioch, which illustrate the assumption of a Christological references in Proverbs 8 early on in the Christian tradition. Young, "Proverbs 8 in Interpretation," 103–4.

15. Athanasius alternates between δημιουργέω and κτίζω in discussion of the creative acts of God or the Son. While these usages may resonate differently with Athanasius' context, I will use "create" to encompass both.

(LXX) and John 5:17.[16] In the John passage, the work of the Son is coordinated with the work of the Father. As it is the Father's work to create, so is it the Son's. It is this creative work which identifies the Son with the nature of the Father, as no creature can create (II.21, 359). Athanasius adds to this argument that the Son alone reveals the Father (drawing on John 14:9,10; II.22, 360) and that the Son receives worship (established through a catena of texts; II.23, 360–361). Through these references, Athanasius grounds Proverbs 8:22, as a passage which makes a distinction between the Father and the Son, in the larger testimony of passages which identify the Father and the Son.[17]

Already in this set of sections Athanasius' tendency to appeal to other passages of Scripture is well illustrated. Recourse to the larger narrative is a mark of *to historikon*, which, for Athanasius, is not confined to the *historia* of a single passage but that of the whole of Scripture. "His highest loyalty is to the central story: the metanarrative of creation, fall, and redemption he finds running through all the particular narratives of the Bible."[18] According to Young, this is emblematic of catholic[19] biblical interpretation in the early Christian period: "discerning the unitive 'mind' (*dianoia*) of scripture was seen as essential to reaching a proper interpretation."[20] This puts the interpretation of Scripture in relation to an understanding of the whole which, for the early church, was expressed in the *regula fidei*.[21] For Athanasius, "the part can be understood only in terms of the whole."[22] Athanasius is not unique in this understanding of Scripture which relates it to the whole; Arius shares this in his own interactions with Proverbs 8.[23]

---

16. O'Keefe and Reno label this the associative reading strategy of the early church fathers. *Sanctified Vision*, 63–68.

17. Pelikan, *The Christian Tradition*, 175.

18. Ernest, *The Bible in Athanasius of Alexandria*, 124.

19. I use this term somewhat anachronistically to denote interpreters held to be orthodox by the church through time.

20. Young, *Biblical Exegesis and the Formation of Christian Culture*, 29.

21. Young, *Biblical Exegesis and the Formation of Christian Culture*, 43.

22. Ernest, *The Bible in Athanasius of Alexandria*, 133.

23. Williams, *Arius*, 230–31. Williams' work focuses on understanding Arius not solely through the writings of his opponents. His exploration puts us on a firmer foundation for understanding Arius' positions. According to Williams, Arius' theological project, including his interpretation of Proverbs 8, illustrates his "seeking, so it appears, for a way of making it clear that the doctrine of creation allows no aspect of the created order to enter into the definition of God." Williams, *Arius*, 231. In this work, Arius is to be conceived of primarily as a theologian, not a philosopher.

Pre-Modern Christian Readings of Proverbs 8

Continuing on, sections 24b–30 maintain focus on what is proper language in relation to the nature of God, the Father, and the Son. Athanasius continues his line of reasoning vis-à-vis the creative act of God and attends to various objections made by Arians to Nicene Christology. He references John 1:3 and notes that the Word is not included in the "all" which was made through him:

> whereas when Scripture speaks of the Word, it does not understand Him as being in the number of "all," but places Him with the Father, as Him in whom Providence and salvation for "all" are wrought and effected by the Father, though all things surely might at the same command have come to be, at which He was brought into being by God alone. (II.24b, 361o)

The last comment initiates a discussion of an Arian argument in which the Son is instrumental to creation, rather than essential to the nature of God. According to the Arians (at least as understood through Athanasius), the Son was created as something of a demiurge, either because God was too proud to be involved in creation or because the creation could not stand direct contact with the Creator. In response, Athanasius argues that God is not proud, but condescends in care for His creatures (II.25, 362). As for the need for a demiurge due to the weakness of creation, the Son as a creature does not solve this problem, for he, too, as a creature, would be unable to withstand the direct impress of God's working (II.26, 362). Contrary to the Arian position, Athanasius asserts repeatedly that the Son does create, which separates him from all created beings, such as Moses (II.27, 362–63). According to Athanasius, some argued that the Son was taught the ability to create; he counters by asserting that if the Son was taught to create, then it was possible that God was also taught this. Additionally, it could then be said that numerous angels and archangels were also taught to frame, which would run counter to Scripture's witness that there is only one creator.

Sections 31–43 form the final set of introductory comments prior to attending to the text of Proverbs 8 more directly. Although the section seems wide-ranging, a common theme is the Word's uniqueness vis-à-vis the creatures. This section begins by asserting that the Son is essential to the nature of God, particularly in relation to God's creative activity, rather than being merely instrumental. His proof of this consists in attending to the structure of Genesis 1 in comparison to other passages in which God speaks. "For when God commands others, whether the Angels, or converses with Moses, or commands Abraham, then the hearer answers . . . but when the Word Himself works or creates, then there is no questioning and answer, for the Father is in Him and the Word in the Father" (II.31, 365). Here it is the uniqueness of God's creative speech versus His speech toward creatures. These remarks also illustrate Athanasius' attention to the order of the words of Scripture, as well as the high value placed on each individual word of Scripture in early Christian interpretation.[24] Next, Athanasius appeals to a catena of texts which he interprets as identifying the Father and the Son together in their essence, focusing on texts which use Wisdom, Word, and Light (II.32, 365–66). These texts are mustered in Athanasius' contention that they are God's words about Himself rather than human words about God; to disagree with them is to argue against God. Further on, human begetting is distinguished from the eternal begetting of the Son (II.35, 367). Next, the difference between human words and the Word of God is explored (II.36, 367). These moves makes sense within the framework which Athanasius has already set up, namely that there are only two categories according to which one can consider the Son: either as a creature or God.

And yet, he must also ward off an Arian contention that Christ was merely one creaturely manifestation of God's eternal wisdom and power. In other words, having argued fiercely that the Son is God, Athanasius must now argue that Christ is this Son, thereby maintaining a Nicene doctrine of God. While God has spoken many words, there is one Word which took on flesh. "Wherefore of Him alone, our Lord Jesus Christ, and of His oneness with the Father, are written and set forth the testimonies, both of the Father signifying that the Son is One, and of the saints, aware of this and saying that the Word is One, and that He is only-Begotten" (II.39, 369). Athanasius also appeals to the baptismal formula, which mentions the Father and the Son, as evidence of the unity of the Father and the Son (II.41, 370). This appeal illuminates Athanasius' frame of reference as Nicene Christianity. He seeks to interpret the Bible in general, and Proverbs 8 in particular, as bearing witness to the ontology manifest in the Nicene Creed. He certainly believes that this is the correct reading of Scripture.[25] However, his

24. The particular way of attending to each word and the order of the words in Scripture shown by Athanasius, and other patristic interpreters, shares much with both Greco-Roman and Jewish literary cultures. See Young, *Biblical Exegesis and the Formation of Christian Culture*, 76–81; Bartholomew, *Introducing Biblical Hermeneutics*, 171.

25. James Ernest concludes that Athanasius viewed the Christian shape of Scripture (bearing witness to the incarnation of the eternal Word for the redemption of humanity) as "in a dialectical way both the result and the criterion of the correct interpretation of Scripture." Ernest, *The Bible in Athanasius of Alexandria*, 150.

confidence comes from a position other than one informed by an historical awareness of the development of thought over time, which has been a prime hallmark of much modern biblical study.[26] Athanasius' conception of God is unapologetically framed within the context of the Christian tradition, including its worship.[27]

Having laid a foundation for the proper speech of the Father and the Son, Athanasius moves into considering Proverbs 8 itself, focusing on verse 22, in sections 44–82. The first six and a half sections of this effort interpret the phrases "He created me" and "a beginning of the ways" as statements of the saving mission of the Incarnate Word. At the outset, Athanasius acknowledges that his argument up to this point has been to provide the framework for a "right explanation" of the text (II.44, 372). The nature of the passage as proverbs requires greater attention to its witness, beyond a "naked" or plain reading. Within the framework established, Proverbs 8:22 cannot mean that Wisdom was created. Therefore it must relate to something other than the surface level meaning. The reader must "inquire into the person" (II.44, 372). Such an inquiry is in keeping with Athanasius' interpretive efforts elsewhere in his writings, by which the reader must attend to the occasion (καιρός), person (πρόσωπον), and the matter (πραγμα) for which a passage is written.[28] As Proverbs 8 relates to the person of Wisdom, "certain things that are necessarily true about the Wisdom of God must be read into this text."[29] Thus, Athanasius looks further on in Proverbs to chapter 9, verse 1 (II.44, 372). The house which Wisdom declares she has built is interpreted as the incarnate body of Christ. To buttress this point, Athanasius looks to how Scripture elsewhere uses the term "created."[30] He acknowledges that creatures are created, but there are other usages within

---

26. As noted in the opening chapter of this section, Krister Stendahl's essay "Biblical Theology, Contemporary" provides a paradigmatic statement for a characteristically modern approach to biblical studies, in which one must distinguish between what a text "meant" and what it "means." In contradistinction from the approach which Stendahl represents, "For the exegetes of the fourth century the issue of distinguishing the 'original' or authorial meaning of the text from other meanings did not arise." Young, "Proverbs 8 in Interpretation," 112. For a postmodern approach toward reclaiming aspects of Athanasius' premodern approach, see Lash, "What Might Martyrdom Mean?"

27. It is likely that Athanasius' opponents would make the same claim. This only strengthens my point that the issue is the proper *Christian* reading of the text.

28. See *Contra Arianos* I.54. Ernest, *The Bible in Athanasius of Alexandria*, 136–37.

29. Ernest, *The Bible in Athanasius of Alexandria*, 139.

30. Athanasius, like the majority of the early church, used the LXX, which uses the verb κτίζω. Modern Old Testament scholarship prefers the Hebrew text, which uses קנה, which has its own semantic range.

Scripture which do not mean "made from nothing." Psalm 102:18 (LXX), Psalm 51:12, Ephesians 2:25, Ephesians 4:22, as well as Jeremiah 31:22 each use the term to mean "renew." Within the context of Proverbs 8, Athanasius notes that Wisdom is not called a creature. Rather Wisdom is the object of the verb "created." He keys in on this as indicating some meaning other than the ascription of creaturehood to Wisdom. He also again appeals to the broader witness of Scripture, which he outlined in his framing comments.

> Such then being the difference between "the creatures" and the single word "He created," if you find anywhere in divine Scripture the Lord called "creature," produce it and fight; but if it is nowhere written that He is a creature, only He Himself says about Himself in the Proverbs, "The Lord created me," shame upon you, both on the ground of the distinction aforesaid and for that the diction is like that of proverbs; and accordingly let "He created" be understood, not of His being a creature, but of that human nature which became His, for to this belongs creation. (II.46, 373)

This human nature which He took upon Himself was for the purpose of renewal and salvation, which he expounds upon in section 47. Additionally, that the passage goes on to speak of the begetting of Wisdom (verses 24 and 25) is significant for Athanasius' interpretation, for this clarifies that the creation spoken of in verse 22 relates to offspring rather than a creature. His logic is that "what is made is of a different nature than the maker. What is begotten is always of the same nature as the begetter."[31] Athanasius also attends to the next phrase of verse 22, which speaks of Wisdom as "the beginning of the ways" (II.48, 374). Again appealing to Genesis 1, Athanasius argues that creation was brought into being all at once rather than incrementally. That Wisdom is created as a beginning and prior to the rest of creation[32] must, in Athanasius' logic, mean that this Wisdom is something other than a creature. Otherwise, the rest of creation would be simultaneously brought into being. Even Wisdom calling God "Lord" speaks of the mission of salvation upon which Christ was sent; he says "Lord" for the sake of the creatures, that the creatures "might have confidence to call Him by grace Father, who is by nature our Lord" (II.51, 376).

In sections 51b through 56, Athanasius explains how "for the works" (Prov 8:22b LXX) influences the reading of the text to speak of the economy

---

31. Weinandy and Keating, *Athanasius and His Legacy*, 19.

32. Presumably Athanasius is drawing this point from Proverbs 8, however he does not specify.

of salvation rather than the essence of Wisdom. According to the pattern of Scripture, one is brought into being before they are given a task: Adam, Noah, and Moses are all examples of this pattern. Thus, in Proverbs 8, that the creation of Wisdom is "for the works" must mean that Wisdom was already in existence; "but when the works were created and need arose afterwards of the Economy for their restoration, then it was that the Word took upon Himself this condescension and assimilation to the works; which He has shewn us by the word 'He created'" (II.51, 376). Such a pattern of speech is itself also repeated in relation to the Son: when the Incarnation of the Son is spoken of, the purpose is specified; when Scripture speaks of His essence, no such purpose is given (II.53–54, 377). Thus Athanasius attends to the patterns of speech in Scripture, holding them to bear witness to divine intentionality.

In sections 57 through 72a, Athanasius interprets the distinction between offspring and work through a lens of grace. He contends that Proverbs 8 participates in a broader scriptural differentiation between a work, which is a creature, and the Offspring, which is proper to the essence of the Father (II.57, 379). Various texts are called in to support this argument. While there are points at which human beings are called God's offspring, or referred to using the language of begetting, Athanasius argues that the ordering of those texts (he specifically works with Deuteronomy 32) makes it clear that creation occurred first, after which Israel was begotten, or adopted, as God's children. By contrast, in Proverbs 8 Athanasius reads verse 25b as guarding against an understanding of the Word being created first and then begotten. According to Athanasius, verse 22 states the reason for which the Word took on flesh, but then verse 25b serves to teach that the Word existed before being created (that is, taking on a body). Athanasius then launches into an extended discussion (sections 62 through 70) of the title Firstborn, which is not explicitly mentioned in Proverbs 8, which leads to further meditations on the nature of the gospel message and what it teaches about the nature of God. He argues that, even though the Son is referred to as both only-begotten (μονογενης)[33] and firstborn (πρωτοτοκος), "μονογενης is used absolutely . . . correct, because it characterizes the Son's relation to the Father; whereas πρωτοτοκος . . . is to be interpreted in terms

---

33. Modern scholarship has tended to argue that there is a linguistic difference between μονογενης (unique) and μονογεννητος (only-begotten). See Moody, "God's Only Son," 213–19. Athanasius uses μονογενης (see II.37, 48, 54, 62, 74, 78, and 80). However, this distinction does not change the import of Athanasius' argument; he is passionately asserting that the Son is uniquely related to the Father through eternal generation. For more, see Giles, *The Eternal Generation of the Son*, 104–18.

Wisdom in the World

of relationship to the created universe."³⁴ His aim is again to reinforce that it is inappropriate to speak of the Son as a creature. In section 71 he returns to Proverbs 8, noting that "He has said with exact discrimination, 'for the works'; as much as to say 'The Father as made Me into flesh, that I might be man,' which again shews that He is not a work but an offspring" (II.71, 387).

The lack of sharp distinction between theology and exegesis is a hallmark of early Christian biblical interpretation. For Athanasius, "Interpretation is in the first instance not explication of a text but explanation of a reality" and in this task, Athanasius was "interested in theological meaning, not terminological [or methodological] consistency."³⁵ The text is understood to participate fully in the revealed reality of God, proclaimed through the church's Rule of Faith, and read in all the Scriptures. As a consequence, the whole of Scripture lies as one interwoven tapestry.

The final argument of Athanasius' *Second Oration*, sections 72b through 82, is concerned with Proverbs 8:23b, which Athanasius renders, "He founded me before the world" (II.72b, 388). It seems that Athanasius draws attention to a potential contradiction in the text of his own accord,³⁶ as he "how can He who founds be founded?" (II.73, 288).³⁷ Once again, Athanasius explains this as referring to the incarnation of the Son. This foundation was for the sake of the works, for their salvation, as the foundation upon which the church may be built (II.74, 388). This founding can be said to occur before the world because other passages of Scripture speak of salvation willed before the world began.

In summary, Athanasius' work begins by laying the ground rules for proper speech about the Son vis-à-vis God. These are founded upon a holistic reading of Scripture and the church's received faith.³⁸ The parameters could largely be summarized as "Whatever is said of the Father must be said of the Son." With this conception of the subject matter explained, Proverbs 8 is interpreted as referring not to the essence of God but of the economy

---

34. Ernest, *The Bible in Athanasius of Alexandria*, 165.

35. Ernest, *The Bible in Athanasius of Alexandria*, 165, 166.

36. Unlike other arguments in *Contra Arianos II*, Athanasius does not here quote or make reference to an Arian position.

37. O'Keefe and Reno refer to this as the dialectical reading strategy of the early church. O'Keefe and Reno, *Sanctified Vision*, 56–63.

38. Rowan Williams contends that Arius was more the theological conservative, at least with regard to language of God, whereas Athanasius perceived that, in order to maintain the church's faith there needed to be innovation in the language used to speak of God. Williams, *Arius*, 234–35.

of salvation. Such a reading is grounded in references to the structure and order of other portions of Scripture compared with that of Proverbs 8, along with attention to the ordering of the words in the chapter itself. Even though his interpretation can be said to relate to a broader understanding of the whole of Scripture, it is difficult to understand how it can be integrated with the remainder of Proverbs 8, particularly verses 26–31. Like Marcellus' interpretation, which had preceded Athanasius' in reading these verses in relation to the economy of salvation, there appears a need to shift the sense in which Wisdom is being spoken when the text begins to speak of the time during creation.[39] However, it is possible that this critique stems from a set of assumptions different from those shared by Athanasius and the context of early Christian interpretation. It is to this possibility that we now turn.

Hermeneutical Reflection on Athanasius' Reading of Proverbs 8

Christopher Seitz writes of his surprise, when he first began to interact with Athanasius' writing on Proverbs 8, of "the impossibility of extracting a page or two . . . the discussion went on for over fifty single-spaced pages."[40] The length and depth of Athanasius' reading is only one facet of his argument which can strike the modern reader as odd. Paul Joyce is representative when he writes, "it is nevertheless hard to escape the sense that the biblical text is being distorted and even abused in such Patristic exegesis. Proverbs 8 is hijacked and manipulated to suit the demands of the internal conflicts and polemics of developing Christianity."[41] According to an historical-critical reading of Proverbs 8:22–31, the passage refers to "a quality or feature of God, his wisdom, which is here personified. A *plain reading* suggests that this is simply a literary motif, a vivid way of describing the wisdom exercised by God in his creative activity, rather than a positing of an agent in any sense distinct."[42] Wisdom is not to be read in any as bearing witness

---

39. Dowling, "Proverbs 8:22–31 in the Christology of the Early Fathers," 114.

40. Seitz, *The Elder Testament*, 204.

41. Joyce, "Proverbs 8 in Interpretation," 89. To be fair to the fullness of Joyce's argument, he returns to and re-evaluates "the severe criticisms we made earlier of the Patristic interpretations of Proverbs 8." Joyce, "Proverbs 8 in Interpretation," 99. He advocates something akin to moving from the first to the second naivete in a contemporary approach to the text, in which one honors historical criticism but also seeks something more than the "original" meaning of a passage.

42. Joyce, "Proverbs 8 in Interpretation," 93. Emphasis added.

to the reality of God; it is "simply a literary motif." And this is the plain reading.

This term that Paul Joyce uses, and which I have highlighted in the quote from him, draws out a central concern in the history of interpretation: reading according to the "plain sense" of Scripture. An historical-critical approach has asserted that the plain sense is rendered when a text is read within its originating setting, whereby one can account for its location in the history of ideas and guard against distorting the text to fit one's own ends. Guarding the integrity of the text is a worthy goal. However, reading Athanasius, and learning that his interaction with the text was not novel or unique, raises some questions as to what constitutes the "plain" reading of the text. After all, if Athanasius' style of reading Proverbs 8 was, for the most part, common, would that not be a "plain reading" for his day? Or could it be that Scripture is such that "plain reading" is intrinsically more demanding that many modern discussions envisage?

If one can see past the conclusions and arguments which can seem so foreign to a modern reader, Athanasius addresses many concerns that are similar to a modern approach to Scripture. He is not as distant from us as one may first suppose. He pays attention to the genre of the text, noting that Proverbs 8 is poetic rather than prosaic, which necessitates the adjustment of one's reading strategy (II.44, 372). He allows for words, such as κτιζω, to have a range of meanings, and seeks this range within material of a common genre, as in Psalm 51:18 (52:18 LXX) (II.46, 373). The syntax of the particular phrases receives attention, as he notes whether a term is used absolutely or relative to another object (II.51b, 376). He likewise has a place in his argument for context, as he must address how his interpretation of verse 22 fits with verse 23 (II.72b, 388).

Even having marked these methodological convergences, Athanasius is different from a modern reader. And yet, he was not so strange to his contemporaries, as I have noted above. Athanasius read and interpreted Scripture within a milieu for which the Bible was cryptic, but which nevertheless had a message for every Christian.[43] Reading Scripture aware of our historically effected consciousness does not raise this critique in order to advocate a return to pre-modern exegesis. Such a return is not possible for us, as even doing so would necessarily involve an awareness of development and distance in the history of ideas. However, encountering such a different style of reading, which nevertheless was standard for its day in

---

43. Kugel, *How to Read the Bible*, 14–17.

the church, invites the reader to raise questions about their own reading. That is, it invites us to query regarding the plain sense: plain to whom, and according to what standards?

In raising this question, we return to issues which Gadamer sought to address in *Truth and Method*. "A person who is trying to understand a text is always projecting. He projects a meaning for the text as a whole as soon as some initial meaning emerges in the text. Again, the initial meaning emerges only because he is reading the text with particular expectations in regard to a certain meaning."[44] The kind of meaning that emerges from the text is related to the expectations brought to the text by the reader. Foregrounding one's expectations are a helpful way of accounting for this, thereby aiding in a better reading of the text. However, these expectations are not only methodological questions which can easily be formulated. In an argument similar to Gadamer's, Rudolf Bultmann notes the need to be knowledgeable of the subject matter in interpretation: "a particular understanding of the subject matter of the text, *grounded in a life relation to it*, is always presupposed by exegesis; and to this extent no exegesis is without presuppositions."[45] Our expectations are our explicit questions as well as the way one's life has interacted with those questions and the subject matter to which they gesture.

To return to the conversation on the plain sense of Scripture, what is plain can be seen to be dependent on our particular expectations, manifested in the kinds of questions we ask of a text, as well as our life's relation to those expectations. It is not that reading Scripture in a mode which foregrounds the development of thought over time is antithetical to such an understanding of the plain sense. Rather, with this reflection, one might realize that these are one set of questions, one mode of reading, which certainly has value for our understanding of Scripture, but that other questions can be brought to the text. As Joyce writes near the conclusion of his essay, "Might it be that having learned lessons both about the value and the excesses of historical criticism we can feel our way to a position that respects the otherness of the original whilst also being open to the power of texts to generate fresh interpretations in later reading situations?"[46]

---

44. Gadamer, *Truth and Method*, 279.

45. Rudolf Bultmann, "Is Exegesis Without Presuppositions Possible?," 149. Emphasis added.

46. Joyce, "Proverbs 8 in Interpretation (1)," 99.

Integrating these concerns into our approach to reading the Bible does not necessarily lead one to some form of anarchic relativism. Rather, it raises the need to read the text aware of our responsibility to the text, but also to ourselves as readers and the contexts in which we read. Frances Young recommends attending to a tripartite responsibility, drawn from ancient rhetorical theory: the λόγος of the text (the Scripture), the ἦθος of the speaker (the reader), and the πάθος of the audience.[47] Within the contemporary frame, might these be recast as a responsibility to the world behind the text, the world within the text, and the world in front of the text? Within such an approach, critiques can still be made, and reason operates to test the validity of arguments within similar contexts and horizons of expectation.[48]

If we bring this question to our reading of Athanasius, questions other than those of the development of ideas are offered for us to ask of Proverbs 8. For Athanasius, the plain sense of the text is that Proverbs 8 participates in and bears witness to the divine being of the Triune God. The ordering and use of words does not primarily bear witness to the socio-economical or religion-as-social-phenomenon reality behind the text, but to a theological and eternal reality. He reads Scripture in a way that the whole Bible was one book, wherein literary and historical differences are secondary to a common theological subject matter.

Modern historical study of the Bible complicates these commitments for a contemporary reader. Historical tools, which represent a respect for the historical development of thought, provide for us one avenue for protecting the integrity of the text. Nevertheless, reading Athanasius raises to a Christian reader's awareness the need to be responsible to the church's Rule of Faith when reading the Bible *as Christian Scripture*. Thus, one line of questioning needs to be how this text bears witness to that faith and speaks to a contemporary Christian, who comes to the text to hear the voice of God. Studying Proverbs 8, attentive to the development of thought over time, can be received as a tool for sharpening our appreciation for the nature of theological talk. Through reading Athanasius, a Christian exegete can be moved to foreground Nicene Trinitarian theology as a factor to which one bears responsibility as well as to the lived life of the church.

---

47. Young, "Proverbs 8 in Interpretation (2)," 114.

48. For a deeper exploration of how reason operates within such horizons, see Charles Taylor, "Explanation and Practical Reason," 34–60.

Matthew Henry's Exegesis of Proverbs 8

In the history of Christian interaction with the Bible, Matthew Henry's *Commentary on the Holy Bible* marks a inflection point.[49] Henry, who lived from 1662 to 1714, offers in his commentary "the first English commentary aimed at Christian believers in general, not the learned pastors or other church workers, and that sought to comment on every phrase in the text, rather than consisting of a series of annotations."[50] The intended lay audience of the commentary and its attention to each phrase mark it out for our attention in this study of Proverbs 8. To be sure, Matthew Henry was not the only Christian write on Proverbs 8 since Athanasius in the fourth century. In the Protestant tradition, Phillip Melanchthon commented on the passage in his *Explicatio Proverbiorum Salmonis* (1555) and John Owen, a Puritan like Henry, did likewise in his *Vindiciae Evangelicae* (1655). In the Roman Catholic context, Cornelius à Lapide published his Great Commentary, which includes comments on Proverbs, in 1681. However, Matthew Henry's method and intended audience offer a distinct piece of exegesis in the history of interpretation.

As noted above, Henry's commentary was intended for a lay audience with an eye toward applying the insights of the Bible to the lives of his readers. Application was an important feature of Puritan exegesis and preaching,[51] and Henry manifests this tendency throughout his writings.[52] However, as will be apparent in the survey following, it was done without "a sense of the difference between the culture of their day and that of Biblical times."[53] While Henry shares with his fellow Puritans this sense of immediacy with the text as well as the concern for application, he is distinct in his hesitance to engage too much in polemics.[54] This avoidance of polemics will be seen in his treatment of Proverbs 8:22–31. As will be noted, that the meaning of these verses was controversial was not unknown in this period. However, Henry merely offers the traditional reading and moves to application.

49. Henry, *Commentary on the Holy Bible*. References to page numbers in Henry's commentary will be given in parentheses throughout this paper.

50. Harman, "The Legacy of Matthew Henry," 187.

51. Lea, "The Hermeneutics of the Puritans," 272.

52. Oliphant Old, "Henry, Matthew (1662–1714)," 522.

53. Lea, "The Hermeneutics of the Puritans," 273. Lea notes that this has benefits and disadvantages. I will engage in a similar evaluation in the conclusion of this section.

54. Old, "Henry, Matthew (1662–1714)," 522–23.

After surveying Henry's work, the conclusion of this section engages in reflection on the nature of reading the Bible as Scripture and applying a text to contemporary life.

Comments on the Poetical Books of the Old Testament

Matthew Henry's commentary sets out to read the text of the Bible in a way that edifies the people of God (v). The poetical books "have in them the very sum and substance of religion, and what they contain is more fitted to our hand, and made ready for use than any part of the Old Testament" (vi). Henry begins the third volume of his commentary on the whole Bible with a preface to the poetical books, in which he introduces the genre of poetry and contemplates differences between these books and the preceding historical books. He acknowledges that poetry can be more difficult to understand than the history books which have come before in his study. Consequently, application to the Christian life is also more complicated;

> here we are advanced to a higher form in God's school, and have books put into our hands, wherein are many things dark, and hard to understand, which we do not apprehend the meaning of so suddenly and so certainly as we could wish; the study whereof requires a more close application of mind, a greater intenseness of thought, and the accomplishing of a diligent search, which yet the treasure hid in them, when it is found, will abundantly recompense. (v)

The method by which the treasure of these books is unearthed is to proceed from that which is most easily understood to that which is more difficult; beginning with "those things are which are most necessary to salvation, and of the greatest use" (v). Those things necessary to salvation are the subject matter of the faith. Like the Christian interpreters who came before him, Henry seeks to read the Bible within the framework of the Christian faith. He writes of the poetical books that "We have here much of natural religion . . . much of God . . . here is much of Christ. . . . Here is that also which, with a divine light, will bring into the soul the heat and influence of the divine fire, will kindle and inflame pious and devout affections, on which wings we may soar upward, until we enter into the holiest" (vii). As these texts can be difficult, the reader must have a solid foundation of faith (that which is easily understood) and can then proceed into that which is more difficult, those things in the text which challenge and push the reader to maturity (entering "into the holiest").

Henry's orienting comments have much in common with the general approach of the early church. In those earlier centuries, Scripture was read in the context of the church's received faith, the *regula fidei*, and difficult passages were understood in the light of clearer passages.[55] This latter method did not dissuade the reader from wrestling with complexities in a particular text; the Fathers often exercised dialectical reading in which these troubles were sought out in order to submit one's faith to the correcting power of Scripture.[56] The Bible was read as providing a united and non-contradictory account of God; therefore, even as the Bible was read within the context of the church's faith, Scripture exercised authority over that faith as held by the reader.[57] Henry stands in line with this approach to the text.

Henry's second point for introducing the books of poetry notes that these books (along with the prophets) have to do with doctrine and devotion rather than history (v). While this notation of difference in genre is not so different from the early church,[58] in early Christian interpretation each passage, no matter its genre, had the potential to render doctrinal and devotional content, through the reading strategy which came to be known as the Quadriga. Matthew Henry stands in the Protestant tradition, which rejected multiple senses in a text and instead emphasized a single and clear meaning for each passage.[59] He therefore alerts his reader that different considerations will be at work in poetry than in his expositions of the historical books.

An additional aspect of Matthew Henry's introduction to the poetic books illustrates his particular place in the history of interpretation. He

---

55. For a discussion of the *regula fidei* in the context of the early church see O'Keefe and Reno, *Sanctified Vision*, 119–28. Richard Muller cites post-Reformation Protestant interpreters' frequent use of the analogy of Scripture and analogy of faith as tools for understanding the meaning of Scripture. Muller, *Post-Reformation Reformed Dogmatics*, 485.

56. This reading strategy "begins with tensions and contradictions. . . . It seeks out puzzles that do not just tease the mind but also torture the reader with the possibility that a beloved text is corrupted by impossibilities and contradictions." O'Keefe and Reno, *Sanctified Vision*, 56.

57. Kugel, *How to Read the Bible*, 14–16.

58. See, for example, Athanasius' *Contra Arianos II*, XIX.44, in which Athanasius comments on Proverbs 8:22, "since, however, these are proverbs, and it is expressed in the way of proverbs, we must not expound them nakedly in their first sense, but we must inquire into the person, and thus religiously put the sense on it." *Contra Arianos II*, 372.

59. Muller, *Post-Reformation Reformed Dogmatics*, 487–88.

surveys a discussion ongoing in his time of the relative age of poetry in ancient cultures, versus narrative or historical writing. His contribution to the discussion is to point out that "the most ancient composition that we meet with in scripture was the song of Moses at the Read Sea, (Exod. xv.) which we find before the very first mention of writing, for that occurs not until Exod. xvii. 14 when God bade Moses write a memorial of the war with Amalek" (vi). Henry illustrates the growing awareness of a text's history. He does not relate this to a discussion of the authorship of various portions of Scripture, as will become common in biblical scholarship later. However, that he notes this as a possible difference in the time of composition shows an incipient awareness of the impact of Renaissance humanism on biblical studies.[60]

Comments on Proverbs 8

As is his standard approach, Matthew Henry offers a proleptic summary and outline of Proverbs 8 before he proceeds to comment on each section of the chapter. According to Henry's reading, Proverbs 8 establishes a two-fold sense of the word of God as wisdom. In the first sense, "Divine revelation is the word and wisdom of God, and so is that pure religion and undefiled, which is built upon it" (493). This is a more practically oriented understanding of wisdom. Henry sees this first sense as derived from verses 1–21 of Proverbs 8. The second sense is the Christological sense: "The Redeemer is the eternal Word and Wisdom, the Logos; he is the Wisdom that speaks to the children of men in the former part of the chapter: all divine revelation passes through his hand and centres in him; but of him as the personal Wisdom, the second Person in the Godhead, in the judgment of many of the ancients, Solomon here speaks, v. 22–31" (469). The second segment of the chapter establishes the Christological sense, but not in isolation from

---

60. A keynote call of Renaissance humanism was *ad fontes*, "back to the sources." In biblical studies this resulted in "reaching behind the Vulgate to the Hebrew and Greek texts and behind medieval commentators to the church fathers." Bartholomew, *Introducing Biblical Hermeneutics*, 195. It also led to an increasing appreciation of the historical context of a text. The tools of the Renaissance led Lorenzo Valla, in 1440, to argue that the *Donation of Constantine* was a forgery. What is significant here is the application of critical tools which suggest an originating context other than the one purported in the document itself. One can see here the seeds of historical-critical study. See Stanglin, *The Letter and Spirit of Biblical Interpretation*, 114–15.

the earlier verses. The final third of the chapter offers a charge to the reader "to attend to the voice of God in his word" (469).

The first section of verses to which Henry gives his attention covers verses 1–11. He draws three main points from these verses: that the "things revealed are easy to be known," that the "things revealed are worthy to be known," and knowledge of these things revealed "is to be preferred before all the wealth of this world" (469–70). In the midst of his expository comments on these points, Henry frequently alludes to or quotes New Testament passages that offer a parallel between Wisdom and Jesus. For example, Wisdom's public cry is paralleled with Jesus' standing in the midst of the crowd and crying out at the Festival of Tabernacles (cf. John 7:37). In addition to these, Henry often draws in other portions from Scripture, both Old and New Testament. For example, Wisdom stands ready to direct at the gate of the city because, according to Ecclesiastes 10:15, the foolish man "knows not how to go to the city." Henry's commitment to a verse-by-verse or phrase-by-phrase style of commentary does not restrict him from drawing in other passages of Scripture. In his view, the Triune God is the subject matter of all Scripture, as such passages can inform one another even if they come from distinct books, testaments, and/or moments in the historical development of the Bible. Once again we can note continuity between early Christian reading of Proverbs 8, at least as seen in Athanasius,[61] and Matthew Henry's commentary.

In addition to bringing the words and meaning of Proverbs 8:1–11 into relationship with other portions of Scripture, Henry also applies these to the life of the reader. So, just as Wisdom cries aloud for all to hear, so "God's ministers are appointed to testify to people, both publicly, and from house to house" (493). Wisdom's addressees are the children of men (Prov 8:4), "not to you, O Jews, only, that Wisdom cries, or to you, O gentlemen, or to you, O scholars; but to you, O men, O sons of men, even the meanest" (493). Reflecting on Wisdom's offer of excellent things (Prov 8:6), he writes, "Though they are level to the capacity of the meanest, yet there is that in them which will be entertainment for the greatest" (494). Henry also comments on the rightness of Wisdom's guidance.

> All the dictates and directions of revealed religion are consonant to, and perfective of, the light and law of nature, and there is nothing in it that puts any hardship upon us, that lays us under any undue restraints, unbecoming the dignity and liberty of the

---

61. See the interaction with Athanasius above.

human nature; nothing that we have reason to complain of: all God's precepts concerning all things are right. (494)

Henry alludes to conversations regarding natural law which were ongoing in the seventeenth and eighteenth centuries. Similarly, his reflection on the social makeup of Wisdom's audience resonates with his time of writing.

The next section of Proverbs 8 that Henry marks off is verses 12–21. He writes "Wisdom here is Christ, in whom are hid all the treasures of wisdom and knowledge; it is Christ in the word, and Christ in the heart; not only Christ revealed to us, but Christ revealed in us" (494). Under this heading, he draws four points from the verses. First, Wisdom provides discretion for the right order of conversation. It also leads one to discover "witty inventions" (the translation given by Henry for Prov 8:12b), good for the proper understanding of God and to safeguard against Satan's devices. Henry applies these descriptions to Christ as one who dwells with prudence, whose witty invention is the way of our salvation and recovery. The second point of Henry's is that wisdom gives men good hearts; Wisdom's hatred of what is evil is applied to the reader. On the froward mouth he writes, "peevishness towards others, God hates, *because it is such an enemy to the peace of mankind, and therefore we should hate it*" (494, emphasis added). There is nothing in Proverbs 8 about why such a thing is worthy of hate; Henry provides his own rationale. While his comments are not necessarily unreasonable, they do resonate with the desire for a more peaceful society which characterized eighteenth-century Europe.[62]

Third, Wisdom "has a great influence upon public affairs, and the well-governing of all societies" (494). Through following Wisdom, an individual will be guided in all difficult situations and their way will be made plain. On a civic level, the verses are taken to show that Christ is the one who provides the power and authority of government. Moreover, religion "is very much the strength and support of the civil government; it teaches subjects their duty, and so by it kings reign over them the more easily; it teaches kings their duty, and so by it kings reign as they ought; and they decree justice, while they rule in the fear of God" (495). Many commentators have marked some discomfort with the unqualified statement that "by me, rulers rule" (Prov 8:15). Henry shows how the text can be taken to apply to ruler (kings), ruled (subjects), and rule (decrees) in order to bring about effective rule.

---

62. Taylor, *A Secular Age*, 127.

Henry provides the most extensive reflection on this section in his fourth point, which address verses 17–21: "it will make all those happy, truly happy, that receive and embrace it" (495). Wisdom's promise to love those who love her and be found by those who seek her early (Prov 8:17–18) is interpreted as a promise from Christ, and correlated to similar promises in the New Testament. He spends more time on the promise of wealth. Wealth and honor will come to those who love Wisdom, or at least as much "as Infinite Wisdom sees good for them" (495). The wealth which religion can bring about is wrought honestly, from "God's blessing on their industry," and it is durable (495). Henry has a place for both divine sovereignty and human responsibility in these comments. Whatever wealth one has must have been seen as good for them by Infinite Wisdom (God), and God is taken to be the ultimate cause of the wealth. However, the efficient cause is a person's industry.

Regardless of whether one has worldly riches, they can have that which is better: Wisdom's fruit, which is the guidance to walk in the way of God. This blessing in the present also leads one to their future glory, which is Henry's interpretation of Wisdom's promise of inheriting substance; "but, let the treasures of the soul be ever so capacious, there is enough in God, and in Christ, and heaven, to fill them. In Wisdom's promises believers have goods laid up, not for days and years, but for eternity; and her fruit therefore is better than gold" (495). On a literal level, Proverbs' interest in life after death is confined to a desire to avoid Sheol; there is no passage in Proverbs that unambiguously corresponds to a blessed afterlife for the righteous. In Proverbs 1–9, the way of wickedness leads to Sheol. The sinners and the adulterous woman lead people on to its way (Prov 1:12; 5:5; 7:27; 9:18). The alternative to the path of Sheol is the path of life. This path of life is not explicitly extended to a reward after death. The potential of the text to speak to this possibility rests in a broader canonical context of reading it. When Proverbs' teaching on life is read in a context which does affirm some sort of life after death for the righteous, such as the Christian faith, then these words can be read as participating in that reality. Even in this latter case, however, attention to the wording of Proverbs maintains a focus on life before death. In this way, even though for some Henry's application of Wisdom's promises to a heavenly afterlife may seem a stretch, his reading context does allow for such an extension of the logic of the book of Proverbs.

The fourth section of Matthew Henry's commentary on Proverbs 8 addresses verses 22–31. These verses offer Henry an opportunity to justify the identification of Wisdom with Jesus Christ. His case could be summarized as asking, "Who else could this be?"

> That it is an intelligent and divine Person that here speaks, seems very plain, and that it is not meant of a mere essential property of the divine nature; for wisdom here has personal properties and actions: and that intelligent divine Person, can be no other than the Son of God himself, to whom the principal things here spoken of wisdom are attributed in other scriptures, and we must explain scripture by itself. (495)

It is not necessarily the case that Solomon had a conception of the Trinity, or of the Son of God. But the Spirit led him "to such expressions as could agree to no other than the Son of God, and would lead us into the knowledge of great things concerning him" (495). Henry's comments regarding what Solomon knew show him to be downstream of Renaissance humanism, as he is concerned to return to the source (*ad fontes*) of the original author's intent.[63] Nevertheless, Henry still has space for a divine authorial intent, apart from what was historically possible for the original human author.[64]

Henry puts forward an interpretation of the passage's relation to the Son of God which is in line with Nicene orthodoxy. He does so in a non-polemical way, without engaging in a debate with alternative readings.[65] These conclusions are that the Son of God has his personality and distinct subsistence, "one with the Father, and of the same essence, and yet a person of himself" as shown by Wisdom being the object of divine actions (495). The passage also shows the eternity of the Son through the passage's "insistence" that Wisdom was brought forth before all worlds (495). Henry's description of the eternal origin of the Son is redolent of Athanasius: "Before the earth was, and that was made in the beginning, before man was made; therefore the second Adam had a being before the first, for the first

---

63. See Stanglin, *The Letter and Spirit in Biblical Interpretation*, 116–17, 133.

64. Muller writes that a central problem which faced Protestant orthodoxy in the post-Reformation period was "the problem of moving from the text to doctrinal statement and even to theological system without the battery of tools readily available to the medieval doctors." *Post-Reformation Reformed Dogmatics*, 484.

65. This is a clear difference between Henry's commentary on Proverbs 8 and John Owen's interaction with Proverbs 8, in which he exposits the text to controvert the argument of the Socinians. See *Vindiciae Evangelicae*, 243–45.

Adam was made of the earth, the second had a being before the earth, and therefore is not of the earth" (495–96).

Henry argues that the passage also establishes Wisdom's agency in the creation of the world. Henry reads אָמוֹן as "one brought up with him" which agrees in substance with the idea of a nursing child (495). Even so, he still understands that Wisdom, as Christ, "was present, not as a spectator, but as the Architect, when the world was made" (496). Henry does not argue so much as he assumes this role for Wisdom through the similarity between Proverbs 8 and other portions of the Bible. He overlays the description of creation in Proverbs 8:22–29 on the first three days of creation in recorded in Genesis 1. Wisdom claims she was there and Henry concludes she was active.

Henry also notes the delight that God shows for Wisdom in this section of Proverbs 8. "As by an eternal generation he was brought forth of the Father, so by an eternal counsel he was brought up with him; which intimates not only the infinite love of the Father to the Son, who is therefore called the Son of his love, (Col. i. 13) but the mutual consciousness and good understanding that were between them, concerning the work of man's redemption" (496). Henry gives no indication of anything in the text that raises the topic of redemption. Proverbs 8 at this point is concerned with Wisdom's presence with God at creation. And yet, Henry argues the passage also applies to redemption. One likely explanation is that Henry is engaging with the church's reading tradition without explicitly noting it. As discussed earlier, Athanasius read Proverbs 8 as having to do both with the eternal generation of the Son as well as the redemptive work associated with the Incarnation.[66]

Henry understands Wisdom's delight in mankind (cf. Prov 8:31) as Christ's joy in the remnant of humanity which he has saved through his suffering.[67]

> Though he foresaw all the difficulties he was to meet with in his work, the services and sufferings he was to go through, yet, because it would issue in the glory of his Father, and the salvation of

---

66. See, for example, Athanasius, *Contra Arianos* II.51.

67. The restriction of a general audience in verse 30 to the remnant in Henry's interpretation illustrates how decisions and doctrines not addressed by a text can nevertheless shape what we believe is possible in reading any text. A similar phenomenon is observable in Henry's understanding that Wisdom is Christ. In Christian doctrine, who else could it be? So here, within Henry's theological system, who other than the elect could be the object of Christ's delight?

those sons of men that were given him, he looked forward upon it with the greatest satisfaction imaginable, in which we have all the encouragement we can desire to come to him, and rely upon him for all the benefits designed us by his glorious undertaking. (496)

Proverbs 8:22–31 offers real encouragement to Christian believers today. Henry's application to a believer's desire to come to Christ and relate to him as their savior aligns with Proverbs 8's conclusion, which invites the reader to relate well to Wisdom.

Henry's last section covers the remaining verses of Proverbs 8, verses 32–36. Henry's interpretation of these verses relate them to a call for the reader to reform their lives. "We have here the application of Wisdom's discourse ... to bring us all into an entire subjection to the laws of religion, to make us wise and good, not to fill our heads with speculations, our tongues with disputes, but to rectify what is amiss in our hearts and lives" (496). First in fulfilling this is the readiness to submissively listen to the voice of Wisdom in every aspect of life. "See here what a good house Wisdom keeps, for every day is dole-day; what a good school, for every day is lecture-day. While we have God's works before our eyes, and his word in our hand, we may be every day hearing Wisdom, and learning instruction from her" (496–97). The hearing of Wisdom's voice must lead to obedient action.[68] Doing so leads one to happiness, which consists in the knowledge of one's salvation in Christ and the good-pleasure of God (497). Finally, those who reject Wisdom embrace their own ruin, judgment, and punishment (497).

Hermeneutical Reflections on Matthew Henry's Reading of Proverbs 8

Matthew Henry's intent to exposit Proverbs in order to edify the people of God was noted at the outset of this section. Throughout his comments on the genre of poetry in the Old Testament and his commentary on Proverbs 8, Henry reads the text with this aim in mind. He draws out implications for the daily life of his readers. His approach conforms to what can be observed in many other Puritan exegetes: "Puritan preachers excelled in expounding

---

68. Beeke and Lanning note that this kind of application was common in Puritan sermons as well. They summarize it as "Practice what you have heard. 'Live out' the sermons you hear. Hearing that does not reform your life will never save your soul. Doers of the Word are the best hearers. Of what value is a mind filled with knowledge when not matched with a fruitful life?" Beeke and Lanning, "Reading and Hearing the Word in a Puritan Way," 73.

how the Word must be used as a means of personal transformation."[69] Henry's own take on this in his work on Proverbs is his statement that "The best comment on those rules [contained in the book of Proverbs] is to be ruled by them" (469).

In many ways, this approach is no different from that of interpreters who came before Matthew Henry. Early church interpretation took place in a context which sought a "morally edificatory" application from every passage of Scripture.[70] However, a distinct feature of Matthew Henry vis-à-vis the tradition is his intent to inform the lives of a lay, non-scholarly audience. Throughout his commentary, rather than engaging in various options for understanding the text, Henry puts forward a single meaning which is most often directed toward the practical lives of Christians.

For example, in his comments on Proverbs 8:22–31, Henry does not even acknowledge other possibilities for understanding the passage's relation to Christ. As quoted above, Henry writes of this passage:

> That it is an intelligent and divine Person that here speaks, seems very plain, and that it is not meant of a mere essential property of the divine nature; for wisdom here has personal properties and actions: and that intelligent divine Person, can be no other than the Son of God himself, to whom the principal things here spoken of wisdom are attributed in other scriptures, and we must explain scripture by itself. (495)

Henry was classically educated and aware of the church's tradition, presumably including its doctrinal struggle over the nature of Christ and this passage's role in that struggle.[71] As such, he was likely aware that the meaning of this passage was not "very plain" but contested.[72] Nevertheless, he provides a single, simple meaning of the passage which agrees with Nicene orthodoxy.

In addition to seemingly ignoring alternatives, Henry also does not ask certain questions of the text that are commonplace in modern

---

69. Beeke and Lanning, "Reading and Hearing the Word in a Puritan Way," 67.

70. Young, *Biblical Exegesis and the Formation of Christian Culture*, 81.

71. For Henry's background and education, see Old, "Henry, Matthew (1662–1714)," 520–24.

72. While Matthew Henry may or may not have read John Owen's work on Proverbs 8, Owen's work, among other writings of the post-Reformation era, makes us aware of the presence of doctrinal debates during this time. Owen's work on Proverbs 8 is written to combat Socinianism, whose teaching on the nature of Christ mirrors that which Athanasius opposed in his writings in the fourth century.

commentaries. He does not address the possibility that Proverbs 8:22–31 is using a figure of speech and should therefore be understood in a different register. He likewise does not explore any implications of the feminine gender of Wisdom vis-à-vis her witness to the Son of God. Nor does he explain how Wisdom could be understood as an active agent in creation. Many modern commentaries see this facet of Wisdom as depending on the translation of אָמוֹן in verse 30.[73] If this word is translated as an artisan it communicates Wisdom's active agency in the Lord's creative work.[74] If, however, it is translated adverbially (faithfully, constantly) or as a nursling child, Wisdom's agency is either ruled out or not in focus.[75] Henry reads אָמוֹן as "one brought up with him" which agrees in substance with the idea of a nursling child, but nevertheless argues that Wisdom is an active agent in creation (495). The absence of these kinds of discussions can be surprising to a modern scholar.[76]

The differences between Henry's commentary and one written in the modern era highlight for us the role of context and purpose in commentary writing. As for the context, Henry was writing to a Christian audience at a time when Christian faith and experience were much more uniform than they are in the late-twentieth and early twenty-first centuries.[77] Henry was forthright about his commitment to read Proverbs in the light of the church's doctrine; he advised and expected that readers be well formed in this doctrine prior to reading more advanced passages and books (v). He was also explicit about his purpose to render a reading which was profitable for the reader's life of faith (v). Much of his commentary illustrates that this profitability was at least partially understood vis-à-vis the practical life of the Christian: "The best comment on those rules [contained in the book of Proverbs] is to be ruled by them" (469). However, given the doctrinal debates of the era, it is likely that the beliefs of the reader were also in the background of Henry's concerns. The absence of alternative readings of Proverbs 8:22, for example, deprive these viewpoint any exposure to Henry's non-academic audience. The conclusion that this passage speaks of

---

73. See, for example, Fox, *Proverbs 1–9*, 285–87.

74. Murphy, *Proverbs*, 48, 52–53; Longman, *Proverbs*, 196, 207.

75. See discussion in chapter 2, "Reading Proverbs 8 in Its Literary Context."

76. We should note that at other times these questions have been asked of the text. Athanasius addresses the figural nature of Proverbs 8:22 in his work. See *Contra Arianos* II.44. John Owen does the same in *Vindiciae Evangelicae*, 243–45.

77. Charles Taylor offers a compelling account for the differences for faith in the modern frame in *A Secular Age*.

the Son of God in a "very plain" way buttresses a confidence in the church's traditional teaching.

Matthew Henry openly acknowledged his reading of the text as a Christian and sought to shape the lives of Christians through his work (v). We have noted how his comments were influenced by this context and purpose. As biblical studies proceeded, there was a greater awareness of and concern for the ways in which a reader's context and faith may sometimes distort the message of the text. However, acknowledging this should not detract from what can be learned from Henry's work. Within the Christian tradition, Scripture is taken up to speak to the church at a particular moment in a way which may be distinct from other moments in time or place. Doing so moves past reading the Bible according to the world behind the text and the world within the text in order to encounter its message in the world in front of the text. The issue is how to do this such that the full potential of the Bible as Scripture is realized.

5

Modern Historically Oriented Scholars

IN THIS CHAPTER, WE move to the modern era of scholarship on Proverbs 8. As before, my interest is to attend to how the efforts surveyed offer a reader different perspectives on the text in the light of the differing questions asked, and differing assumptions brought to bear. On the other side of the shift toward reading the Bible according to its background in the world behind the text, Craig Bartholomew categorizes three changes, or turns, in the study of the Bible.[1] The first is the literary turn, which interprets literary features of the text not in relation to a purported world behind the text but as literary technique and artistic intention. A second turn which Bartholomew notes is the postmodern turn which "insists that particular epistemologies and views of history underlie the practice of historical criticism. If such views are to be maintained, then their basis must be argued for: the basis cannot just be assumed."[2] The influence of this turn is most often seen in introductions to commentaries on Proverbs, in which a scholar may stake out their theological commitments or social location. A third turn that Bartholomew tentatively categorizes is a theological turn: "an increasing number of scholars are arguing, in response to the postmodern turn, that we need a *theological* hermeneutic in biblical studies, and nowadays works in what is fuzzily called theological interpretation are springing up all over the place."[3] As Bartholomew intimates, there is little agreement

---

1. Bartholomew, *Introducing Biblical Hermeneutics*, 237.
2. Bartholomew, *Introducing Biblical Hermeneutics*, 243.
3. Bartholomew, *Introducing Biblical Hermeneutics*, 245. Emphasis original. Bartholomew's title for this section is "Amid Contemporary Pluralism: A Theological Turn?," hence my statement that he tentatively offers this as a third turn. It is unclear to me from whence this arises, as he is able to give plenty of examples of scholars who are going

on what a theological turn would mean. He also wishes to be clear that this turn does not seek to ignore those other facets of reading the text (historical, literary, ideological). Bartholomew specifically cites von Rad's *Wisdom in Israel* as an example of a reading steeped in historical criticism and yet producing a theological reading of the Old Testament's material relating to wisdom.[4] Nevertheless, there is a new energy around reading the text of the Bible theologically, in some way or another. In the latter portion of this section, I will attend specifically to scholars, including von Rad, who are reading Proverbs 8 within a self-professed theological mode. First, however, in this next portion I will survey scholars who do not share this commitment, but wish to read Proverbs 8 solely in historical and literary modes.

A Survey of Interpretations of Proverbs 8 According to the World of Ancient Israel

The aim of my overall project is to bring forth a transformative reading of Proverbs 8, read in the recontextualized setting of Christian faith. To do so with honesty requires that one "protect the text from a premature appropriation by the reader."[5] Placing the text in its historical context and attending to its philology, structure, and composition (in other words, approaching the text using classical historical-critical tools) puts safeguards in place for an honest reading. As such, I will first survey the field of scholarship on the passage coming from those who operate without an expressed theological interest. These scholars may or may not be people of faith; irrespective of that commitment, they are writing in such a way that does not foreground it. Next I will interact with those who explicitly approach the text as Christians or with an aim towards some form of Christian application. The following survey is not meant to be exhaustive. Rather, I hope to offer a representative sample of the moves scholars have generally made when interpreting Proverbs 8 in the modern era of biblical interpretation. My goal is not only to learn from them but also to acknowledge and illustrate something of the vast amount of energy which has been put into the "world behind the text" and "world of the text" of Proverbs 8.

---

about this work. Perhaps it is the lack of agreement on all that theological interpretation entails.

4. Bartholomew, *Introducing Biblical Hermeneutics*, 245.
5. Schneiders, *The Revelatory Text*, 171.

Sprüche Salomos by Otto Plöger

Otto Plöger writes the Proverbs commentary in the *Biblischer Kommentar Altes Testament* series.[6] In his interpretation and commentary on the text of Proverbs 8, Plöger attends to the world behind and the world within the text, that is, its historical and literary dimensions. Of these two, it is the literary aspect of the text which predominates in his discussion. He consistently acknowledges the dynamic in the text between the words of personified Wisdom and the "Wisdom teacher." Additionally, his close reading leads him to address connections and tensions within the text.

His opening comments on Proverbs 8 address the form of the chapter. The chapter features a shift in speaker, "Denn hier läßt ... der Weisheitslehrer ... die Weisheit als seine Lehrmeisterin wiederum selbst zu Worte kommen" (87). Plöger notes the differences in form between Proverbs 8 and other speeches in the book: "den paränetische Elemente finden sich nur in der Einladung des Eingangsabschnittes (v. 4–11) und in der abschließenden Ermahnung (v. 32–36), mit der auch der Weisheitslehrer seine Mahnreden zu beenden pflegt, die hier aber von der Weisheit selbst vorgenommen wird" (87). He concludes that the chapter should be considered a "Selbstempfehlung" (87).

With this designation, Plöger moves on to address the vocabulary and meaning of Proverbs 8. In his remarks, his attention is repeatedly given to the purpose of certain moves made in the construction of the passage. For example, in Proverbs 8:1 wisdom is in the singular (חָכְמָה), whereas in the first instance of personified wisdom in the book, the term is plural (חָכְמוֹת, Prov 1:20). Plöger attributes the singular of chapter 8 to "insight" (תְּבוּנָה), in parallel with "wisdom," also being in the singular: "vermutlich veranlaßt durch die zur Weisheit in Parallele gestellte 'Einsicht'" (88). This early example illustrates Plöger's concern to understand what the text is doing, and often looking for an answer in literary or structural purposes. Plöger's attention to the world of the text retains dynamism, in that the text is not reduced to "mere" structure. Rather, the text is interpreted to construe a living world. For example, Plöger observes two differing approaches between the voice of Wisdom and that of the teacher; Wisdom addresses the wider public, whereas the teacher is content to speak to "die Einzelperson oder an einen kleineren Hörerkreis ... Dieser Öffentlichkeitsanspruch erklärt

---

6. Plöger, *Sprüche Salomos*. As in previous sections, references to this work will be placed in parentheses throughout this summary and evaluation.

es, daß die Weisheit auch dort, wo sie werbend einlädt, eher dekretiert als ermahnt, auch wenn ihren Worten das paränetische Element nicht fremd ist" (88). Plöger connects two features of the text (varying audiences, varying styles of address) in a way that enriches one's reading of the text in that now these two features take on great significance as understood in relation to one another.

Plöger titles verses 4–11 of the chapter "Die Einladung der Weisheit" (88). Within this section, Wisdom gives her invitation to all people by enumerating the "kostbaren Gaben" of Wisdom (88). These gifts embrace both intellectual and ethical qualities. "Diese Gaben gehören dem ethisch-religiösen Bereich an, wie es die Verse 7ff. deutlich zu erkennen geben. Aber die Verknüpfung intellektueller und ethisch-religiöser Kategorient ist von der Sache her gefordert, um die Qualität dessen, was die Weisheit darbietet, zu durchschauen" (88). Within his comments on this section, Plöger again notes a difference brought about by the use of personified wisdom, over against the voice of the teacher: "Gewiß könnte so auch der Weisheitslehrer geredet haben, und die Verse 10 und 11 nehmen modifiziert auf, was er in 3,14 und 15 selbst gesagt hat. Aber im Munde der personifizierten Weisheit, die wie Jahwe zu reden vermag, gewinnen diese Worte an Hoheit und Würde" (89). Plöger does not explicitly break into reflection on the world in front of the text. However, he reads and interprets the literary points of view ("literarisch gesehen" [89]) in a way that illustrates an appreciation for the art of the text.

Plöger's attention to the rhetorical effect brought about by the text's construction continues as he considers the next section. "In diesem Abschnitt . . . redet die Weisheit in einer Sprache, derer sich der Weisheitslehrer nicht bedienen könnte, wenn er nicht als anmaßend erscheinen will" (89). Once again, the text's presentation through personification is marked as difference-making, expressed here through its effect on the message. However, his energies are not solely dedicated to the rhetorical elements of the passage. Within his comments, Plöger considers four terms and their meaning in the context of Proverbs 8:12–21: עָרְמָה, מְזִמּוֹת, עֵצָה, and צְדָקָה. The first two of these terms are generally used negatively. In Proverbs 8 they are deployed in a positive light. Of the first, עָרְמָה, he writes: "In V. 5 als Lebensklugheit verstanden, erfährt die der Weisheit benachbarte, mit ihr in ständigem Kontakt lebende 'Klugheit' eine besondere Note, indem sie in der zweiten Vershälfte in Parallele gesetzt wird zu Verhaltensweisen, die sich durch kluge Besonnenheit auszeichnen" (89). With regards to מְזִמּוֹת,

"So wird man den meist im Sinne von 'Ränken; und 'Intrigen' aufzufassenden Plural מְזִמּוֹת hier (und ähnlich in 2,11 sing.) verstehen dürfen: Zur lebensklugheit gehört umsichtige Besonnenheit" (89). For the meaning of the word עָתֵק in verse 18, Plöger grounds his understanding in "von der Grundbedeutung des Stammes עתק ('sich weiterbewegen') ausgeht, ode rein 'alterwürdiges' Vermögen, das von Beständigkeit getragen ist" (90). The last term which attracts his attention is צְדָקָה: he suggests that it can best be understood as supporting the idea of constancy expressed through עָתֵק, thus rendering Proverbs 8:18b as "ein durch Gerechtigkeit erworbenes und darum beständiges Vermögen" (90).

The connections which Plöger notes between this passage and other portions of the Old Testament are a further illustration of his interest in the world of the text. The description of Wisdom's benefits in 8:12–16 are analogous to Job 12:13–25. Plöger further marks the similarities between this section and Isaiah 11:2: "Deshalb hat der Hinweis auf die Idealgestalt des messianischen Fürsten in Jes 11,2 ... gewiß nicht im Sinne einer Abhängigkeit, schon eine gewisse Berechtigung, auch wenn hier von einer Geistbegabung unmittelbar nicht die Rede ist. Anstelle der Geistbegabung steht hier die Weisheit selbst" (90). The text of Proverbs 8 exists within a world of other texts, most especially those other works which make up the Old Testament.

Plöger's analysis progresses to verses 22–31, the uniqueness of which leads him to consider the world behind the text. He notes the work of Donner and Kayatz, who argue for an Egyptian origin or dependency for the personification of wisdom (91). Plöger does not engage in a debate as to the accuracy of these arguments. Rather, he moves to consider their effect.

> Doch erhebt sich die Frage, ob eine solche Anlehnung an fremdländische Vorstellungen, in welchem Ausmaß sie auch immer geschehen sein mag, in dem Augenblick erfolgte, als die Beschäftigung mit der Weisheit in Israel eine Grenze erreicht hatte, die zu überschreiten nur mit Hilfe fremden Gedankengutes möglich war, oder ob es sich eher um ein Veranschaulichungselement handelt, um der nun einmal personifizierten Weisheit ein schärferes, aber auch nicht ungefährliches Profil zu verleihen. (91)

This is indeed a crucial issue raised by the proposed foreign origins of the figure of personified wisdom. However one chooses to respond, Plöger notes that Israel has made its own contribution to the figure, that is, it was not transferred wholesale without modification.

Die sich selbst vorstellende Weisheit bleibt identische mit der
Weisheit, die im Eingangsstück von Kap. 8 die Menschen anredet,
und dies in einer Weise, einladend und auch drohend (vgl. 1,20ff.),
die im Bekenntnis Israels bislang nur mit Jahwe verbunden wurde,
eine Verhaltensweise, die nach meiner Kenntnis der ägyptischen
Maat fremd war. (91)

The inclusion of this figure and the particularity of its presentation takes on a distinct profile when brought into relationship with what has already been written of this Wisdom earlier in Proverbs.

With these observations, Plöger takes up the relationship between Wisdom and the LORD of Israel. Through the various phrases and expressions of Proverbs 8:22-31, Plöger argues she is "nicht schöpfungsimmanent, sie kann aber in ihrer Herleitung von Jahwe ein 'kreatürliches' Element nicht völlig abstreifen" (93). In his reading, Wisdom is clearly subordinated to the LORD. The shift of speaker at verse 22 attests to this: "Sie läßt die Einzigartigkeit Jahwes unangetastet, indem sie, die bislang redendes Subjekt war, sich im Verhältnis zu Jahwe zum Objekt macht" (92). Additionally, Plöger understands the variety of expressions of Wisdom's origin to communicate derivation and subordination to the LORD (92). The sense of subordination works to create a unique status for Wisdom. "Denn ist sie von der Schöpfung her gesehen näher an Jahwe zu rücken, von Jahwe her gesehen verbleibt ihr eine stärker Affinität zu Schöpfung" (93). She is a bridge figure, existing, as it were, between creation and the LORD.

As to how best characterize her role, Plöger addresses the contested term אָמוֹן, which he readily acknowledges is by no means clearly understood (94). He wades into this conversation with some expressed reserve: "Es widerstrebt mir, die Kette der zahlreichen Vorschläge um ein neues Glied zu vermehren" (95). He notes that verse 30 contains three clauses, the second and third of which end with "einer allgemein gehaltenen Zeitangabe" (95). On this basis, he advocates an understanding of "constant" for the word. He allows that the alternative understanding of "foster child" is accounted for by the sense of the verse. However, he does not find space for an active role for Wisdom in creation. "Als Demiurgin jedenfalls wird die Weisheit nicht vorgeführt; ihr Anteil am Schöpfungswerk ist eher indirekt zu verstehen" (95).

Plöger's understanding of Wisdom and her relationship to the LORD is historical. It arises out of a desire to articulate how the pursuit of wisdom relates to the "Gott des Bekenntnisses" (98). The presentation of Wisdom in Proverbs is one articulation along the history of ideas; Plöger notes that while personified Wisdom shows up in Sirach and the Wisdom of Solomon, in these "Sie selbst redet nicht und lädt auch nicht ein und wird nicht zu einer Gesprächspartnerin, und damit entfallen wesentliche Motive zu ihrer Personifizierung" (98). Despite this later development, under Plöger's historical lens, Wisdom of Proverbs 8 is a child (thus special creature) of the Lord who delights in God's creative work and shares her unique knowledge of creation with those who love her (95–96). As such, she stands in between the student and the Lord, mediating knowledge to the enquirer.

Plöger reads the final few verses of chapter 8 as a final admonition ("Die Abschlußermahnung der Weisheit" [96]). He once again notes the world behind the text by mentioning a proposal for a different order of verses 32–36, one which is based on the LXX. However, as is characteristic of his approach to the whole chapter, he turns from this to the world of the text. "In jedem Fall folgt die Weisheit einer Gepflogenheit des Weisheitslehrers, einer belehrenden Rede eine abschließende Ermahnung folgen zu lassen" (96). With that being said, Wisdom's admonition is distinct when compared with those which have come from the teacher. Wisdom expresses affection for humanity and promises life to those who love her: "Sie versäumt nicht, auch in diesem Zusammenhang auf ihre Verbindung mit Jahwe hinzuweisen" (96). The structural similarities to other forms in the book highlight a difference, which in turn discloses, within the world of the text, the kind of close relationship between the Lord and Wisdom which this passage has articulated.

In his summary, Plöger argues that the major contribution of Proverbs 8 is not what it says about wisdom and creation, but its extended personification and what this says about Wisdom and the Lord of Israel. With regards to the portions of the chapter which speak of creation, he writes, "Um den Beitrag der Weisheit zum Schöpfungsthema umfassender zu würdigen, wird man anderweitige Texte heranziehen müssen, die einen weisheitlichen Zielen unterstellt worden sind, wie etwa die Gottesreden im Hiobbuch oder bestimmte Psalmen" (97). He is more concerned with the phenomenon of personification and finds the proposal of loans from non-Israelite cultures to stop short of the more interesting question, "warum sich die Weisheit in Israel solcher Anleihen bediente" (97). He notes that personification occurs in Proverbs "wenn die ... Affinität der Weisheit zu Jahwe vorgeführt werden soll" (97). According to Plöger, the primary function of this personification is to "das Verhältnis der Weisheit zu dem Gott des Bekenntnisses zu veranschaulichen" (98). In his summary he does not expand upon how personification aids one's understanding of the relationship between God and Wisdom. Based on his earlier comments one might surmise that the personification communicates an intimacy between God and the wisdom proclaimed in Proverbs. His final words on the chapter urge caution in developing any further theological claims regarding wisdom, as he warns that attempting to find in the personification a constitutive meaning should only be undertaken with great caution (98).

The exegetical work of Otto Plöger on Proverbs 8 is primarily focused on the world of the text, as he attends to the structure, vocabulary, and rhetorical effect of the passage. The result is a rich reading that draws the reader into an appreciation of the nuances of the longest speech of personified Wisdom in the canon of the Old Testament. For the purposes of the present study, Plöger is a welcome conversation partner and companion. His attention to the difference personification makes is particularly suggestive. He displays a dissatisfaction with grounding the meaning of the passage, and more particularly personified wisdom, solely in an ancient Near Eastern setting.

Die Sprüche by Arndt Meinhold

Arndt Meinhold's 1991 commentary[7] displays shared characteristics with that of Otto Plöger in that both focus on the world of the text. Distinguishing Mienhold's commentary from Plöger's is how Meinhold's analysis of the structure of Proverbs 8 shapes his interpretation of its meaning. In the following summary, I will attend to these features of his commentary.

Meinhold begins by addressing the structure of the entire poem; he acknowledges that all three sections within verses 4-31 have the character of Wisdom's self-praise. His tendency to closely link structure and meaning is illustrated by his observation that the first word of each of the three sections helps to distinguish their particular contribution to the whole: "Das erste Wort von V.4-11 ('euch') faßt die Angesprochenen und Eingeladenen ins Auge; das erste Wort von V.12-21 ('ich') deutet an, daß es in diesem Abschnitt vor allem um die Weisheit selbst geht; das erste Wort von V.22-31 ('JHWH') verweist darauf, daß nun der unmittelbare Bezug JHWHs zur

---

7. Meinhold, *Die Sprüche*. As with the other surveys of interpretation, page numbers for Meinhold's commentary will be provided parenthetically.

Weisheit und umgekehrt zur Debatte steht" (135). He pursues these in more depth when he exegetes each section.

Prior to moving to each section, he takes up the issue of ancient Near Eastern influences for the figure of personified Wisdom. Again, the structure and particularities of the text take precedence: "Die Verhältnisbestimmung zwischen der Weisheit und JHWH schränkt die religionsgeschichtlichen Herleitungsversuch der personifizierten Weisheit bzw. Ihre Vermittlung von außerhalb Israels ein" (135). Meinhold maintains that personified Wisdom's relationship with the LORD God of Israel must be taken seriously, and remain the major focus for understanding Proverbs 8.

Moving into his more detailed exegesis of Proverbs 8, one example can be drawn from his comments on each of the three main sections of Wisdom's speech which illustrates how structure shapes meaning. In the first section (vv. 4–11), he notes its symmetrical structure: "Zwei Zeilen mit vier Bezeichnungen für die Adressaten (V.4f.) und zwei Zeilen mit vier Bezeichnungen für Kostbarkeiten, die anstelle der Weisheit nicht erworben werden sollen bzw. einen Vergleich mit ihr nicht aushalten (V.10f.), rahmen vier Langzeilen mit acht Aussagen über die Güte ihrer Rede (V.6–9)" (137). He then notes an objection to the originality of verse 11. He adjudicates this debate by appealing to the regularity of structure in these verses, arguing that it must have been made by the same author.

His comments on the second section of Wisdom's speech (verses 12–21) offers another illustration. Meinhold remarks that this section could be divided into two on the basis of the repetition of "I" (אֲנִי) at verses 12 and 17. Each of these "I's" "bezeichnet den Beginn der jeweils fünf Langzeilen umfassenden Teilabschnitte" (139). On this basis, he argues that verses 12–16 address rulers, whereas verses 17–21 address common people. Other commentators have sought to unify these audiences. Plöger, for example, interprets the reference to royalty as an illustration: "Was den Fürsten, insofern sie Liebhaber der Weisheit sind, gelingt in ihrem guten Regiment, verheißt die Weisheit mutatis mutandis allen ihren Liebhabern."[8] Meinhold acknowledges that the general audience is the main focus of the passage (139). Nevertheless, his interpretation keeps them separated because of the structure of the section.

A third and final example of the prioritizing of structure for meaning is found in Meinhold's interpretation of verses 22–31. As with the other sections, Meinhold begins by analyzing the arrangement of the section. The

---

8. Plöger, *Sprüche Salomos*, 90.

verses speak of three phases: "vor, während und kurz nach der Erschaffung der Welt" (143).[9] Within this structure, Wisdom's role develops:

> Zunächst war sie völlig passiv, den an ihr geschah Schöpferhandeln (V.22–26); dann war sie anwesend, als JHWH die Welt mit den Großgeschöpfen Himmel und Erde geschaffen und die Wasserversorgung geregelt hat (V.27–30a), und schließlich nahm sie eine aktive, erheiternde Rolle wahr, die den Schöpfer vergnügt und auf andere Weise auch die Menschen einbezog (V.30b–31). (143)

Meinhold discerns this development by the grammar and style of each division. As he moves into comments on each of these much debated verses, he does not engage in detailed refutation of opposing views. Thus, regarding the meaning of קנני, he writes "trotz zahlreicher Einreden schwerlich in Zweifel stehen, daß das Verb 'kaufen/erwerben' ... hier im Sinne von 'erschaffen' gebraucht ist" (144). Similarly, he does not substantially engage with others on the proper understanding of אמון in verse 30, only noting in the footnote of his translation, "Wenn 'Werkmeister' tatsächlich gemeint wäre, käme auf Grund der Verse 22–29 nur JHWH, nicht aber die Weisheit, in Frage. Wahrscheinlich ist aber das passive Partizip des Verbs 'mn in der Bedeutung 'Pflegekind/Pflegling' zu veranschlagen" (134 fn 31). One possible conclusion from this lack of engagement is that, at least within the context of this particular commentary, Meinhold leans on structural analysis to determine the meaning of constituent verses.

The above summary sought to illustrate one facet of Arndt Meinhold's commentary on Proverbs 8. These comments on the chapter's structure are insightful for a close reading of the poem. They exemplify how the tools of literary study as developed within the modern period of biblical study, can be applied to the text.

---

9. This delineation of the section is similar to that of Weeks, "The Context and Meaning of Proverbs 8:30a." Weeks, however, does not restrict the last section to only a short time after the creation. Rather, the third section (verses 30b–31) "should be understood with reference not to a brief interval in the past but to the whole subsequent period" Weeks, "The Context and Meaning of Proverbs 8:30a," 438.

Wisdom in the World

The Anchor Yale Bible Commentary on Proverbs by Michael Fox

In the Anchor Yale series of commentaries, Michael Fox pens the volume on Proverbs.[10] Fox offers a stimulating and well-researched investigation into Proverbs. He includes sections regarding words used for wisdom and folly, the origins of the book, and numerous excursuses which offer extended meditation on various topics raised in the flow of the commentary. Fox refers to not only ancient sources and modern commentaries, but also regularly interacts with Jewish commentaries on the text from the ninth to nineteenth century C.E.

Fox's comments on Proverbs 8 concentrate primarily on the literary features of the text. He notes parallels in other OT passages, wrestles with the definitions of particular words, and pushes past what may seem as an obvious reading in an effort to connect with a more holistic picture. An example of the latter is in his interaction with first verse of the chapter:

> the sentence premises that *something* is calling, some voice is heard. But whose? It is, the author declares, surely Wisdom whose voice we hear everywhere, loud and clear—unless we perversely choose to stopple our ears. In naturalistic terms, wisdom's call is the power of reason, heard within the mind. (265, emphasis original)

This exposition illustrates Fox's tendency to move from a verse of the poem to a broader picture. Also present is his view of the text as present to the reader; he states that *we* hear Wisdom's voice unless *we* choose to stopple our ears. These are aspects of the world in front of the text; an integrated sense of a whole passage brought to the attention and world of the reader. Notwithstanding these hints and forays into this world, Fox remains focused on the passage as a text placed in the canonical collection known as the Hebrew Bible and sourced in the ancient Near Eastern world. The location of this text in the ancient past is primary; even though it has produced a tradition of interaction from which the modern interpreter can draw in the mode of a classic, it remains an artifact of the history of ideas.

Fox divides the chapter into five sections. The first three verses, written in third person, form an introduction. After this comes an exordium (vv. 4–11), a self-commendation (vv. 12–21), an exposition of Wisdom's origins (vv. 22–31), and a final invitation (vv. 32–36).

---

10. Fox, *Proverbs 1–9*. For the remainder of this section, citations from this work will be provided in parentheses.

Modern Historically Oriented Scholars

In his comments on the introductory verses, he looks to other OT usage of terms in order to establish personified Wisdom's location. He concludes that the verses are not intended to communicate a single location or instance of speech. Rather, what is being communicated is "an ongoing, typical occurrence" (267). The introduction functions to place Wisdom in "every city, and even the entirety of the inhabited world. Ancient Near Eastern mythology often represented the cosmos as a city, and some cities were regarded as microcosms of heaven and earth" (267).

Verses 4–11 form an exordium, in which Wisdom addresses, exhorts, and motivates her listeners (267). Her address is deemed significant because of its gracious and inclusive character. With regards to the first, Fox sees in Wisdom's address to all of humanity a sign of graciousness: "However lofty her origins and status, Wisdom cares about people, even the less worthy, and seeks them out" (267). We might also add the lofty nature of her location on the heights. That she calls even to those otherwise considered hopeless illustrates an inclusiveness to her message. Fox remarks upon the rare form for "men" (אִישִׁים, v. 4) as a Phoenicianism (268). Medieval Jewish interpretation handled the two terms for humanity mentioned in 8:4 in various ways (the rich and the poor; the honorable and the dishonorable; the Torah-educated and those not). Fox demurs from recommending these, but he does note "the two expressions together do connote totality" (267). Like Plöger, Fox interprets Proverbs 8:5 not as a limitation of Wisdom's audience, but as a clarification that even these, the simple, are addressed (268). He moves to integrate this inclusiveness with a broader OT picture of a prophet; "But perhaps Lady Wisdom, like a prophet, is morally obliged to deliver her message even to those who will not or cannot absorb it (cf. Isa 6:8–10; Ezek 2:3–5; 3:7)" (268). His comments on these two verses nicely illustrate his hermeneutical tendencies to focus primarily on the world of the text through recourse to other canonical contexts, to refer to the world behind the text via linguistic evidence, to acknowledge the history of interpretation, and to integrate the message of a verse or verses into a coherent thought.

Fox's exposition of the next section of Proverbs 8 illustrates that these priorities persist throughout the commentary. He advocates translating Proverbs 8:12a (אֲנִי־חָכְמָה) "I am Wisdom," rather than an appositional "I, Wisdom," due to his reading of ANE self-identification inscriptions (271). Fox takes some time to clarify the meaning of Wisdom inhabiting cunning[11]

---

11. Fox includes a helpful section early on in his commentary exploring words used

(שָׁכַנְתִּי עָרְמָה); "Wisdom does not say that she *is* cunning, but that she 'inhabits' cunning; in other words, she has an abiding connection to it but is not precisely equated with it" (271, emphasis original). These comments serve to clarify what is and is not meant by the text and how it relates to its various concepts so that the reader might profitably understand. He goes on to disagree with Sa'adia, the tenth-century Jewish commentator. "Sa'adia defines *'ormah* here as understanding and cleverness in obedience to God"; Fox finds this interpretation "pietistic" (271). Fox's final comment on verse 12 is his first mention of his view that Wisdom is presented as the ideal wise human (272).

One of the helpful features of Fox's work is the space he takes to explore the inner dynamics of the text, both in the confined context of Proverbs 8 and in relation to the wider canonical context. Near the end of his exposition of verses 12-21, he has two brief excursuses: one on reciprocal love in the book and another on seeking and studying. In the former he remarks upon the emotional requirements placed upon the student by the book. The student of wisdom must love wisdom, which Fox interprets as the love of learning (275, cf. Prov 4:6; 7:4; 29:3; 8:34).[12] He pushes beyond a simple affirmation to ask the more difficult question: what does it mean for Wisdom to return love? He expands upon this in a way that reveals his understanding of Wisdom as a cognitive faculty (something he explicitly states in numerous other places of the commentary); "As one progresses in learning, the vastness of knowledge is even more evident, but lines of organization begin to appear, and interconnections emerge that facilitate memory and comprehension . . . a learner may have the sensation that the field of knowledge is cooperating in clarifying itself" (276). In the conclusion of this chapter, I will attend to Fox's assertion that Wisdom is equated with a cognitive faculty.

The second of his excursuses in this section asks and answers, "What does it mean in practice to seek wisdom?" (276). Fox calls upon Egyptian parallel material which affords him greater insight into this process in the world behind the text. On this basis, along with evidence in Ben Sira, he

---

for wisdom and folly in the book (28-43). In this section, he argues that עָרְמָה is best understood as "cunning," which is a morally dubious term. Used in the book of Proverbs, the word "and the cognate verbs refer to cunning used legitimately." Fox, *Proverbs 1-9*, 35.

12. Fox's description is reminiscent of the activities of students in *yeshivot*. See "Yeshiva" in *The New Encyclopedia of Judaism*, 807-9.

concludes that reading Israel's scriptures (including the book of Proverbs) as well as "the entirety of literature" constitutes this task (277).

The penultimate section of the poem is the most controversial. Fox recognizes the debates surrounding Proverbs 8:22 in the Christian tradition. However, the solution to the proper translation of קנה is clear: "In my view, the question is moot. The word's *lexical* meaning, the semantic content it brings to context, is 'acquire,' no more than that" (279). Surprisingly, after this strong assertion, Fox avers that here in Proverbs 8:22, the verb should be translated "created," to avoid misapplying pre-existence to the idea (as is present in the English term "acquire") (279). That the term needs clarification because of the nuance of meaning between the languages operates on the logic of recontextualization. However, no attention is given to this phenomenon in its broader application. The use of the verb קנה is another instance of Wisdom as an example of the human quest for wisdom, as noted above in verse 12. "The verb *qanah* is chosen to designate divine acquisition of wisdom to show that this is the prototype of human acquisition of wisdom, even though they gain wisdom in quite different ways" (280). Fox does not expand on how this may serve as a model for attaining wisdom even though such acquisition occurs by starkly different ways.

Verses 24–29 relate to the created order and, in order to assist the reader, Fox offers a brief sketch of ancient Near Eastern cosmology. References to other Old Testament texts support the presence of these views within Israel at various points in its history. That they do so does not mean Israel had unified their understanding of said order, nor that it persisted without change throughout Israel's history: "Prov 8 exhibits some unusual notions and need not be assimilated to other biblical texts" (282).

Verses 30–31 contain "one of the great puzzles of the Hebrew Bible because of its theological implications" (285) namely the phrase וָאֶהְיֶה אֶצְלוֹ אָמוֹן. Fox's reasoning through this debate corresponds to the priorities already illustrated; he looks to other OT usage, he interacts with Hebrew syntax, he refers to the interpretive tradition, and he appeals to the broader sense of the passage. He finds the proposal for "artisan" unconvincing; Wisdom is "in none of these roles during creation" (286). He rules out "constantly" because "the root '-m-n 'be firm' is not productive in the G-stem. . . . Moreover, the N-stem would be expected in the proposed sense" (286). He settles on "growing up with," in which the term is an infinitive absolute "serving as an adverbial complement. . . . It requires no emendations and accords with the morphology of the Hebrew word" (287). The joy, delight, and play of the following verses affirm his interpretation. He takes a few lines to address what it means for Wisdom to play, concluding that her play "expresses the joy of intellect: exploring, thinking, learning" (289). Such play then interprets the activities of scholars and wise students who seek Wisdom; they are to understand that they, too, are playing before God.

The final section of the chapter (vv. 32–36) mark a shift in tone from the preceding one. Now Wisdom speaks in her maturity (289). In this section, Fox integrates this picture of joyful Wisdom to the purpose of the chapter which is to exhort the reader to seek and obey her. The language of these verses furthers this purpose through allusion to desire, an allusion also prevalent in Proverbs 7. "Prov 8:34 implies a contrast between waiting at Wisdom's door and that of a seductress. The attraction of wisdom is erotic in its power, and the wise pursue her as ardently as a lover does his beloved" (290). Fox's reflection on verse 36 continues this theme, as the verse presents a relationship with Wisdom which is personal and emotional, "love and devotion versus offensiveness and hatred" (291).

After his verse by verse exposition, Fox integrates his exegetical comments so as to present a holistic purpose of the chapter. This purpose is to commend wisdom to the reader, and the chapter accomplishes this by appealing to the desire of the reader. The benefits of wisdom, the antiquity of it, and the emotional appeal all contribute to this purpose.

The final section relating to Proverbs 8 is comprised of six observations related to personified Wisdom in the chapter. These are: human wisdom is external; wisdom is a unity; wisdom speaks wisdom, not God's word; wisdom is energy; wisdom is fun; and wisdom loves humanity (293–95).

Fox addresses the relationship between Wisdom and the LORD both in the commentary proper and in a later excursus. Within his commentary Fox concludes that "Wisdom is portrayed as an entity proceeding from God (according to 2:6, from his *mouth*) and intermediate between him and the world" (293, emphasis original). In Fox's reading, Wisdom is derived from the LORD and subordinated to him. The force of verses 22–31 is to add to Wisdom's resume as a guide for the student qualified by her presence at creation and preeminence over it. The portrayal serves Proverbs 1–9's wider purpose, which is to increase the reader's desire for wisdom. Wisdom is "a child dandled on the knee" of the LORD, playing while the LORD creates, and exploring the products of the LORD's creative acts (287–89).[13]

---

13. Fox emphasizes that there is no dialogue recorded between Wisdom and the LORD, therefore Wisdom is not "discussing the aeon in retrospect" but joyfully studying and learning from that which God has created. Fox, *Proverbs 1–9*, 289.

According to Fox, the Wisdom who speaks in Proverbs 8 is more than a textual phenomenon; she is an "entity" (293). Fox credits Gerhard von Rad with "an important insight by describing Lady Wisdom as representing a real and independent power in the world and beyond it" (353). This power is external to the human mind, making it an object in the universe (293).

> Lady Wisdom symbolizes the perfect and transcendent universal, of which the infinite instances of human wisdom are imperfect images or realizations. Like a Platonic *idea*, the wisdom-universal exists objectively and not only as an abstraction or mental construct. It dwells in special proximity to God—"before him," present to his mind—while maintaining a distinct and separate existence. (356)

Wisdom is thus a special creation of God, intimately connected with the LORD God, but still a creation. When through study human minds come into contact with Wisdom, this objectively existing mental power, they are connected to a being who is close to the mind of God. This proximity was and is temporal; Wisdom only knows of created things. However, she is eminently qualified to teach and guide inquirers because she has existed since the foundation of the world.

Fox's study offers in depth interaction with the text, philologically and theologically. He regularly engages with the history of interpretation, focusing primarily on the Jewish interpretive tradition. He treats these with respect, often drawing on them for insights into the dynamics and reality of the text. His study is a great aid to any student.

The Hermeneia Commentary on Proverbs 1–15 by Bernd Schipper

In the *Hermeneia* series, Bernd Schipper authors the commentary on Proverbs.[14] Schipper locates himself within an interpretive tradition at the start of his commentary. He begins with a brief history of research on the book of Proverbs "in order to situate the commentary within the broader history of research" (1). He does this because each commentary and interpretation "stands within a particular exegetical tradition, and its particular approach must be made explicit prior to the verse-by-verse" exposition (1). That Schipper foregrounds this history with these comments acknowledges a world before the text, that is, a complex context in which all interpretation

---

14. Schipper, *Proverbs 1–15*. Citations from this commentary will be in parentheses through this section.

takes place. It is a refreshing acknowledgement, if not surprising given the parameters of the series (ix).

Interestingly, the history of research provided by Schipper begins in the mid-nineteenth century with the work of Ernst Bertheau (1847). He divides the time between then and the publication of his own commentary between "the time before the discovery of ancient Near Eastern wisdom literature, the time immediately following this discovery, and the more recent period" (1). All three of these periods could be characterized by attention to the world behind the text, even as knowledge of that world shifts and changes (exhibited by the demarcating event of discovering ANE parallels). As such, they fit the broader agenda of the commentary series. Still, Schipper reads this history with an eye to learning how to approach the text. He defines his approach in line with the general trends of each of these periods: from the first period, he highlights the connection between Proverbs and other biblical texts, particularly Deuteronomy; drawing from the middle period, he "takes into account the Egyptian wisdom instruction" as uncovered by archaeologists; and finally from the more recent works, Schipper "inquires into the overall function of the book in the formation of the moral self" (4–5). In this order, it appears that Schipper attends to the world of the text (canonical context), the world behind the text (Egyptian literature), and the world in front of the text (formative function of the moral self). Unfortunately, the last of these three is under-developed, as the introductory essays and exegetical work on Proverbs 8 leave the formative potential of the book in the past, within Israel's history.

The introductory essays explore the redactional history of the book of Proverbs, the relationship of the book to ANE parallels, and finally the concept of wisdom within the book itself. Through these extensive treatises Schipper draws on the world behind the text via extant parallel documents and textual criticism. He attends to the world of the text through canonical resonances, allusions, and quotations. He does not draw conclusions that represent the text as more than its parts. For example, in his comments regarding the seven superscriptions within the book, he marks the mention of Hezekiah as intriguing; "Why is Hezekiah—who is not associated with sapiential thought anywhere in biblical historiography—mentioned here?" (7). His answer traces an increasing significance of this Judean king through the Second Temple period. That Hezekiah is mentioned because he was increasingly important during the putative time of the book's development places the meaning squarely in the world behind the text, without then moving to in-text or in-front-of-the-text conclusions. In his next set of essays, Schipper treats the relationship between Proverbs and other ANE parallels. One of his conclusions is that, within ANE wisdom texts, the father and son dynamic need not be taken literally. Rather, it refers "to a special relationship between the wisdom teacher and the wisdom student in which the student is introduced to a form of knowledge that is not available to all but must be learned through rigorous study of sapiential writings" (14). This language is evocative of Alistair MacIntyre's evaluation and proposal for the mode of tradition as an approach to moral inquiry.[15]

Schipper's subsequent section addresses the concept of wisdom within the book, an exploration that is characterized by attention to the vocabulary, structure, and canonical allusions and connections. He does penetrate beyond a surface level reading to reflect on deeper dynamics at work within the text. For example, the variety of terms used to refer to the broad concept of wisdom "point to an educational process that seeks to instill practical skills" aimed at the heart, "the organ that guides human behavior" (25). Schipper explores Proverbs 4:20–27, the first references to the heart in the book, as developing a "sapiential instruction on the body" (26). These are fascinating insights which expand wisdom from solely a cognitive or rational capacity to include "know-how" and even how one bodily inhabits the world. Following on these comments, Schipper argues that the sapiential vocabulary of the book "ultimately relates to the individual in society" (26). These various concepts cut against a strand of anthropology which construes human beings as atomistic, thinking things.

Yet another suggestive section of these early essays of Schipper is "Wisdom and *Torah*." On the basis of linguistic and conceptual links between Deuteronomy and Psalm 119 (among other texts), he argues that there is a relationship set up between these important ideas within the Old Testament. He does additional work within the exegesis of individual passages. However, his initial survey offers one way to understand the trend within Jewish interpretation to equate wisdom and Torah, as we see in Ben Sira, the Wisdom of Solomon, and Philo. With that being said, he does not integrate his reflections into a coherent message. According to his analysis, the book contains divergent understands of how wisdom and Torah relate; Proverbs 2 and Proverbs 30 offer two sites to which he points for varying understandings of the usefulness of Torah for the knowledge of God (39).

---

15. MacIntyre, *Three Rival Versions of Moral Enquiry*.

He does not then move to reflect on a meaning from the final redactional phase which left these two views unresolved within the text itself.

The final section of his general introduction explores the textual history of the book, in which Schipper interacts primarily with Michael Fox and his *The Hebrew Bible: A Critical Edition* (2015). Schipper's main point of contention with Fox is the latter's tendency to emend the MT to the LXX. Schipper notes how Fox's sense of the whole influences his approach to textual criticism: "Since Fox assumes an originally 'secular' understanding of wisdom and evaluates theological statements as later additions, he proposes, for example, that Prov 8:13 and 19 do not belong to the original Hebrew text but are later 'pietistic insertion[s]'" (41). Schipper begins his commentary by acknowledging that every interpretation stands within a certain tradition (see above). It is surprising that within these comments he objects to another's interpretation, it would seem, on the basis of a similar (if not identical) dynamic. He does not then remind the reader of his own prior commitments, nor acknowledge the contingent nature of all interpretation in relation to the reader's sense of the whole. Rather, what follows are list of factors by which Schipper advocates the MT as the better guide to the Hebrew *Vorlage*.

Turning now to his comments on Proverbs 8, Schipper acknowledges the vast amount of literature related to the chapter. Instead of aiming for an exhaustive reading, he focuses on three facets of the chapter: the distinct audience named in chapter 8 vis-à-vis Proverbs 1–7; the connections in 8:22–31 to Genesis 1; and the way "the poem develops the idea that personified Wisdom is not only a wisdom teacher but also Yhwh's 'first work of creation'" (284). Following on from this final point, Schipper argues the "personified Wisdom takes on a position between God and humanity that, in Deuteronom(ist)ic theology, is reserved for God's word—the *torah*" (284). Schipper's exposition of the chapter with regard to these three points displays the same priorities as his introductory essays; an attention to the cultural background, the history of the text's development, and the literary elements within and alluded to by Proverbs 8. As with those earlier examples, Schipper does not attend to a possible cohesive message for the chapter in interaction with the contemporary world.

In his analysis of the structure of Proverbs 8, Schipper emphasizes the unity of the whole chapter on the basis of, among other aspects, key words being repeated throughout the various sections. Such features tie the passage together to make "a coherent text that explains the significance of wisdom, its origins, and its authority through fundamental statements and also takes on the character of an instruction through the closing section" (288). This position guides Schipper's analysis of the verses often debated as later additions. For example, he regards Proverbs 8:13 as "an important clarification and is thus a meaningful part of the overall composition and not a secondary element" (302).[16]

His next section addresses the background of the chapter. In it, Schipper focuses on intertextuality, reception history, redaction history, and ancient Near Eastern parallels. As Proverbs 8 draws on Genesis 1, alludes to Isaiah 11, and shares similar vocabulary with Deuteronomy 30:15-20, Schipper concludes that Wisdom takes on the "decisive authority for how to direct one's life to God," over against Torah or the king (290). He next argues that notable passages that are "*torah*-oriented" presuppose and receive Proverbs 8 and its teaching regarding Wisdom (290). He detects three stages of development behind the text:

> (1) That which originally described the *torah* in Deuteronomy 30 was (2) applied to personified Wisdom in Proverbs 8, which was so closely associated with Yhwh that there was no room left for an independent concept of *torah*, before (3) the attributes of personified Wisdom were "inverted" and applied to the sapientially conceived *torah* in Psalms 19 and 119. (291-92)

Schipper does not discuss how a reader might understand and appropriate this multi-faceted teaching on the relationship between Wisdom and Torah. A third subunit in his comments on background briefly brings this proposed "second-stage" into conversation with Schipper's view on the redaction of the book of Proverbs. In his view, Proverbs 1:20-33 and 3:13-20 succeed chapter 8 in the development of the book. Proverbs 8 was therefore recontextualized in such as way that "its claims to authority became more and more attenuated" (292). Finally, Schipper views the chapter through the lens of extant ancient Near Eastern parallel literature. He concludes that the phenomenon of personified Wisdom was "modelled after certain ideas connected to the Egyptian goddess Isis during the Persian and Ptolemaic periods" (294).

Coming now to the exposition proper of the chapter, I will provide instances of Schipper's priorities, paying particular attention to those most debated features of the chapter. Verses 1-3 describe the initial call of

---

16. It is unclear to me whether or not Schipper allows that an important clarification could be a secondary element.

Wisdom and identify her location. Schipper is attentive to the text as a multivalent reality. For example, he identifies three levels of meaning for verse 2: "(1) the elevated position of Wisdom, (2) Wisdom's speech from this elevated position, which lends her greater authority, and (3) the use of the metaphor of the path, which is fundamental to chaps. 1–9" (295). Schipper does not address whether the various locations of verses 2 and 3 are intended to refer to one place or many. Instead, he notes the archaeological evidence for multi-chambered gates, a point which illustrates his attention to the world behind the text (296).

Schipper identifies verses 4–11 as a subunit of the chapter.[17] Verse 4 contains one of the standout features of the chapter which he singled out in his introduction to the chapter. In this verse, Wisdom's audience is expanded beyond the norm to include "the largest possible audience" including "not only the wisdom students (פְּתָאיִם) . . . but also those who are regarded as unteachable (כְּסִילִים, 'fools')" (296, 297). His conclusion from this expansion comes in his summary comments on the chapter. There, this facet leads him to believe that "chap. 8 resembles the Hellenistic aretalogies of Isis" (317). That such noteworthy features lead him to a world-behind-the-text conclusion is a significant indicator of how Schipper understands the meaning of the text. This focus behind the text persists through his study of verses 4–11. The command "hear!" (שִׁמְעוּ) in verse 6 is likened to Amenemope, Ptahhotep, and the Book of Thoth (297). Wisdom's claim for her integrity in verse 7 is compared to the "Late-Period Egyptian instruction in Papyrus Brooklyn" (298). One should not get the impression that Schipper's interests are solely ancient Near Eastern parallels. He compares the vocabulary and function of Proverbs 8:6 with other portions of the book to surmise that Wisdom is cast as a wisdom teacher (298). He connects the "murmur" (הגה) of Wisdom in 8:7 with various psalms which "closely associates personified Wisdom with the 'righteous person' whose life is guided by God's word, that is, God's truth" (298).

Verses 12–21 consist of the second speech of Wisdom in the chapter. This subunit provides further justification for Wisdom's authority, a conclusion from which Schipper draws two points. First, with regard to the world behind the text, he speculates whether the chapter "was written at a time when the authority of sapiential instruction was no longer taken for granted and had to be furthered justified" (301). Second, he considers possible implications for the redaction of the book, as chapter 8's broader

---

17. Schipper does not title these subunits.

Modern Historically Oriented Scholars

audience and explicitly grounded authority are distinct from chapters 3–7 (301). His approach to Proverbs 8:13 has already been mentioned as an example of how the cohesion of the chapter guides his handling of text-critical questions. However, he also notes the implications of this verse for the world of the text, specifically by positing a distinction between Wisdom and the Lord.[18] Verse 14 and 15 have been noted by many to interlink with Isaiah 11:2. Through this connection, Schipper reads Wisdom as stepping in to two important roles. First, "Wisdom claims for herself that which prophetic literature associates with the future salvific ruler, namely, the divine qualities that, when received by humankind, allow one to lead a successful life before God"; and second, "Insofar as Wisdom bestows the power to rule, she takes over a role elsewhere assigned to Yhwh" (303). Neither in his exegesis nor in his conclusion does Schipper develop further these implications of the text.

In his comments on verses 22–31 Schipper subdivides the section as Wisdom's creation before the creation of the world (vv. 22–23), the temporal precedence of Wisdom over all other created things (vv. 24–26), the Lord's creative acts in Wisdom's presence (vv. 27–29b), and Wisdom's role as an intermediary between the Lord and humanity (vv. 29c–31) (287). Schipper navigates the translation debates of verses 22–23 primarily through references to other texts of the Old Testament: קנה means "to create" on the basis of Deuteronomy 32:6b and Psalm 139:13; רֵאשִׁית is a temporal statement ("beginning") because of its similar use in Proverbs 1:7, 9:10, and Psalm 111:10; קֶדֶם מִפְעָלָיו מֵאָז is translated "at the outset of his deeds" based on numerous references (2 Sam 15:34; Isa 16:13; Ps 93:2; Isa 45:21; Jer 30:20; Lam 5:21; Job 29:2; Hab 1:12; Ps 74:2) (308–9). His concern to relate the text to its historical environment is also evident; he provides Egyptian parallels to the "not yet" formula of Proverbs 8:24 (309). Before moving to his next subunit, Schipper provides a summative statement of these verses: "Building on the statements about the beginnings of the earth in Prov 8:22–23, the description in v. 24 of a time 'when there were no depths' points to a time *before* the creation as described in Genesis 1.... Prov 8:24 has the perspective of 'Genesis 1, verse zero'" (310, emphasis original). These verses which establish Wisdom's temporal precedence do so against the background of common ancient Near Eastern cosmology (310). Verse 27 introduces the section on the Lord's creative acts in Wisdom's presence. They do so in an order distinct from Genesis 1, yet with

---

18. If Wisdom fears the Lord, Wisdom must not be the Lord.

their own literary structure and beauty. Within this section, which extends through verse 29, Schipper continues to detect links between Wisdom and Torah through the text's multi-level meaning: "v. 29 combines two different levels of meaning . . . it refers to the 'foundations of the earth' following ancient Israelite cosmology . . . [and] it echoes terminology relating to Israel's obligation to obey the law and authoritative word of God" (312). From this, "the divine law can be conceived of as part of the order of creation that applies to both the physical world and humanity" (312). The final subdivision (vv. 29c–31) establishes Wisdom's role as an intermediary. Schipper objects to too strenuous a connection between the וָאֶהְיֶה of Proverbs 8:30 and Exodus 3:14; the form appears in many places and its significance should not be overdrawn (312). In the debates surrounding the proper understanding of אָמוֹן, Schipper lands on the side of "constantly." He notes, as others have done, that verse 30's other two clauses end with temporal markers. Additionally, it fits his understanding of the point of the poem. Along with verse 31, this subunit "creates a hierarchy of God at the top, then (even if just below God) Wisdom, and finally humanity" (314). Schipper offers no thoughts as to how a cosmology that differs from the ancient three-tiered cosmology would enter into and appropriate this teaching.

Schipper's exegesis of verses 32–36 emphasizes two points: the verbal connections between these concluding verses and previous units within the chapter; and the application of ideas to Wisdom that were previously only associated with the LORD. The macarism of verses 32–34 is evocative of Psalm 1, in which one is blessed through study of Torah, walking in the way of the LORD, now transposed to following Wisdom (315). Schipper connects the gates of verse 34 to the gates and entrances of the temple, the homes of Israelites (Deut 6), and the Passover (Exod 12) (316). Finally, the two ways of verses 35–36 shape a connection with the two ways teaching in Deuteronomy (316).

Schipper's comments on Proverbs 8 suggest numerous avenues for interpretation and recontextualization in the contemporary world. However, maintaining the parameters of the series, Schipper does not mention any of these. Rather, his reflections remain in the two worlds of behind and within the text. He notes that Proverbs 8 communicates something distinct in the Old Testament by making her "the only point of reference for humankind" and drawing Wisdom "as close to God as possible within a monotheistic worldview" (317).[19] The broader audience at which Wisdom aims her

---

19. This latter phrase brings to mind Christopher Seitz's argument that space be made

teaching in chapter 8, as I have already mentioned, leads Schipper to conclusions regarding the compositional background of the book. Likewise, the relationship between Wisdom and Torah which he has been careful to draw through the chapter serves to provide fodder for subsequent history of ideas, in terms of conversations in the Second Temple period, the Gospel of John, and the Council of Nicaea (318).

Summary Reflections on Interpreting Proverbs 8 According to Its Ancient Context

The above survey of secular interpretations of Proverbs 8 lays out the current field of scholarship on the chapter coming from sources which make no explicit claim for Christian interpretation. These scholars were chosen as representatives of contemporary interpretations of the chapter in major scholarly commentary series. They each relate to the text primarily through the lens of the world behind the text and the world of the text. The methods and conclusions are salutary for any seeking an honest reading of Proverbs 8 as they are deployed to situate the text as a literary document stemming from an ancient culture.

While there are differences between the authors, they are united in the effort to understand Proverbs 8 primarily through its placement in the context of the ancient Near East. For one seeking to read the text in a transformative way, these efforts are beneficial. At various points in the canonical Christian Bible, the reader is made aware of their capacity for self-deception. For example, Old Testament prophets reprimand the people for seeking words which please them and, in the New Testament, Jesus rebukes the Jewish leaders of his day for interpreting Scripture for their own benefit. Christian readers are thus exhorted to seek an honest interpretation which calls for distancing oneself from the text for the protection of its message. An overly hasty appropriation truncates the dialogical reading process and can hallow out the potential challenge of the text. In this effort, historical-critical and literary readings are beneficial.

Even so, these efforts come up short in the goal for Christian transformative reading, which seeks an interaction between the meaning of the text and the world in front of the text. One might reasonably reckon that if the issue resides in the conventions of the contemporary secular university.

---

for the Old Testament's own distinct form of monotheism. Seitz, "Trinity in the Old Testament," 28–40.

Otto Plöger, Arndt Meinhold, Michael Fox, and Bernd Schipper write from the perspective of the academy, not the church or synagogue, even as they may or may not be participants in a Jewish or Christian faith community. To address dimensions of the text that are not developed in their work, we now turn to some contemporary representatives of commentaries written within an explicitly Christian framework, to see what, if any, difference this makes.

6

Modern Historically Oriented Christian Scholars

Historically Oriented Study of the Bible in the Frame of Christian Faith

THIS NEXT CHAPTER CONTINUES the focus on modern interpreters. However, the four scholars surveyed explicitly wrote within a Christian frame of reference and with an eye toward the strengthening of Christian faith. This sets them apart from those surveyed above, who did not share this explicit aim. What will be seen is that the revolution in biblical studies initiated by the Enlightenment set the parameters in which even those writing for faith felt the need to operate. The sense that the past was very different from the present, and therefore ancient texts must be understood in conjunction with their place in the history of ideas, is prominent in these scholars. The sense of historical distance contrasts with the pre-modern interpretations surveyed earlier; for Athanasius and Matthew Henry the text had an immediacy to Christian life and faith. As we shall see, this immediacy has disappeared in the modern context, even for Christian writers offering their work for the benefit of the church.

The scholars selected for this survey come from various contexts. The first two come from the modern German context: Franz Delitzsch and Gerhard von Rad. The second two, Tremper Longman and Daniel Treier, write and teach in North America. There is also a span of time in this selection: Delitzsch writes in the late nineteenth, von Rad in the mid-twentieth, and Longman and Treier in the twenty-first century. Each offers a different portrait of the ways Christians have taken up the study of Proverbs 8 in modern biblical studies.

Franz Delitzsch on Proverbs 8

Franz Delitzsch's 1872 commentary on Proverbs is an interesting study for a contemporary reader.[1] The majority of the attention in his text is given to philological issues: proper translation, cognate languages, syntax, morphology, and grammar. In some sense it reads more like a volume in Baylor's *Handbook on the Hebrew Bible* series than part of a commentary series. Whereas modern Christian commentaries do often engage with these textual issues, they also tend to give more space to integrating the witness of one verse into the larger theological context. This is not necessarily a deficiency in his commentary; rather, it is a difference that highlights distinctions between differing periods of interpretation.

Delitzsch's work on Proverbs is part of the joint project, along with Carl Keil, the stated aim of which is to produce commentaries on the whole Old Testament accessible not only to biblical scholars, "besonders aber den Theologiestudierenden und den Geistlichen unserer auf das feste prophetische und apostolische Wort sich gründenden Kirche."[2] Both Keil and Delitzsch sought to counter the influence of critical theories which had, in their view, undermined the authority of the Bible. Delitzsch was convinced that the Old Testament related to the reader "the history of God's involvement in human history in order to achieve the salvation of the human race."[3] The significance of Delitzsch view, when compared with that of Keil, was that "it enabled him to see the Old Testament as the unfolding story of divine involvement in human affairs, as opposed to the static approach of Hengstenberg and his school (including Keil)."[4] This particular position regarding God's involvement in human history provides a framework by which we can understand Delitzsch's philological work, which, as will be shown, dominates his interaction with Proverbs 8.

The general approach of Delitzsch in this commentary is to introduce sections with a short paragraph relating the current passage with that which has come before. Much of the commentary is taken up with verse by verse exposition. Delitzsch notes which verse is under his consideration

---

1. Delitzsch, *Proverbs, Ecclesiastes, Song of Solomon*. Throughout this section of the book, references to Delitzsch's work will be in parenthetical citations.

2. Wagner, *Franz Delitzsch*, 319.

3. Rogerson, "Keil, Carl Friedrich (1807–1888) and Franz Delitzsch (1813–1890)," 606.

4. Rogerson, "Keil, Carl Friedrich (1807–1888) and Franz Delitzsch (1813–1890)," 607.

and offers one to two sentences summarizing its message. A translation is then offered, followed by comments, largely philological in flavor. He heavily interacts with textual variants and older translations. Delitzsch will oftentimes relate a Hebrew word to a Greek, Latin, or Arabic cognate to offer a fuller picture of its use.

Delitzsch titles all of chapter 8 "A Discourse of Wisdom Concerning Her Excellence and Her Gifts" (172). This chapter brings the reader back to the voice of Wisdom first heard in Proverbs 1:20. Proverbs 8:22 begins a section of self-testimony in order to establish "her right to be heard, and to be obeyed and loved by men" (182). The poem of verses 22–31 presents her nobility and her unique relationship to God.

As already seen in earlier sections, a *crux interpretum* is found in the opening words of verse 22, particularly regarding the proper translation of קָנָנִי. Delitzsch notes that older translations render this verb "partly by verbs of creation ... partly by verbs of acquiring" (182–83). He acknowledges the Christological controversy of the early church, in which the Arian party argued on the basis of the Greek that the Son began existence before the world but in time, whereas the Athanasians insisted that the Son is eternal with the Father and verse 22 only relates to "the position, place of the Son" (183). Delitzsch argues for neither position, but prefers a translation of "brought me forth" on the basis of two factors. His first reason for translating קָנָנִי as "brought me forth" has to do with his view of the reality toward which the personified wisdom points. "Wisdom is not God, but is God's; she has personal existence in the Logos of the N.T., but is not herself the Logos; she is the world-idea, which, once projected, is objective to God, not as a dead form, but as a living spiritual image" (183). This is contrary to the Athanasian position, as Athanasius read verses 22–31 as relating to the incarnation of the Eternal Son, the Logos of God.[5] Delitzsch disagrees on developmental grounds: "the further progress of the revelation [rather than the text of Proverbs 8 itself] points to her [Wisdom's] actual personification in the Logos" (183).

Delitzsch's use of the term "world-idea" (183), along with the developmental scheme, seems to resonate with his own historical moment. Beginning as far back as Leibniz in the late seventeenth and early eighteenth century, through Herder, Humbolt, Fichte, and Ranke there runs a stream of thought related to the importance of ideas in developing history.

---

5. See discussion of Athanasius' position above.

According to Fichte, the divine idea is the absolute, God or eternal life itself, which manifests itself in all nature and history; it is the ground of all the appearances in the sensible world. The task of the scholar is to know the idea, to trace its development in the natural and historical world, and to communicate it to others.[6]

For Ranke, the idea has two related meanings: first it is the dominant idea of an epoch, and second it is the "characteristic nature of a state or nation."[7] While it may be difficult to ascertain the specific influence of these individual historical scholars, Delitzsch's use of the term along with his strong sense of development connects with the intellectual environment of his day.

Delitzsch's second reason for his preferred translation of קָנָנִי as "brought me forth" is the claim that Wisdom's creation prior to that of the world equates to an eternal existence: "to be before the world is to be before time" (183). The text connects Wisdom's creation with that of the creatures (רֵאשִׁית דַּרְכּוֹ קֶדֶם מִפְעָלָיו מֵאָז), but for Delitzsch this is only because Wisdom's beginning is the *a priori* for the creation of the world. However, "the power which was before heaven and earth were, and which operated at the creation of the earth or the heavens, cannot certainly fall under the category of creatures around and above us" (183). If Wisdom was active in creating all these things, as Delitzsch assumes, she cannot then be counted among them as one created.

One aspect that is surprising is how little Delitzsch supports his assertions. In the present, twenty-first-century context, his first assertion would be strongly contested. And yet, Delitzsch simply states this position regarding the relationship between personified Wisdom and the divine Logos without further comment or argumentation. Searching through his introduction and other portions of the book (such as Proverbs 1:20ff and 3:19–20) reveal no more interaction on this point. The remainder of his commentary is marked by great attention to details, philological, lexical, and grammatical. It may be that he thinks his focus on these linguistic issues will demonstrate the truth of his position.

As an example of his philological concerns, to determine the meaning of קָנָנִי Delitzsch draws on the Arabic *ḳnâ* and avers that both come from the same general idea of forging (184). However, unlike ברא, the verb in Proverbs 8:22 is not marked by the commencement of time, that is, it is not asserting the creation of an object out of nothing. "קנה comprehends

---

6. Beiser, *The German Historicist Tradition*, 283.
7. Beiser, *The German Historicist Tradition*, 282.

in it the meaning to create, and to create something for oneself, to prepare, *parare* (*e.g.* Ps. cxxxix. 13), and to prepare something for oneself, *comparare*, as κτίζειν and κτᾶσθαι, both from *kshi*, to build, the former expressed by *struere*, and the latter by *sibi struere*." In the space of a few sentences, Delitzsch deploys Arabic, Latin, and Greek to understand a Hebrew word usage. He concludes that Proverbs 8:22a is best translated and interpreted "Jahve brought me forth as the beginning of His ways" (182, 184).

Delitzsch displays sensitivity to the nuances of various terms. In Proverbs 8:23, he settles on a translation of "I was set up" from נִסַּכְתִּי: "I was woven" "does not commend itself, for רֻקַּם (Ps. cxxxix. 15), used of the embryo, lies far from the metaphorical sense in which נָסַךְ = Arab. *nasaj, texere*, would here be translated of the origin of a person, or even of such a spiritual being as Wisdom" (184–85). He also parses the various temporal terms in the verse: "מֵעוֹלָם points backwards into the infinite distance, מֵרֹאשׁ into the beginning of the world, מִקַּדְמֵי־אָרֶץ not into the times which precede the origin of the earth, but into the oldest times of its gradual rising" (185). These differences are not supported by any evidence, but his account offers reasons for why diverse terms are used in this verse.

Delitzsch also gives attention to grammatical issues. Regarding verse 24, he notes that "נִכְבַּדֵּי־מָיִם (abounding with water) is a descriptive *epitheton* to מַעְיָנוֹת, which, notwithstanding its fem. plur., is construed as masc." (186). He also rejects the form of the first term under question here, asserting that the word should instead be written with *Patach*, thus נִכְבַּדֵּי.

In verse 27 it is again noteworthy what Delitzsch does not discuss. He translates the verse "When He prepared the heavens, I was there, when He measured out a circle for the mirror of the multitude of waters." Immediately prior to offering this translation he asserts that Wisdom's existence not only preceded creation but "she was also actively taking part in the creative work" (187). It is remarkable that there is no other comment in relation to this. It is as if he expected his translation to offer final and indisputable proof that Wisdom was active. Again, in contemporary commentaries, Wisdom's role in creation is highly debated. What does receive attention by Delitzsch is the apparent *Naturwissenschaft* of the verse, particularly the impression given in the text that the earth is surrounded by waters. Delitzsch writes "This idea of the ocean girdling the earth is introduced into the O.T. without its being sanctioned by it" (188). Through attention to the contextual usages of תְּהוֹם he assures the reader that this verse refers not to waters in the heavens but "seas, fountains, rivers, in which the waters under the heavens spread over the earth" (188). In this allocation of exegetical interest it is apparent that concerns other than those prevalent in the twenty-first century drive Delitzsch's exegesis.

Despite the differences noted between contemporary commentaries and Delitzsch, the nineteenth-century commentary shares a concern for the proper understanding for אָמוֹן in Proverbs 8:30. Two options seem viable to Delitzsch: that of Wisdom as foster-child and of Wisdom as architect. He ultimately steers away from the former for two reasons. Delitzsch agrees that Wisdom is elsewhere presented as God's child, but "on this very account, because this is further said, we lose nothing if אמון should be interpreted otherwise" (190). Additionally, a problem with this reading is that it actually works against the later assertions that Wisdom's is God's child, not that of another: "but the designation אמון would make Him to be the אֹמֵן of Wisdom; and the child which an אֹמֵן bears, Num. ix. 12, and fosters, Esth. ii. 7, is not his own" (190). The alternate understanding comes from אָמַן, meaning to be firm or strong in one's art. It does not occur in the feminine because "handicraft (אוּמָנוּת) belongs to men, and not to women" (191). Delitzsch sees this option as answering the question as to God's purpose for bringing forth Wisdom as well as clarifying her role in the creation of the world:

> it was she who transferred the creative thoughts originally existing in the creative will of God, and set in motion by His creative order, from their ideal into their real effectiveness, and, as it were, artistically carried out the delineations of the several creatures; she was the mediating cause, the demiurgic power, which the divine creative activity made use of. (191)

This summary position is interestingly close to the Arian reading, at least as it is presented by Athanasius; "they [the Arians] say concerning Him, that 'God willing to create originate nature, when He saw that it could not endure the untampered hand of the Father, and to be created by Him, makes and creates first and alone one only, and calls Him Son and Word, that through Him as a *medium*, all things might thereupon be brought to be.'"[8] What is perhaps most interesting about this similarity is that, up to this point, Delitzsch has followed Athanasius in certain translation options. Like Athanasius, he does not see verse 22 as referring to a creation out of nothing, but rather an eternal production or revealing. And yet Delitzsch ends with a position in which Wisdom is a "demiurgic power," a phrase that

---

8. Athanasius, *Contra Arianos* II.24, in *NPNF* 361. Emphasis added.

would mean, in Athanasius' ears, a lesser being to God. We can conclude that Delitzsch's sense of the progression of thought leads to this position, for his perspective is that "wisdom the poet here personifies; he does not speak of the personal Logos, but the further progress of the revelation points to her actual personification in the Logos" (183). In other words, the text is restrained by its own historical moment in the history of thought. This is in contrast to Athanasius for whom the text of Scripture participated in the divine life outside of history. These contrasts highlight how methods exist embedded in a broader understanding of reality.

Gerhard von Rad on Proverbs 8

Roughly a century after Delitzsch's commentary was published Gerhard von Rad published a work devoted entirely to the phenomenon of wisdom in Old Testament Israel.[9] As we shall see, the pair provide an interesting contrast of methods. Delitzsch is attentive to the minutest details, noting even where he believes an accent has been misplaced in the text; von Rad gives little room for such notes, preferring investigation into the broader picture inspiring the texts related to personified wisdom. This preference may be representative of von Rad's later career, as his works on wisdom literature move "away from exclusive tracing of Yahweh's redemptive history to warn against excessive emphasis on history."[10] However, even in earlier work such as his *Old Testament Theology*, one has the sense that von Rad is pushing back against an atomism that was prevalent in early twentieth-century biblical studies[11] in order to emphasize the lived reality of faith within the community of Israel.

Von Rad addresses texts in canonical and intertestamental literature in which wisdom is personified in his chapter "The Self-Revelation of Creation." In this study, von Rad is concerned to elucidate "what this idea [of personified wisdom] . . . really means in the context of Yahwism" (144). That is, he wants to get a sense of how this concept was perceived in the life of ancient Israel. Such a concern is in line with von Rad's scholarly reputation

---

9. Von Rad, *Wisdom in Israel*. Throughout this section of the commentary, references to this work will be provided parenthetically.

10. Crenshaw, "Rad, Gerhard von (1901–1971)," 845.

11. Crenshaw, "Rad, Gerhard von (1901–1971)," 843. For a fuller evaluation of von Rad's life and work, see the entirety of Crenshaw's article, and the many works he references in the article's bibliography.

as one interested in the tradition-history of the text, representing a certain species of *Sitz im Leben*, one not centered necessarily on the cult, but attentive to the theology which produced and passed on such texts.

Von Rad discusses Job 28 prior to Proverbs 8 and a few of his comments are repeated when he comes to the Proverbs text. A brief notice of this prior discussion will usefully introduce the discussion of Proverbs 8. First, according to von Rad, the author of Job 28 is not concerned with precise definitions: that "wisdom" stands in parallelism with "understanding" in Job 28:12, 20, and 28, leads him to this conclusion. Contrary to the aim of the text defining the precise referent for the reader, "what is meant is already known to the reader or listener" (146). There is a reality behind the words of the text toward which "wisdom" and "understanding" gesture and the goal of Job 28 is to put discovery of this reality outside of the reach of human grasp.

A second comment of note is that von Rad reads Job 28 as teaching that wisdom is created and yet has a special status. "The imprecise expressions—he 'counted it out', he 'established it', he 'searched it out'—include, however, the idea that he created it." He immediately follows this statement with "At any rate, it is contrasted with God and was subject to his ordering activity" (147). He supports his assertion that wisdom is subordinate to God, if not created by God, through the structure of the text: "God's actions in relation to rain and wind on the one hand and to wisdom on the other are simultaneous" (147). Remarkable to von Rad is the tension present in the text between wisdom as something created yet separate from creation. He concludes that "This 'wisdom', this 'understanding' must, therefore, signify something like the 'meaning' implanted by God in creature, the divine mystery of creation" (148). His position as to the immanence of wisdom, that is, its place as within the created order will resurface in his discussion of Proverbs 8.

Von Rad is distinctly concerned with the theological background of the text. Near the end of his comments on Job 28 he writes "A vast amount of experience and of solid thought must have preceded such a poem before it could have come into being at all" (148). Von Rad appreciates that ideas arise from contexts, traditions of theology and practice. Combined with his earlier assertion that readers/listeners already knew of what Job 28 spoke, we are led to see this text, at least, as an articulation, an effort of bringing-to-speech that which is already in the background or social imagination of the believing community.

Given his focus on how personified wisdom was integrated with Yahwism, Proverbs 8:22–31 is an important text for von Rad. These verses speak of wisdom's "mysterious origins which reach back to the time when the world was created" (151). He subdivides the passage into four parts of which the first and fourth relate to wisdom herself (vv. 22f.; 30f.), the second portion is set prior to creation (vv. 24–26), and the third set of verses speak of the Lord's creative acts (vv. 27–29).

In a move illustrative of von Rad's concerns, an offset paragraph quickly addresses textual debates such as the proper translation of קָנָנִי and אָמוֹן. Judging from space given to this aspect of the text, he desires to quickly get past these issues to other topics. Regarding the former Hebrew term, von Rad comments "that the verb in v. 22b [קָנָנִי] means 'create' is scarcely questioned. But what difference would it make if one abandoned this meaning? Wisdom belongs, in any case, to the sphere of that which is created" (152). Read in isolation, one might accuse von Rad of assuming the outcome of his exegesis too early. However, he has already addressed this issue in Job 28, as we saw above. He seems to carry the conclusion regarding wisdom's created-ness over from that passage. Regarding the latter debated term, אָמוֹן, von Rad rejects "work-master" based on lack of clear support and a perceived conflict with the "playing" in which wisdom engages in verses 30 and following.

The limited space given to the above debates allows von Rad to focus on what he perceives as a greater concern: how this idea is related to Yahwism. He is not satisfied by postulations that Israel borrowed this material wholesale from neighboring cultures. He allows "in vv. 22–29 the style of a specific Egyptian divine proclamation has clearly been borrowed and that in vv. 30f. the Egyptian idea of a deity caressing personified truth (Maat) has somehow, though not without internal modifications, found its way into our didactic poem" (153). However, the transfer of the style and wording has resulted in a new meaning in the context of Israel's faith. Within this faith context, wisdom is a creation, "an entity which belongs in the world, even if it is the first of the works of creation, the creature above all creatures" (154). Von Rad hereby acknowledges the interrelation of ideas and practices; he resists any attempt to flatten Israelite faith into an imitation of that of its neighbors.

An appreciation for contingency is apparent in the next portion of von Rad's argument, which addresses the idea that the concepts expressed in Proverbs 8 are late and speculative. Von Rad is responding to the charge that these reflections on personified wisdom are divorced from lived religious experience and are "the products of an intellectual, creative genius which is capable of making abstract deductions" (154). Over against this, von Rad argues a position redolent of mid- to late-twentieth-century philosophical hermeneutics, that early wisdom aphorisms are predicated on a sense of the whole: "on what basis did the persistent attempts to determine individual orders operate—especially the tracing of analogies in different spheres of life—if not on the presupposition of a great all-embracing order including everything that exists, an order which can, however, never be grasped any more than only partially?" (154) That is, those proverbs which populate the book starting in chapter 10 are reliant on an overall sense of the whole. Therefore, even though passages such as Proverbs 8 and Job 28 may be late in Israel's history, they nevertheless articulate something long present in the tradition.

Continuing his objections to this wisdom being speculative, "what is being spoken of in Prov. 8 is an event, something which happens to man in the world and is actually brought upon him by the world" (154). The world impinges on the lives of these ancient Israelites in such a way, and in interaction with their tradition and the traditions around them, to produce a fresh articulation. Von Rad ties the articulation in Proverbs 8 to Job 28. Wisdom continues to be something within creation, an attribute of the immanent realm rather than a divine attribute. However, this fresh expression does modify the tradition. "The most interesting feature of what is new is that this world order turns, as a person, towards men, wooing them and encouraging them in direct address" (156). Although the direct address, call, or summons of the natural world has overlap with "the nature religions," Yahwism's distinctive framework shapes it: "Israel did not agree to the mythicization and deification of the first principle of the world" (156). The context of Israel's faith contours the natural call to give rise to a unique expression, not found in any other of Israel's religious neighbors.[12]

Von Rad further stresses the contingency of this wisdom concept within its expression in Israel, more specifically its personification.

> But this personification is anything but a freely chosen, decorative, stylistic device which the reader who is skilled in rhetoric could easily have replaced by a completely different one, with the sole aim of simplifying understanding. Rather, this form of speech was

---

12. See von Rad, *Wisdom in Israel*, 153.

determined by the subject in question and could be fixed in words only in this way without incurring loss. (157)

Over against those who might wish to see this as "mere" literary ornamentation, von Rad understands the personification as carrying something essential to proper articulation. Alternate renderings for this idea such as "primeval order," "world reason," or "Logos" lose something of the personal element present through personification (157, 161).

Attention to the tradition behind the text continues throughout the remainder of von Rad's chapter as he explores the nature of this call from wisdom, as well as the feature of love given and required by wisdom. Exploration moves beyond just Proverbs 8 to include other wisdom literature, including Sirach. In this enquiry, the theological experience of the tradition explains the features of the text.

As to the call of Wisdom, "It was obviously the opinion of the teachers that man is addressed from creation by a desire for order from which he cannot escape" (158). No corner of life, no topic was removed from this voice, from the mundane to the rule of government. To ignore this voice was to invite dire consequences, as Proverbs 1:24-31 illustrate. "Here, too, we have the presentation of something that actually takes place" (161). That is, what is expressed in Proverbs 8 and other wisdom texts arises from encounters with the world that are here brought to speech using the resources of the tradition.

Von Rad maintains throughout that this voice calling to humanity is not as such that of the LORD. "This call from the mysterious order to men is, as we have seen, perfectly clear; although it is actually *a voice speaking out of what has been made* (and speaking of Yahweh in the third person, Prov. 8.13), it nevertheless bears all the marks of a divine address" (163, emphasis added). Features of this voice are akin to priestly and prophetic revelation, but are also different. To account for this, von Rad looks to the socio-historical situation surrounding the monarchy, which "ushered in a period of specific individualization in which the individual's interest in Yahweh was questioned much more urgently than in the era of older Yahwism" (164). The tradition did not adequately equip or prepare the Israelite for this; the teaching of the self-revelation of creation was the contribution of the wise men to the crisis brought on by this lack of preparation (165).

Other than the call of Wisdom, the other facet of the self-revelation of creation that draws von Rad's interest is the facet of love. Throughout Proverbs and Sirach this theme is present in various ways: through wisdom cast as a woman inviting people into her home, in the contrast between her and the seductive foreign woman, and in the calls to love wisdom and wisdom's promise of love in return. Again, von Rad seeks to ground this in the lived experienced of the ancients. The inquiring minds sets out on a journey for knowledge of the world,

> It encounters an opposite, indeed it is at once overtaken by the voice of the divine, primeval order, for this voice is already directed towards men; it is already on the way to them and addresses them from the place for which reason is, in fact, searching, but which it can never reach by its own efforts (Job 28). And because the mystery of the world moves toward man and seeks his ear, for this reason wisdom must, indeed, may now be loved by man. (167–68)

Von Rad casts this story in terms of an ancient Israelites' experience of search and encounter. Living out of the tradition of Yahwism led one to a particular encounter with the world. This encounter led early on to the older practical wisdom of the short sayings. However, through making this encounter itself the object of thought, and reaching for further resources in her neighbors, Israel brought forth personified wisdom, the doctrine of the self-revelation of creation (174). This address of creation to humanity, leading to a point of decision, "is attested only in Israel" and von Rad explicates this in terms of the lived experience of Israel's faith in its ancient Near Eastern theological context (175).

Von Rad's approach again displays a concern for the context of the faith in the lived experience of the Israelites. His narration of the crisis brought about by the scrutiny on the individual is winsomely written. However, as he acknowledged earlier, even though these reflections must arise from a "vast amount of experience . . . nothing of that has been preserved for us" (148). Without some record of that experience, von Rad's narrations cannot escape the charge of speculation. However, speculation need not be a condemning charge. All interpretation occurs against a background, some sense of the whole. Without the background, words dissolve into marks on a page. Responsible interpretation is aware of the background and allows it to be challenged, corroborated, or corrected by the text. Von Rad's narration offers us a possible window into the interaction between ancient Israelites and the world brought about by their faith, and it is a window facilitated by von Rad's own horizon as a twentieth-century Christian Old Testament scholar.

MODERN HISTORICALLY ORIENTED CHRISTIAN SCHOLARS

The Proverbs Commentary in the Baker Commentary on the Old Testament Wisdom and Psalms Series by Tremper Longman III

The distinguishing features of the Baker Old Testament Commentary on the Old Testament Wisdom and Psalms are, according to the series preface, a focus on the biblical book and attention to the distinctive contributions of the OT wisdom books.[13] The preface acknowledges that each of the books under discussion in the series (Psalms, Proverbs, Job, Ecclesiastes, and Song of Songs) is "harder to fit into the development of redemptive history and requires more effort to hear their distinctive message" (12). Although the various authors of the commentaries will be different, the structure of each in the series is intended to be similar. An introduction covers issues such as authorship, date, structure. Section by section commentary follows, focusing on "the meaning of the text in its original historical setting" (13). After each section, theological implications are explored: "connections with other parts of the canon, both OT and NT, are sketched out along with the continuing relevance of each passage for us today" (13). One may note at the outset that, prima facie, familiar modern scholarly concerns receive much more space and weight than issues of "continuing relevance ... for us today."

Tremper Longman III serves not only as the series editor but also as the author of the initial installment in the series.[14] His understanding of Proverbs 8 is heavily influenced by earlier studies reflected in his work *Fictional Akkadian Autobiography*.[15] He divides the chapter into an introduction in verses 1–3, an exordium found in verses 4–11, a formal autobiographical introduction in verses 12–21, a teaching on her relationship with the LORD in verses 22–31, and in verses 32–36 a final autobiographical note which turn explicitly to the audience (197–98).

Longman devotes a comparatively large amount of space to discussing ancient Near Eastern cosmology, particularly in relation to verses 24–29 of Proverbs 8. Egyptian, Mesopotamian, and Canaanite creation beliefs are noted for the importance of water in creation, as in Genesis 1. Yet Wisdom claims precedence before these primordial waters, as well as the mountains

---

13. Longman, "Series Preface" in *Proverbs*, 12. The remaining quotations from the preface are cited in parentheses throughout the opening paragraph.

14. Longman, *Proverbs*. Citations for this work will be provided in parenthetical in-text citations throughout the remainder of this section.

15. Longman, *Fictional Akkadian Biography*.

and the rest of God's creation (206). The language of this passage is noted as redolent of the Babylonian creation myth, the *Enuma Elish*. In the poetic description of the passage, "by allusion to Gen. 1 as well as the broader ancient Near Eastern tradition of creation, we are being told of Wisdom's presence during these primordial events" (207).

Longman acknowledges the "interplay between exegesis and theology" as a part of his comments on his translation (204). Many scholars want to avoid certain translations because of theological commitments. Strikingly, Longman claims that "the only real reasons for moving away from [a rendering of אָמוֹן as 'craftsman' in 8:30] are theologically motivated" (196 n. h). Longman contends that our reading is always influenced by our prior theological understanding. He does not, however, probe the possible complexities within, or possible objections to, this contention. Consider, for example, the translation of 8:22. Longman argues that verses 22 "describes the begetting of Wisdom by Yahweh" (204). He opts for translating קנה as "begot" due to the presence of other birth imagery in verses 24 and 25. This birth of Wisdom takes place at the start of time and in relationship to the rest of God's acts of creation. Verse 23 supports this assertion that Wisdom was "brought into being at the beginning, before other acts of creation" (205). As already noted, however, Athanasius made similar notes regarding the relative nature of Wisdom's beginning. Both Athanasius and Longman bring a Christian theological understanding to the text, but its impact greatly differs. Athanasius claims "for if He says that He was created 'for the works,' He shews His intention of signifying, not His Essence, but the Economy which took place 'for His works,' which comes second to being."[16] Athanasius sees this qualification as indicating another meaning for "create" in the verse rather than "came from nothing," and is found among his arguments that this verse is a reference to the incarnation of the Son rather than His eternal being. The difference between Athanasius' reading and Longman's is striking, given that both read within a Christian theological understanding. This illustrates the complex nature of theological understanding and the role it plays in interpretation.

In verse 30, the term אָמוֹן is a *hapax legomenon*. Longman allows that his translation, "craftsman," is only probable (207). However, he sees it as "appropriate to the context and implies that Wisdom was not only present but also involved in creation as a guiding force" (207). The final verse of this subunit of the poem evokes the celebration of creation and paints

---

16. Athanasius, *Contra Arianos II*.51, 376.

Wisdom as "a child sporting in a new environment" (207). The dual direction of Wisdom's delight presents her as a mediator between the human and the divine. In his exploration of the theological implications of the poem, Longman summarizes the teaching of Proverbs 8:22–31: "She was there before anything else was created and then witnessed the creation process itself. Indeed, the implication is not only that she was present but that she also participated in the creation. Her references to herself as a 'craftsman' (8:30) may indicate that she helped in the project" (209).

Longman's interpretation of Woman Wisdom illustrates the view of Wisdom as a personified attribute of the LORD (33, 212). As such, personified Wisdom is a literary stand-in for the LORD, or a feature of the LORD's character. Like Plöger and Fox, Longman values reading the passage against the background of its proposed originating historical context (101–2). However, Longman acknowledges that Christian faith influences the interpretation of the passage. Longman accounts for this influence in terms of chronological development; "it was the coming of Jesus that revealed a deeper meaning within the holy writings of Israel, . . . his coming clarified the earlier revelation" (102). His interpretation of Wisdom rests on reading the location of Wisdom's house (cf. Prov 9:3) as a poetic move to identify her as the LORD. "Here we need to transport ourselves back into the world of the original text, where we discover that the building on the high point of the city is the temple. This was true throughout the ancient Near East" (33). The house of Wisdom functions as a literary synecdoche, joining "a long list of other metaphors for God's relationship with his people, including warrior, shepherd, father, spouse, king and more" (33). Additionally, Longman cites a parallel with the ancient literary genre of fictional biography.[17] In light of these sources, Longman understands the relationship between Wisdom and the LORD as literary, referring to the personal being of God, not to an entity other than the LORD.

Longman notes both the development of Wisdom theology in the intertestamental period as well as its application to Christ in the NT. However, the connections between Wisdom and Jesus should not be over-extended.[18] An example of such a mistake is found in Arius, the fourth-century interpreter (212). Arius and his followers pressed "literally the language

---

17. See his *Fictional Akkadian Biography*, on which he draws in his commentary on Proverbs for the Baker Commentary on the Old Testament Psalms and Wisdom.

18. He is similarly cautions about overemphasizing the connections between Wisdom and Torah. *Proverbs*, 212.

that Wisdom (Jesus) was created or brought forth as the first of creation" (212). Longman does not mention the response of Athanasius or other pro-Nicene figures. Rather he asserts that the passage is "not a prophecy of Jesus or any kind of literal description of him" (212); Wisdom is not "a preincarnate form of the second person of the Trinity" (213). His position is grounded in the poetic genre of Proverbs; as this is poetry, images and figures should be understood metaphorically.[19] Again, Longman takes on an interpretive strategy of Athanasius but comes to different conclusions. Athanasius argued against the Arian reading on the basis of genre:

> For what is said in proverbs is not said plainly, but is put forth latently.... Therefore it is necessary to unfold the sense of what is said, and to seek it as something hidden, and not nakedly to expound as if the meaning were spoken "plainly," lest by a false interpretation we wander from the truth.[20]

At the risk of oversimplification, between the two interpreters (Athanasius and Longman) there is a certain similarity in method, accompanied by a certain caution. Nonetheless their readings differ greatly.

Longman openly affirms the conditioned and contextual nature of his knowledge through his claim that theology and exegesis cannot be separated. In this regard, Athanasius and Longman share common core theological convictions; both would affirm the Nicene Creed, both affirm that Scripture is God's word and reveals the God of Christian faith.[21] The formation toward which Longman gestures must run deeper than these explicit theological formulations. Without an extended treatment of the matter, we can make certain observations about their operating imaginaries. Longman has a high view of the ancient historical context as seen through his references to ANE cosmology and creation myths as likely explicators for portions of Proverbs 8. His reliance on his previous work, *Fictional Akkadian Autobiography*, offers another instance of this. He sees the poem as finding its meaning in relation to historically contemporaneous works and customs. Acknowledging the genre of Proverbs moves one to seek likely

---

19. He does not engage in the conversation regarding whether or not metaphors can refer or are merely ornamental.

20. Athanasius, *Contra Arianos* II.44, 372.

21. For Longman's views on the latter, see his comments in "Series Preface" in *Proverbs*, 12–13. I am assuming his views on the Nicene Creed based on presentations I have heard as well as the statement of faith for Westmont College, where Longman taught for nineteen years.

historical references for each image and metaphor. These historical sources "push" the meaning as they are part of the poem's background. Within Longman's Christian framework, God's work of revelation is found through these lines of influence. To use Charles Taylor's terminology, the conception here is located within the immanent frame.[22]

In comparison to Longman, Athanasius' social imaginary appears as one that moves more easily toward the transcendent. Scripture participates in a higher reality and its meaning need not be tied to its historical context. When Athanasius acknowledges the genre of Proverbs, this leads him not to the historical environment, but the theological reference of Scripture, understood by him to be the Nicene confession of the Triune God.[23] Athanasius lived in a world dominated by metaphysical realist cosmology; a cosmology lived out in practices, even those of reading Scripture. The comparison between these two exegetes highlights their differences.

The Brazos Theological Commentary on Proverbs by Daniel Treier

Of the various commentary series reviewed in this project, the Brazos Theological Commentary is the most distinct. In contrast with the others' focus on textual concerns, the series preface of this series embraces theological tradition as an aid in interpretation. "The central premise in this commentary series is that doctrine provides structure and cogency to scriptural interpretation."[24] The task of biblical interpretation is taken to be a complex one in which guides are needed in order to gain a Christian understanding of the text. "The way forward must rely upon a tradition of reading that Irenaeus reports has been passed on as the rule or canon of truth that functions as a confession of faith" (x). The series editor, Reno, contrasts this approach with a modernist one, represented by Benjamin Jowett. The reading has a different relationship with postmodernism. Reno appreciates postmodernism's encouragement to criticize the critics (x). However, he understands postmodernism primarily in somewhat Nietzschean form: "We read Athanasius and think him stage-managing the

---

22. The immanent frame can also be open to the transcendent, but the conditions of such belief have changed over time. I am not accusing Longman of lacking a sense of divine purpose in the text. Rather, his framework for understanding this interaction is one shaped by the present secular age. See Taylor, *A Secular Age*, 539–93.

23. See Young, *Biblical Exegesis and the Formation of Christian Culture*, 29–45.

24. Reno, "Series Preface" in *Proverbs and Ecclesiastes*, xiv. References to the preface will be found in parentheses throughout my comments on it.

diversity of scripture to support his positions against the Arians" (xi). As such, he wishes to distinguish the series' approach from postmodernism. Rather than understanding tradition as obscuring, the Brazos Theological Commentary series approaches it as "a clarifying agent for our minds fogged by self-deception" (xii). As such, the scholars engaged to write the works of the series are selected because they are theologians, as an attempt to reunite the disciplines in service of the church.

Daniel Treier authors the Brazos Theological Commentary volume on Proverbs and Ecclesiastes.[25] Treier acknowledges at the outset of his comments on Proverbs 8:22–31 that the passage has a long history of Christological reading. However, he wants to clear the air so that his readers do not assume such a relationship is without complication: "one should not get the idea that Prov. 8 would be simple if we kept Jesus out of it; problems of translation and interpretation abound in any case" (45). The five topics he wishes to address in this vein are the meaning of the verbs in 8:22–26, the meaning of אָמוֹן in 8:30, the timing of various acts, the literary function and identity of Wisdom, and, finally, any Christological relevance of the passage (45).

Treier first addresses the meaning of the verbs in verses 22 through 26. He follows Longman and others in preferring an understanding of קנה as "beget" in verse 22. Verse 23's verb נסכתי could mean either "installed" or "woven," and Treier opts for the latter to go along with the metaphors in verses 24–25 (46). Those verses use the verb חלל, "to bring forth," which "highlights divine agency, unquestionably introducing a birth metaphor" (46).

Next, Treier turns to the meaning of אמון in Proverbs 8:30. Treier sees problems in translating this word "artisan": the support of Jeremiah 52:15 seems itself disputable, and the possible conceptual analogy of Proverbs 3:19 "could also entail no more than Wisdom serving as God's instrument" (47). He does not see the alternative reading of "child" as attractive for grammatical reasons, but more importantly because "child" lacks the gravitas that the rest of the poem seems to have. Treier favors the adverbial readings of Bruce Waltke and Stuart Weeks, such that the line would read "and I was beside him constantly" or "faithfully" (47).[26] This reading introduces

---

25. Trier, *Proverbs and Ecclesiastes*. Throughout the remainder of the review of Trier's work, page numbers will be provided in parenthetical citations.

26. We should note that Weeks' analysis of the structure of verses 22–31 lead him to translate this verse in the present tense, "I have remained at his side faithfully," rather than in the past tense. See Weeks, "The Context and Meaning of Proverbs 8:30a," 441–42.

for Treier the possibility of an intertextual allusion in Revelation 3:14, in which Christ asserts that he is a "faithful and true witness."

Treier then addresses the timing of the various acts in Proverbs 8:22–31. His comments challenge a superficial reading of the passage as meaning that Wisdom is a creature. Verses 30 and 31 are often read with "Wisdom beside God during creation, with the delight of 8:31 presumably being subsequent to this act or process of creation itself" (48). However, based on the *inclusio* of "I was there" in verse 27 and "I was beside him" in verse 30, along with the link between 8:30–31, it is better to understand Wisdom as present with God during creation and delighting in that presence ever since. Working backwards, the assertion of the poem that Wisdom preceded some features of the cosmos is compatible with John's Gospel and Nicene Christology. With regard to verse 22, "A nonliteral understanding of begetting is entirely consistent with the poetic nature of the passage and the symbolic force of household imagery throughout Proverbs. Classic Christian theology rightly highlights the text's metaphorical establishment of Wisdom's divine pedigree" (48). Even the claim that Wisdom is the Lord's first act from of old does not necessitate an understanding of Wisdom as a creature. "The phrasing gives every appearance of trying to convey Wisdom's distinctiveness, not her fit within creaturely patterns" (49).

The fourth topic of Treier's attention is the literary function and identity of Wisdom. He recognizes that the personification of Wisdom is "a literary motif in the middle of a passage that takes poetic license" (49). Be that as it may, as the text presents it, Wisdom cannot be solely identified with a divine attribute or the book of Proverbs. The distinctions between the Lord and Wisdom mitigate against the first. The associations between Wisdom and the divine argue against the latter. Treier does not want to tell Jewish readers how to read their scriptures. However, he does argue that "it is understandable how readings by the early (Jewish) Christians would naturally involve the messianic hopes, connected to future divine self-revelation, that were now thought to reach fulfillment" (49). Christian identification of Christ with Wisdom is based on these hopes, as well as mysteries laden in the text. Wisdom "clearly is beyond just another created reality ... while not solely identifiable with God either" (49). Treier acknowledges that Jesus Christ is not present "directly on the text's surface" but that does not rule out a Christological reading. Wisdom serves as a mediator between God and the world and "is God present, teaching and ruling through not only kings and priests but also parents and nonhuman creatures" (50). The logic of Wisdom in the book, including in chapter 8, offer a parallel logic to the New Testament presentation of Christ.

Treier transitions smoothly into discussing the Christological relevance of Proverbs 8. On his reading, Christ presents "the resolution of a mystery latent in the text, though not always clearly recognized" (51). Treier engages with the writings of Athanasius through this last section. Arius' interpretation of the passage threatened God's simplicity, as if God had to create wisdom in order to be wise. Additionally, Arius believed that God could not engage with creation and therefore created the Son to do this work. Yet, this "presumes what Prov. 8 counteracts, namely the idea that God cannot be directly engaged with the cosmos but must create through an intermediary to avoid getting his own hands dirty" (52). Treier defends Athanasius' interpretations up to this point. However, he separates himself from the Alexandrian bishop on his exegetical conclusions that refer the begetting of verse 22 to the incarnation. Such a reading would reverse the expected sequence of existence and economy. It also ignores the strong link between each section of Proverbs 8:22-31. "Athanasius' interpretation at this point is an unnecessary expedient if we dismiss 'created' from our translation of 8:22a or even simply accept that such poetic license would not entail an Arian ontology in any case" (53). Regardless of this difficulty, Treier believes that Athanasius "points toward the fundamental issue that determines how to read this text" (53). This issue is how to understand Wisdom's relationship with God and creation. Treier then surveys how Proverbs 8 (the entire chapter) casts Wisdom in terms qualitatively distinct from creation, as well as those relate her to the divine. He also explores how New Testament texts such as John 1, Colossians 1, and Matthew 11 allude to this passage. In conclusion, Treier believes that understanding this passage as having Christological relevance encourages readers to hold redemption and creation together. "Covenant life means the renewal of creation, while creaturely life is ultimately designed for covenant fellowship with God" (57).

Treier's commentary accords well with the standards outlined by Reno's preface. It is theologically explicit without letting the theological tradition necessarily lock the interpreter into one conclusion. Treier feels free to acknowledge that other readings are possible as well as to disagree with Athanasius as certain points. He models a helpful appropriation of the tradition. He is unashamed of his embeddedness in a theological stream and fulfills the requirements of the series.

Hermeneutical Reflections on Modern Historically Oriented Scholars

Each of the four scholars surveyed above write with a concern for the enduring significance of the Old Testament text for the Christian faith. And yet, each approaches the passage in a distinct way. Delitzsch deals with the text philologically and in great detail, only touching lightly on the theological issues raised by Proverbs 8. Gerhard von Rad is interested in the larger theological background of faith required to produce such a text, and dispenses with the textual sticky wicket of Proverbs 8:22 and 31 in a short paragraph so that he can get on to the broader theological content. Tremper Longman's approach illustrates a contemporary application of the comparative method in biblical studies, as he coordinates the phrases and ideas of Proverbs 8 with surrounding ANE cultures. While his conclusions differ from scholars like Plöger and Fox, his methods are indistinguishable from them. Daniel Treier offers a way of reading Proverbs 8 that bears a family resemblance to pre-modern interpreters like Athanasius, thereby providing a pathway for a reading of the text in line with traditional Christian theology.

Having acknowledged their differences, all show their location in the broader historically oriented approach of modernity by respecting the text's original context. For Delitzsch this is made manifest in his philological moves of comparing words to cognate terms in other languages, preferably those roughly contemporaneous with the Hebrew in question. For von Rad it is the traditio-historical context which best explains the text. It would appear to be a strong sense of the historically contingent nature of Proverbs 8 that leads both authors to disagree, implicitly and explicitly, with the premodern interpretation of this passage represented by Athanasius and Matthew Henry.

Tremper Longman and Daniel Treier represent something of the variety present in late twentieth- and early twenty-first-century biblical scholarship on what it means to interpret the Bible theologically. Based on his reading of Proverbs, Longman might best be characterized as reading the Bible as the development of increasingly clearer revelation. Proverbs' witness is tied to its originating location in time and place; its genre and meaning are primarily associated with Akkadian literature rather than the canonical context. This viewpoint shares much in common with those who write from a non-faith perspective. For Longman, like Plöger, Fox, and Schipper, the differences and distances between the originating context of Proverbs 8 and other contexts exercise significant influence on possible meanings.

Dan Treier, however, represents a viewpoint in which these differences are emphasized less. What takes on more prominence is Proverbs 8 as Christian Scripture, that is, as taken up in the two-testament canonical collection of the Christian church. While most commentators note the history of interpretation, Treier gives this history more attention and seeks to address how it can be helpful for a contemporary reader. As noted above, he does not feel bound by this tradition, even as he evaluates it positively. Treier is not able to engage with as much depth with the scholarly conversations about the ancient context. This is likely due to the constraints of the commentary series vis-à-vis size and focus. This lack may leave one, even a Christian, suspicious of an overly hasty appropriation of the text within the Christian tradition, even as they are thankful for a reading of the text which honors those who have come before in that same tradition.

The differences between these four Christian interpreters illustrate some aspects of the debates in the modern era over the roles of faith and history in the interpretation of the Bible within Christian practice.

Hermeneutical Reflections on Modern Commentaries on Proverbs 8

In 1860, Benjamin Jowett called for the Bible to be read like any other book.[27] His attitude was paradigmatic for much of the academic study of the Bible for roughly a century. However, in the latter half of the twentieth century, and now into the twenty-first century, the landscape has changed. At the outset of this chapter, we acknowledged Craig Bartholomew's analysis of three turns in modern biblical studies.[28] These turns have produced what at times can be a cacophony of interpretative methods. In regards to Proverbs 8, much of the recent work has maintained the classic focus on the world behind the text, and incorporated insights into the world of the text. The benefit of this focus is that the text can be guarded against overhasty appropriation. The critical phase of interpretation which attends to the world behind and the world of the text can deepen the appropriation

---

27. Jowett, "On the Interpretation of Scripture," 482.
28. Bartholomew, *Introducing Biblical Hermeneutics*, 237–45.

of the text by opening up for transformation areas that would otherwise have been ignored.

What remains less developed is sustained attention to the world in front of the text; few offered much in terms of a fruitful dialogue between the text and the present world. Nor did it appear to be a priority for any of these commentaries, regardless of faith commitments, to offer an articulation of a mode of being-in-the-world opened up by the text. In this we can sense the loss between these modern and the pre-modern commentaries surveyed. In pre-modern commentaries, there was a sense of nearness between the text and the life lived by readers in the world. Modern scholarship, initially desiring to recover a reading of the text which bore more similarity to its original historical audience, has increasingly been removed from the sort of applicability displayed by those of the pre-modern world.[29]

The main focus of the next section of the book is the world in front of the text. However, at this point we can offer one example of how attention to the interaction between the reader and the text can beneficially foreground certain discussions, and therefore open the reader up to a deeper challenge stemming from the text.

In the survey above, Michael Fox's categorization of wisdom as primarily cognitive was highlighted. In his essay on wisdom in the personification passages, Fox writes, "Lady Wisdom is a strange being, a personification of a *mental power* who claims to have preceded creation and to exist in a daughterlike relationship to God."[30] This statement of wisdom as a mental power is echoed in other places in the essay and throughout the commentary. In the same essay Fox concludes that "Wisdom is like a living, sentient organism, requiring interaction *with other minds* for its own vitality and realization."[31] According to his introduction, wisdom "is the power of the human mind, both in its intellectual faculties and in the knowledge it can gain, hold, and transmit. Wisdom both transcends the individual mind and resides within it"; the book displays a firm conviction in "the ability of the human mind, for all its frailties, to illuminate the darkness and guide us aright."[32]

As noted above, Fox's description of wisdom and what it means to pursue wisdom is in certain ways reminiscent of the activities of students

---

29. See the comments of Steinmetz, "The Superiority of Pre-Critical Exegesis," 27–38.
30. Fox, *Proverbs 1–9*, 352, emphasis added.
31. Fox, *Proverbs 1–9*, 357, emphasis added.
32. Fox, *Proverbs 1–9*, 3.

in *yeshivot*. To be clear, pointing out this similarity is not an exercise in ideological unmasking, as if showing that Fox is influenced by his tradition somehow invalidates his conclusions. Fox's understanding of wisdom can be understood as one possibility of construing the text. Nevertheless, my point is that not engaging with the world in front of the text and contemporary appropriation forecloses certain discussions which would make this commentary more helpful for ascertaining the enduring significance of Proverbs 8. Fox assumes an overlap between his own understanding of wisdom, influenced by his tradition lived in the contemporary frame, and that of ancient wisdom; he repeatedly argues that Proverbs' conception of the human being prizes the intellect. Even if this is the case, we may wonder how a world influenced so heavily by Cartesian dualism (either in favor or objection) may differ from the ancient one. If the meaning of each chess piece changes based on the presence of other pieces on the board, how might the presence of a Cartesian demarcation between the internal and the external make a difference for a mental conception of wisdom? Again, it is not that Fox's reading is necessarily wrong. Rather, this example points to one place wherein a dialectical relationship could be explored between the text and a reader in the Cartesian-influenced modern era. Even if Fox is more influenced by his awareness of *yeshivot*, his commentary is written for a general audience, many of whom do not share this practice and background. Instead of the interpretive task being only concerned with descriptions of the past, ideally there would be movement between a critical self-understanding in the present and the text of the past, by which they might "inform, enable, correct and enlighten each other."[33] Attending to the dialectical interaction between the world in front of the text and our own can open up these sorts of dialogues, and thereby increase the transformative potential of the text.

---

33. Lash, "Interpretation and Imagination," 25.

Summary of Section 2

IN THE PAGES ABOVE, I surveyed the history of interpretation of Proverbs 8 over a span of roughly seventeen hundred years. The summaries of commentaries illustrate the changes which have taken place in that time in the general approach to biblical interpretation and the specific reading of Proverbs 8. Looking back, what was lost and what was gained through these changes?

The earlier commentaries, which come from the pre-modern era, illustrate a sense of immediacy between the text of the bible and the life of the reader. Athanasius read Proverbs 8 as speaking directly to the controversy over the doctrine of Christ. Matthew Henry did the same with the life of the Christian in the eighteenth century. It would be untrue to say that they had no sense of history, but their sense of it did not impress upon them any gulf between the words on the page and the world in which they lived and moved and had their being. As one progresses into and through the modern era, this sense of immediacy fades away. Scholarly energy became dedicated to placing this text in the distant past. Even commentators writing with an explicitly Christian framework, for the most part, sought to relate Proverbs 8 to its historical context and then offered only tangential implications for the Christian life. When those applications were expounded it was without a robust interaction with the world in which Christians live. The loss here is the capacity of the commentaries to guide the church into a different way of being in the world.

With this being said, we can be appreciative of the developments in biblical interpretation over the centuries. As has been noted on several occasions, the critical phase of interpretation is important for generating a challenging and transformative reading of the text. It is true that the Bible is made up of ancient documents, Proverbs 8 being one of them. Locating the text within the history of ideas makes the reader aware that the words on the page may not mean what they think they mean. The relation of Proverbs 8 to ancient sources makes the passage strange to the modern reader and can invite a more robust dialogue between the reader, or at least the reader with scholarly inclinations, and the text. Surveying the history of interpretation, as Michael Fox and Dan Treier do with the Jewish and Christian traditions, respectively, can show how this passage has been read differently and to different ends, thereby offering the reader alternatives to what may otherwise be an obvious application.

"Beyond the desert of criticism, we wish to be called again."[1] In the next section, we will attend to the world in front of the text and its capacity to speak into the Christian life today. But this capacity of the text is buttressed by a healthy historically informed reading of it. The past two hundred years of interpretation can only be described as a desert insofar as they often left the reader without an obvious pathway to reading the Bible as Christian Scripture. Aside from this, they offer tools for the contemporary reader to move from the first naivete, and thereby deepen the potential of the second naivete. It is to this call back across the desert that we now turn.

---

1. Ricoeur, *The Symbolism of Evil*, 349.

SECTION 3

Toward a Renewed Christian Reading of Proverbs 8

IN THE FIRST SECTION of the book, Proverbs 8 was studied in its literary context, using standard tools in biblical study. This work provided a firm basis for understanding the passage in its nature as a literary document. However, we noted that more was needed in order to understand Proverbs 8 as Christian Scripture. As such, in section 2 we attended to selected examples of how this passage has been read through the history of interpretation, from the fourth century to the present. Doing so raised for our awareness the many and varied ways Proverbs 8 has been understood within a Christian frame of reference. Interacting with interpreters from different contexts raised questions that might otherwise not occur to a modern reader. We now turn to reading Proverbs 8 as Christian Scripture, by which we seek to articulate and appropriate a mode-of-being offered by the text, one that is faithful to the presence of God in the world.

This section begins by engaging two significant contemporary thinkers: Paul Ricoeur and Charles Taylor. The work of each of them enriches our sense of the world in front of the text, and provides a chance to re-think biblical interpretation. The section then moves to present a contemporary conception of Wisdom as a heuristic for fuller engagement with the text. As noted in the introduction to section 2, reading takes place within a tradition. This tradition may be theological, but it need not be. One's conception of various topics mentioned in the text come in to play as one reads. As Proverbs 8 relates to wisdom in general, we begin by foregrounding a contemporary conception of wisdom. The section ends with three first attempts at a renewed Christian reading of Proverbs 8. The first reads Proverbs 8 existentially, that is, as relating to the way one lives in the world. The second focuses on Proverbs 8:22 and its possible concurrence with Nicene Trinitarian theology. The third attempt reads Proverbs 8 with canonical intertextuality in relation to the theme of light in the Gospel of John.

Engaging Significant Thinkers for a Renewed Christian Reading

HAVING READ PROVERBS 8 as a literary document (world of the text) we come now to the text as a living, scriptural document (world in front of the text). Earlier in the book, the concept of the world in front of the text was introduced. In the approach to reading the Bible advocated by Sandra Schneiders, the text projects a possible mode of being for the reader to appropriate. This perspective derives from the work of Paul Ricoeur, who is a significant thinker outside of biblical studies who nevertheless offers perspectives which can enrich biblical interpretation. Alongside Ricoeur, Charles Taylor is another figure whose work provides an opportunity to re-think the task of biblical interpretation. In this chapter, I will offer an account of the work of Ricoeur and Taylor, and then reflect on the specific difference the Christian privileging of the Bible as Scripture makes for reading the text.

Ricoeur and Taylor: Two Significant Thinkers and Biblical Interpretation

Is attention to the world projected in front of the text essential to the task of interpretation? Or is it too subjective for the academic interested in the literal-historical meaning of the text, with the more imaginative elements better left to the preacher? The approach of this section affirms that the world in front of the text, and the concomitant appropriation of that world, is essential to the task of interpretation. The positions of Paul Ricoeur and Charles Taylor together draw the reader's attention to the possible mode of being toward which the text gestures. Ricoeur's contribution to this is his consideration of the impact of the disruption between the text and its author. Taylor's is his position on language as constituting specifically human concerns in a common space between interlocutors. Below I will summarize how both Ricoeur and Taylor endorse and complicate the appropriation of the world projected by the text.

Ricoeur begins by defining the nature of a text. A text is "any discourse fixed in writing."[1] That texts stand in relation to discourse implies various facets of "distanciation." In discourse, there is a distinction between the event of discourse and the meaning of the discourse. The event is the moment of utterance, the meaning is that which endures, expressed in the minimal structure of a sentence. The utterance takes the form of speech (*parole*) which is comprehensible based on its relation to the general system of its language (*langue*).[2] It is the dialectic between specific (speech) to general (language) which produces the distanciation: "Just as language, by being actualized in discourse, surpasses itself as system and realises itself as event, so too discourse, by entering the process of understanding, surpasses itself as event and becomes meaning."[3] Thus we understand the distanciation of the saying in the said to be the dynamic by which event of speech is taken up into the broader system of language in order to be understood.

Ricoeur further argues that discourse is a work, a product of labor by the speaker, such that form is imposed upon material in the application of stylistics. "By introducing the categories of production and labour into the dimension of discourse, the notion of work appears as a practical mediation between the irrationality of the event and the rationality of meaning."[4] In imposing form, thereby becoming a work, discourse opens itself up to objectification, an object of study. Ricoeur is swift to state that "This does not mean ... that explanation can eliminate understanding": the fundamental nature of discourse is that something is said about something, and it is this whole project which is the aim of interpretation.[5] When discourse moves from speech to writing an eruption occurs; the text becomes autonomous from the intentions of the author. "What the text signifies no longer coincides with what the author meant; henceforth, textual meaning

---

1. Ricoeur, "What Is a Text? Explanation and Understanding," 107.
2. Ricoeur, "The Hermeneutical Function of Distanciation," 95–96.
3. Ricoeur, "The Hermeneutical Function of Distanciation," 96.
4. Ricoeur, "The Hermeneutical Function of Distanciation," 99.
5. Ricoeur, "The Hermeneutical Function of Distanciation," 100–101.

and psychological meaning have different destinies."[6] The text interrupts the normal dialogical sequence of speaker to listener, in which the reference to the "real world" can be clarified by the interlocutor to ascertain what Ricoeur has termed the "psychological" meaning. Acknowledging this interruption does not negate an author's influence on the meaning. The nature of discourse as a work means that the author has imprinted a style upon the expressions contained therein. However, these stylistic impressions extend beyond the author's specific speech/writing act as an instance made sensible by the broader category of language. This is the case because whereas speech has a specific audience, the audience of written discourse is anyone who can read, and this is not an accident, but essential to the very nature of writing. So, while speech and writing both relate to discourse, one is not subordinate to the other.[7]

A central difference between spoken discourse and written discourse is reference. In dialogue, "living speech, the *ideal* sense of what is said turns towards the *real* reference, towards that 'about which' we speak."[8] As I noted above, the written text interrupts the referential process of speech. Now there is no longer a common situation of interlocutors, a "real world" toward which the speaker/author can gesture. The text is not "an instance of dialogue."[9] As such, the referential power of the written work is directed toward a world of the text, disclosed by the text, which takes the place of ostensive reference in speech.[10] As quoted above, for Ricoeur the loss of "first order reference" ("real world" reference) opens up "second order reference," a proposed world which is placed before the reader. Ricoeur characterizes this change as freedom: "each text is free to enter into relation with all the other texts which come to take the place of the circumstantial reality referred to by living speech."[11] Written works are hereby seen to be their own species of discourse: literature.

---

6. Ricoeur, "The Hermeneutical Function of Distanciation," 101.

7. Ricoeur, "The Hermeneutical Function of Distanciation," 102. In another essay, Ricoeur writes that, "The psychological and sociological priority of speech over writing is not in question. It may be asked, however, whether the late appearance of writing has not provoked a radical change in our relation to the very states of our discourse." Ricoeur, "What Is a Text?," 108.

8. Ricoeur, "What Is a Text?," 110.

9. Ricouer, "What Is a Text?," 108.

10. Ricoeur, "Metaphor and The Central Problem of Hermeneutics," 139.

11. Ricoeur, "What Is a Text?," 110.

Wisdom in the World

The concept of the world in front of the text arises from the nature of distanciation present in discourse in general and written discourse in particular. As such, it "is not the product of methodology and hence something superfluous and parasitical; rather it is constitutive of the phenomenon of the text as writing."[12] Therefore, reflection upon this world is essential for completing the full arc of interpreting any written work, including biblical texts. Nevertheless, there remains a distinction between this world in front of the text and appropriation.[13] One may be tempted to accede to Ricoeur's treatment in such a way that the task of academic interpretation is simply to describe this world. Ricoeur, rightly or wrongly, does not leave one that room.

According to him, this distinction is not such that they are isolated enterprises; they belong to an arc of interpretation which also includes the descriptive task of explanation. The disruption of the relationship between the author and the text can produce two kinds of reading. "We can, as readers, remain in the suspense of the text, treating it as a worldless and authorless object . . . [or] we can lift the suspense and fulfill the text in speech, restoring it to living communication; in this case, we interpret the text."[14] These two attitudes toward reading function dialectically. Earlier we noted Ricoeur's contention that discourse is a work, and that this facet opened it up to objectification. It is thus accessible to structural and literary analysis. As an instantiation of the broader system of language we can seek to unpack its sense by recourse to this system.[15] In one portion of his work, Ricoeur explores how understanding a metaphor as an event of logical absurdity can provide a guide to understanding a text. For a metaphor to "work" it must evoke a moment of absurdity, otherwise it is dead.[16] Analogously, for us to understand a text, it must be allowed to be alien (*fremd*), discovering or recovering its discordance with our initial naïve understanding. This is the work of explanation. In this portion of the interpretive task the construction of meaning "rests upon 'clues' contained in the text itself. A clue serves as a guide for a specific construction, in that it contains at once a permission and a prohibition; it excludes unsuitable constructions and

---

12. Ricoeur, "The Hermeneutical Function of Distanciation," 102.

13. Schneiders prefers the term "transformative understanding." Schneiders, *The Revelatory Text*, 158.

14. Ricoeur, "What Is a Text?," 114.

15. Ricoeur, "Metaphor and The Central Problem of Hermeneutics," 137.

16. Ricoeur, "Metaphor and The Central Problem of Hermeneutics," 133–35.

allows those which give more meaning to the same words."[17] The previous surveys of biblical commentaries on the book of Proverbs illustrated the proficiency of many scholars in this arena. However, for interpretation to be faithful to the text it cannot stay at this point; it must proceed further to understanding and appropriation.

Ricoeur grounds his assertion (that all interpretation includes understanding and appropriation) in the nature of texts. He has allowed two different attitudes toward reading, as quoted above; that which holds the text's reference in suspense, and that which lifts the suspense.

> It is this second attitude which is the real aim of reading. For this attitude reveals the true nature of the suspense which intercepts the movement of the text towards meaning. The other attitude would not even be possible if it were not first apparent that the text, as writing, awaits and calls for a reading. If reading is possible, it is indeed because the text is not closed in on itself but opens out onto other things.[18]

In our reading of the text, including that which operates in the phase of explanation, the speech (*parole*) of the text is connected to the broader system of language (*langue*) and expressed anew in a new event of discourse. The reader is already involved in the text even at its earlier stages. Explanation brings this first appropriation out into the open, questions it, and works to allow the text to be alien. The work of structural analysis is to unearth the deeper connections within the literary world of the text, evoking with more clarity the underlying question which the text puts to the reader. "Now what we have just said about the depth semantics unveiled by the structural analysis of the text invites us to say that the intended meaning of the text is not essentially the presumed intention of the author, the lived experience of the writer, but rather what the text means for whoever complies with its injunction."[19] Explanation serves understanding and appropriation. It is necessary in order to expose the deeper meaning of the text, a meaning best understood as existential. Texts propose a world which "I could inhabit and wherein I could project one of my ownmost possibilities."[20] The world

---

17. Ricoeur, "Metaphor and The Central Problem of Hermeneutics," 137. Referencing E.D. Hirsch, Ricoeur asserts that "one construction can be said to be more probable than another, but not more truthful."

18. Ricoeur, "What Is a Text?," 120.

19. Ricoeur, "What Is a Text?," 123.

20. Ricoeur, "The Hermeneutical Function of Distanciation," 104.

in front of the text offers to the reader a mode of being in the world for their appropriation.

Appropriation of the textual world corresponds to an answer in spoken discourse. Texts are addressed to someone and the "interpretation is complete when the reading releases something like an event, an event of discourse, an event in the present time. As appropriation, the interpretation becomes an event."[21] The interpretive arc culminates in appropriation, making one's own what is otherwise foreign to them.[22] To return to the analogy of a metaphor, just as metaphors create new meanings out of logical absurdity, so the text proposes a possible world, a new meaning for the reader out of what has been made strange.[23] Both the personal goal of integration and the foreign nature of the text and its world must be held in view with regard to appropriation. As to the former, the text offers a world in front of which the reader is to understand themselves. This is an ontological exercise; not one that is solely descriptive. Neglecting this aspect fails to complete the arc of interpretation and maintains the suspense of explanation: the full capacity of the text is not actualized.[24] As to the latter of the two assertions above, the foreignness of the text reminds us that the world in front of the text is not the reader's world. The complexity of the reader's world must be taken into account for honest integration to take place. The goal of interpretation "is attained only insofar as interpretation actualises the meaning of the text for the present reader," which is completed when "the reading releases something like an event, an event of discourse, an event in the present time."[25] For Ricoeur, event and meaning stand in a dialectical relationship, with meaning being the broader system against which events make sense. For the event of appropriation to make sense it must understood within the horizon of the reader's world, even as it enlarges that world.

Whereas explanation sought the sense of the text, understanding and appropriation relates to its reference. "To understand is to follow the dynamic of the work, its movement from what it says to that about which it speaks. Beyond my situation as reader, beyond the situation of the author, I offer myself to the possible mode of being-in-the-world which the text

---

21. Ricoeur, "Appropriation," 147.
22. Ricoeur, "Appropriation," 147.
23. Ricoeur, "Metaphor and The Central Problem of Hermeneutics," 139.
24. Ricoeur, "What Is a Text?," 120.
25. Ricoeur, "Appropriation," 147.

opens up and discloses to me."²⁶ Ricoeur is not proposing some psychological connection between the author and the reader; the text projects the world and it is that world opened by the text into which the reader is invited. Additionally, the reader is not somehow to project his own subjectivity onto the text. Rather, "the reader understands himself in front of the text, in front of the world of the work. To understand oneself in front of a text is quite the contrary of projecting oneself and one's own beliefs and prejudices; it is to let the work and its world enlarge the horizon of the understanding which I have of myself."²⁷ It is in this way that appropriation is best understood existentially.

Ricoeur advocates an understanding of a text that necessitates an appreciation for its facility to project a world in which a new form of life is offered to the reader. As he bases his view on the nature of discourse, it is not an elective feature of textual interpretation. The work of explanation involves one already in this world as one step along the spectrum toward understanding and appropriation.²⁸ Thus in the study of Proverbs 8, the literary study of the passage contributes to the explanatory phase. It can be appreciated as deepening the possible impact of understanding and appropriateness. At the end of this section, concluding the survey of Ricoeur and Taylor, I will address the aspect of reading Proverbs 8 as Scripture. At this point we can at least claim that doing so involves one in the goal of understanding and appropriation congruent with Ricoeur's proposals.

A key component of Ricoeur's approach is the eruption that occurs at the loss of a common situation once discourse is written. At this point, the text does not have "first-order reference" and makes its own "second-order reference" in the world of the text. We can further understand this dynamic with recourse to Charles Taylor's philosophy of language expressed in his essay, "Theories of Meaning."²⁹

---

26. Ricoeur, "Metaphor and The Central Problem of Hermeneutics," 139.

27. Ricoeur, "Metaphor and The Central Problem of Hermeneutics," 140.

28. Following Lash: "I am only concerned to insist, as a matter of general hermeneutical principle, that understanding what an ancient text 'originally meant', in the circumstances in which it was originally produced, and understanding what that text might mean today, are mutually interdependent and not merely successive enterprises." Lash, "What Might Martyrdom Mean?," 81.

29. Charles Taylor, "Theories of Meaning," 248–92. This will be the major source for this next section, therefore references to this essay will be provided in parenthetical citations.

Taylor articulates an understanding of human language that he contrasts with theories that focus on words designating things and/or encoding information. Taylor offers three interrelated answers to his question, "what are we bringing about in language and essentially through language, i.e. such that it can only be brought about through language?" (256) The three facets are formulation, common space, and human concern. By the first he refers to the capacity of language to bring to our awareness that of which we previously had an implicit sense. Once we have a focus, we can "draw in however rough a fashion its boundaries" (258). Terms are known in relationship with others; by distinguishing our concern we can compare it and contrast it with other terms and thus gain a greater clarity on the term. The second of Taylor's three facets of language is that it "serves to place some matter out in the open between interlocutors" (259). Through language, an item or experience becomes something common, not privately held. This item or experience may have already been known by one, both, or all interlocutors. Once it is articulated it becomes something of common focus; now we share it. The third facet, in addition to formulation and founding common spaces, is language's capacity to serve as the medium for the most characteristically human concerns. Taylor particularly treats our moral standards under this point: "to recognize for instance that some acts have a special status because they meet some standard, we have to have language" (262). Language is essential in order to bring a concern into focus, to place it in "public space," and to know and abide by distinctly human concerns.

Taylor draws three implications with regards to a theory of meaning from these facets of language, two of which get the majority of his attention. As such, I will detail and interact with these, and leave out the third which is only given a paragraph in his argument. First, under the influence of the public and human concerns feature above, language is understood as expressive (263). While a speaker may or may not communicate some information through language, what is always present is expression; the putting into public something of the speaker or the environment for the common focus. Additionally, this expression is a kind of display. It is marked by the speaker through tone, vocabulary choice, style, etc. These stylistic choices are made according to standards of which the speaker is aware.

In his approach, Taylor attends to what we do with language, rather than language in the abstract. Thus, even a hypothetical language developed explicitly to be non-rhetorical would be used for expression and display. The speakers engaged in this language may devise some special context for speaking it, a context dedicated to true depictions.[30] "Of course, the old Adam returns; one has only to think of all the special tricks of argument in which one displays oneself as more authentically a participant in this exchange than one's adversary" (267). As long as humans are involved, language is expressive.

The second implication for theories of meaning is the constitutive dimension of language, in which "there are some phenomena, central to human life, which are partly constituted by language" (270). Our feelings, self-descriptions, and social relations are all constituted by language. The language we use to describe our feelings shapes them, such that changing the words changes the feeling itself.

> Let us say that I am confused over my feelings for X; then I come to a clarification where I see that while I disapprove of some things I admire some quality in him; or after being confused about my feelings for Y, I come to see it as a kind of fascination, and not the sort of love on which companionship can be built. In both these cases, the change in descriptions is inseparable from an alteration in the feeling. (270)[31]

The same phenomenon obtains in our self-descriptions, understanding who we are individually and socially. Our social relations are based on footings, stances we take towards others in a society. Language is essential for an understanding and awareness of these stances. As such, of these will vary from culture to culture, depending on the language used and common social practices which support that language.[32] These illustrate "ways in which the language we use enters into, is an essential part of, our feelings, our goals, our social relations and practices" (273).

Taylor's argument agrees with and augments our understanding of Ricoeur's approach. As Ricoeur wrote of discourse as a work of art so Taylor argues language is fundamentally expressive; it displays distinctly human concerns in a common space. So stated, the style of a work hints

---

30. One is tempted to think of academic conferences with this remark.

31. We could make a case for distanciation of the text from the author on the basis of this change in feeling brought about by articulation/formulation. It is possible that the author of a text does not know that which they intend until the word is chosen and written down. Or that once marked down and set in the context of a whole work, a new meaning occurs to them. Thus the text is distanced from an author's original intentions, although we still see it as a true expression of meaning.

32. Taylor cites Wittgenstein's adage, "To imagine a language means to imagine a form of life." Taylor, "Theories of Meaning," 281.

toward its projection of a mode of being in the world; what is expressed through the style is marked by essentially human values and concerns. A constitutive view of language makes these hints explicit: the text, through its status as alien (*fremd*), offers to the reader a new vocabulary for understanding themselves before the text. This expression arises from its own social context, thus it is open to objectification and analysis. However, objective analysis is not hermetically sealed off from understanding and appropriation; whatever language the commentator uses to describe the text is expressive, marked by display which conforms to values. To produce such a description, the commentator stands in two horizons; that of the text and their own. With regard to the first, they aim to present the text without distortion, avoiding anachronism. With regard to the latter horizon, any statement must be understandable to the interpreter and their audience. To satisfy both of these, the commentator must participate in the horizon of both, the public spaces opened up by each language. Every public space has participants and exists as a result of communication between participants; therefore, "there cannot be a totally non-participatory learning of language" (282). Far from being a neutral objective observer, the interpreter is a participant in a communicative act as a reader of language.

The expressive view of language which Taylor advocates complements Ricoeur's view of a text as discourse. Additionally, another piece of Taylor's work also helps a reader in the contemporary West to appreciate a key step in appropriating a text. As stated above, the complexity of the reader's world must be accounted for if honest appropriation can take place. Taylor's *A Secular Age* is a relevant conversation partner for the task of accounting for the complexity the twenty-first-century North Atlantic milieu.[33] In this book, Taylor asks and explores searching questions of our present cultural moment. His work focuses on the change in the conditions of belief between the medieval period down to the present day; "the change I want to define and trace is one which takes us from a society in which it was virtually impossible not to believe in God, to one in which faith, even for the staunchest believer, is one human possibility among others" (3). The description of medieval experience is less relevant to the present study. What is significant is Taylor's focus on contemporary conditions of belief, which are the operative background understandings.

---

33. Taylor, *A Secular Age*. Through the next several pages references to *A Secular Age* will be provided in parenthetical citations.

A Renewed Christian Reading

The scale of Taylor's argument is architectonic. However, at numerous points along the way he helpfully provides summaries. As he turns in his book from historical narrative to contemporary analysis, he highlights the critical features of the immanent frame of reference, a frame that shapes the conditions of the belief in the twenty-first-century Western setting. As I enumerate these, it is to be remembered that they are descriptive of background understanding rather than conceptualized beliefs. Taylor is gesturing toward the sense of the world embodied by practices that arise in the modern world, which include but are not exhausted by theoretical beliefs. In the subsequent paragraphs, I attempt to concisely summarize Taylor's nuanced, developed, and sweeping commentary on the changes between 1500 A.D. and the present age, noting features that bear on the present attempt to appropriate the world projected by a particular passage read as Christian Scripture, such as Proverbs 8.

A key feature of the immanent frame is disenchantment, a gradual process by which the world is emptied of the experience of spiritual significance. In a disenchanted world, meaning is no longer understood to inhere in objects themselves; meaning is instead understood as human-generated. Background conceptions of self, society, time, and creation (and more) are all caught up and reconfigured by this change. Under the category of understanding of the self, the medieval sense of the self as "porous" (vulnerable to outside forces) is replaced "by the buffered self, for whom it comes to seem axiomatic that all thought, feeling and purpose, all the features we normally can ascribe to agents, must be in minds, which are distinct from the 'outer' world" (539). The buffered self is reinforced by language and practice. Linguistically, in our contemporary world, there is a "rich vocabulary of interiority, an inner realm of thought and feeling to be explore" (539). Practically, new emphases on self-discipline and new arrangements for privacy arise. There is a concomitant increase in one's sense of individuality.

> The social orders we live in are not grounded cosmically, prior to us, there as it were, waiting for us to take up our allotted space; rather society is made by individuals, or at least for individuals, and their place in it should reflects the reasons why they joined in the first place, or why God appointed this common experience for them. (540)

The facets of the buffered self, discipline, and individuality work within the drive to reform society, a society conceived of as changeable and requiring change. This instrumental stance toward the world is then accompanied by a flattened view of time, leaving behind the older conception of "higher times" which interrupt and intersect with the mundane moments of life.[34] Time is now seen as a resource, not to be wasted, as opposed to ordering our lives. A final element of the disenchanted immanent frame of reference is that "this frame constitutes a 'natural' order, to be contrasted to a 'supernatural' one, an 'immanent' world, over against a possible 'transcendent' one" (542). These various facets create the "practical context within which the self-sufficiency of this immanent realm could become a matter of experience" (543). Taylor is not primarily addressing articulated beliefs. Rather, his focus is on the practical context, which shows up as one pays attention to the regular habits and language of the everyday. His narrative takes the year 1500 A.D. as a terminus ad quo and notes how the shape of human mundane experience has changed. His description of the present age arises from this comparison.

Taylor acknowledges that the world need not be experienced as immanent. One of his aims in the book is to contest the narrative of retreating religiosity (533–35). However, even those who are open to the transcendent develop this orientation within the "sensed context" of the immanent frame (549). The shared practices of both believer (open to the transcendent) and unbeliever (closed to it) reinforce this, as background understanding is carried by enacted practices. Thus there is overlap, not bifurcation, between those who experience the world immanently and those who experience it as open to something greater. The gap between the experience of believer and unbeliever is not as wide as a focus on articulated beliefs would suggest, even as there are distinct practices peculiar to each group.[35]

Taylor repeatedly asserts that the changes in conditions of belief arose out of a sense of the world informed by Christianity. Secularism is not solely the work of anti-Christian forces. Rather, the "drive to a new form of religious life, more personal, committed, devoted" contributes significantly to these facets (541).[36] Taylor's exposition of the movements toward the immanent frame helpfully opens up a view of our current age as offering

---

34. An example of higher time is Good Friday, which is conceived of as being closer to the original day of crucifixion than a calendar date closer in time to the worshipper.

35. For a down-to-earth articulation of this, see David Foster Wallace, "This Is Water." Wallace brings attention to the everyday, mundane rituals which make up so much of life. These obtain for both the believer and non-believer and, as both Taylor and Wallace argue in their own way, are the site of so much formation.

36. It is not that things had to go this way. Taylor acknowledges there were and are possibilities other than the matrix of conditions we have today.

possibilities for faith, even as it also presents challenges. For example, many within the church today decry individualism. At the same time, there is an emphasis on each person needing to own their faith, making it personal, even individual. Taylor helps a contemporary reader see the relationship between these and gives pause to an unqualified denunciations. It would be hard, and perhaps undesirable, to conceive of a life of faith void from some form of personal commitment today. As a result, we can understand how both individual devotion and "individualism" exist within a broader framework, arising from Christian concerns and now caught up in varying ways depending on the operating system of dispositions.

Taylor's point that Christians are not so different from non-Christians can make Christians uncomfortable, but it is a double-edged blade. Through Taylor's analysis, the practices of the contemporary frame are shown to have continuity with those of our medieval forebears. In Peter Baehr's article "Purity and Danger in the Modern University," the author addresses a scandal of the London School of Economics accepting donations from the Gaddafi family.[37] In the course of his writing he notes that, in the post-war period, the purpose of the university has changed. Academics "are also expected, in growing numbers, to be social workers to society at large, *a clerisy ministering to the collective soul*. Civic engagement, social entrepreneurship, service learning; these are the new responsibilities that the university must discharge in *its redemptive mission to make society good*."[38] The ecclesiastical terminology stands out. When the school's acceptance of the money was made public, it issued in a scandal. Why was this scandalous? Because, as the title of Baehr's article suggests, universities and their faculty are expected to be ideologically pure.[39] If they are not, they face community backlash. While there are differences between them, there are similar dynamics between this situation and, say, witch trials or the running off of a heretic from a village. In the medieval examples, these were

---

37. Baehr, "Purity and Danger in the Modern University," 297–300.

38. Baehr, "Purity and Danger in the Modern University," 298. Emphasis added.

39. Baehr calls for a re-evaluation of the university's purpose in society because in the current state, "Ideological commitments privilege solidarity over independence of mind. Specialization narrows our vision. Relativism blurs our sense of moral boundaries. Libyans in Benghazi risked all for their independence. University academics, if the recent past is any guide, are unlikely to follow their example any time soon." "Purity and Danger in the Modern University," 300. His last words, couched in the example of martyrdom, resonate with a call to a crusade.

done because the witch and the heretic posed a threat to the corporate well-being.[40] Is this not so with the modern university, which has a redemptive mission to pursue? The breakdown of the perceived impermeable barrier between the Christian and the "secularist," between the modern era and the "dark ages" can discomfort all involved.

As the above two examples illustrate, the path to arrive at the modern frame of reference is more complicated than the standard narrative presents; Taylor brings questions to the settled status quo. Taylor gives language to a broader range of issues of living in the current cultural environment.[41] These include the features of the common background understanding of buffered identity conceived primarily as individual, an instrumental stance toward time and society, and the world as constituted by a "natural" order over against a supernatural one. These features shape believer and unbeliever alike at the level of our unchallenged frameworks, our understandings the world. Among the sources of the "secular age" are Christian history, theology, and practice. As such, "secular," per Taylor's usage, is not a label which can be solely applied to materialist atheists bent on the destruction of the Christian faith. We are all secular, and that is not a totally negative comment.[42]

Considering the task of appropriating a text, Taylor's description of the background operative in our secular age does not dictate the outcome of this move. It is not as if the text cannot say something opposed to these dominant understandings. Rather, attempts to integrate the text should acknowledge these default features for many today and raise to the awareness of the reader challenges particular to a contemporary reading of the text. That the sources of the secular age include Christian theology gives pause in asserting a simple corrective function of the text towards current cultural

---

40. One key difference between the medieval and the modern milieu is that the medieval had the capacity to tolerate some presence of evil in society through its understanding "that there are severe limits to the degree in which sin and disorder can be done away with in this world." In the modern frame, this tolerance is gone, replaced by speech codes for political correctness, and zero tolerance for any chaos or evil. *A Secular Age*, 119, 124.

41. Taylor's approach aids the current study regardless of potential differences between the medieval and ancient senses of the world. I am drawing on Taylor for an understanding of the present, rather than a comprehensive description of the past.

42. For example, as Taylor points out, we can all be glad that public executions are no longer a major form of entertainment.

A Renewed Christian Reading

practices. These complicating moves open up the potential for the reader and the text to "mutually inform, enable, correct and enlighten each other."[43]

Through both Ricoeur and Taylor, we can understand that the language of a text opens up new modes of being for a reader through its stylized presentation of a world in front of the text. Both also fill out what it means to appropriate the world projected by the text: Ricoeur addresses how and why one might do this; Taylor offers a reader in the twenty-first-century Western milieu a possible deeper understanding of the world into which to integrate the world in front of the text. Both scholars articulate their stance in such a way as to make attending to the proposed world essential for a full interpretation of the text.

Reading the Bible as Scripture

In distinct but compatible ways, Ricoeur and Taylor advocate reading texts for the greater reality toward which they gesture. However, neither of them refer to the difference made by recognizing a text *as Scripture*. Such a recognition privileges a text in particular ways. Readers who take up a text in this manner draw upon distinct commitments inherently related to this ascription. One such commitment, helpfully articulated by Walter Moberly, is that "*here* truth about God, the world, and ourselves is to be found."[44] Recognizing a text as Scripture privileges it as bearing witness to these deep existential realities. In the language of Charles Taylor, as surveyed above, the text is taken to gesture toward the presence of God in the world and the shape of life that is in accordance with this presence. Ricoeur helpfully articulates what it might mean to practice the text's enduring significance through appropriating the world it projects. As discussed above, this appropriation involves a dialectical relationship which takes seriously the worlds of both the reader and the text. Therefore, to read the text as Scripture by definition shapes the reading of a text toward a deeper understanding of the nature of God, the world, and human beings.

A second and complimentary commitment of reading a text as Scripture is a general attitude of trust toward the text. In the Christian tradition, trust is integral to reading the Bible as Scripture because one is committed to seeking an encounter with the Triune God, a God whose revelation is best analogized to human relationship. Martin Buber notes that "The relation to

---

43. Lash, "Interpretation and Imagination," 25.
44. Moberly, *The Bible in a Disenchanted Age*, 106.

a human being is the proper metaphor for the relation to God—as genuine address is here accorded a genuine answer."[45] Following Buber, an encounter with God is participatory, rather than observational or evidentiary, and accordingly calls for trust.[46] This trust does not rule out criticism of the text. Rather, criticism is a function of the trust. As Ricoeur articulates, the critical moves undertaken are aimed toward the strengthening of the text's potential challenge to the reader. It is because the reader ultimately trusts the text that critical distancing is appropriate, as it moves the reader past surface level understanding or confusion into a deeper grasp of the text's witness. Buber's analogy to human relationship is helpful, as such a relationship built on trust will move toward greater understanding. And so, even though it is complicated, an element of trust is concomitant to recognizing a text as Scripture. Such trust is not integral to other ways of reading texts, even though one may read them for their world they project.

In the light of these two key commitments to reading a text as Scripture, we can make a helpful distinction between the Bible and other, non-scriptural, texts, and so come to understand something of the difference it makes to read a text as Scripture. Transformation by way of encounter with the Triune God is a first-order expectation of reading a text as Scripture; it is not so with non-scriptural texts. Other genre expectations and commitments accompany non-scriptural texts; when one reads fiction they are expecting entertainment, etc. This is not to say that transformation is not at all a possible outcome of reading other genres. Numerous works have been held to be classics because of their capacity for articulating a powerful mode of being-in-the-world. But one does not read them with the first-order expectation that one will encounter the Triune God of Christian faith within their respective pages. However, when one takes up and reads the Bible as Scripture, such an encounter is anticipated.

In the next section of the book, I will return to Proverbs 8 in order to deploy the insights of Paul Ricoeur and Charles Taylor. Additionally, the commitments I have outlined will be on display, as I am seeking to read the passage in trust that it does bear witness to the reality of God, the world, and human beings.

---

45. Buber, *I and Thou*, 151. Even though I am quoting Buber immediately after making a comment about reading within the Christian tradition, I am aware that Buber was Jewish. However, he offers a way of articulating the nature of reality and life before God that resonates with the Christian tradition. My interaction with, and appreciation for, his work is filtered through Nicholas Lash's book, *Easter in Ordinary*.

46. Moberly, *The Bible in a Disenchanted Age*, 138.

8

A Contemporary Conception of Wisdom

THE ABOVE ENGAGEMENT WITH Paul Ricoeur and Charles Taylor highlighted the role played by the reader's context in appropriating the text. The reader's context is not intended to override the text. Rather, awareness of pertinent factors helps to engage the subject matter of the text, as well as to guard against an overhasty appropriation. As part of canonical Scripture, one could say that the subject matter of Proverbs 8 is God. Nevertheless, the register in which the chapter speaks is couched in the language of wisdom. It is to this concept of wisdom that we devote this chapter, as a heuristic device for engaging the text.[1]

Through explicitly stating a contemporary conception, one becomes more open to the transformative power of the text. Articulation puts a concept "out in the open" and can therefore be a common object of consideration. Through the explication of my understanding of wisdom below, some guesswork is removed for the readers, who can return to critique it on the other side of the interpretive process. An openness to such correction, an understanding of the fallibility of one's positions and the possibility of others, is required for an honest approach which avoids an unrealistic sense of neutrality and a stubborn "dogmatism" in relation to study.[2] In the following pages, my aim is to provide a clear statement of a working view

---

1. Stuart Weeks has articulated an understanding of wisdom, from his study of Proverbs 1–9, which shares much in common with the following construction from contemporary philosophical resources. I will summarize Weeks work and indicate particular areas of overlap later in this chapter.

2. Bultmann, "Is Exegesis without Presuppositions Possible?," 149–50. The work leading up to this point in the book is also a helpful bulwark to safeguard an honest reading of the text.

of wisdom so that the reader is aware of some pre-understandings and can evaluate them in light of the text as the study proceeds.

Wisdom as Embodied Know-How

What is wisdom? The operating definition that will be expanded upon is this: Wisdom is embodied know-how, a practical sense demonstrated in the encounter between an ingrained habitus and a "field," or event of interaction.[3] To be considered wise is to enact a practice by practical sense such that the outcome is deemed good by the inherent disposition of the community.[4] Wisdom thus construed is not commensurate with formulations but is a "quasi-bodily involvement in the world," that is, less understood as a mental activity and more as an embodied understanding.[5]

Many of those contemporary scholars who address the subject of wisdom begin their treatments with comments on the nature of human existence.[6] The importance of the distinction between know-how and formulations (know-that) can only be appreciated (in the opinion of these scholars) by a view of the human being that is embedded in the world. The dominant alternative to such a construal is the human being as a disengaged, rational agent, whose "inner" self is separate from the world "out there."[7] Within this alternative picture, knowledge is an inner representation of an outer reality. Concomitantly, what is not represented is not known.

The place to begin to construct an embedded view of human being is with what humans do in ethical situations.[8] Charles Taylor uses the example of following the rules of the road, such as turning the right direction

---

3. Bourdieu, *The Logic of Practice*, 66.

4. Here I am expanding on the definition offered by Francisco Varela: "a wise (or virtuous) person is *one who knows what is good and spontaneously does it.*" Varela, *Ethical Know-How*, 4, emphasis original. Varela's equation of wise and virtuous along with his use of "good" points to the inclusion of wisdom as a concept in the field of ethics.

5. Bourdieu, *The Logic of Practice*, 66.

6. Bourdieu, *The Logic of Practice*, 52. Charles Taylor, "To Follow a Rule," 169–71. Varela, *Ethical Know-How*, 3–5.

7. This alternative vision can be labelled "Cartesian," "objectivist," or "rationalistic," among other descriptions. Varela, *Ethical Know-How*, 6.

8. The focus on action could be understood as a particular interpretation of Ludwig Wittgenstein's injunction: "don't think, but look!" Wittgenstein, *Philosophical Investigations*, 31. Bourdieu, Taylor, and Varela are each dealing with human activity as it is played out rather than as abstracted from everyday scenarios.

in response to a street sign.⁹ How does a person know to turn the indicated direction? Within the representational school of thought, they know because they frame representations of the rule (statements) and know the correct option from the incorrect options on justifiable, that is representable, grounds. However, as "any explanation leaves some potential issues unresolved, it stands in need of further explanations to back it up."[10] This may necessitate constant regress. "If I have exhausted the justifications I have reached bedrock, and my spade is turned. Then I am inclined to say: 'This is simply what I do.'"[11] The recourse offered by Wittgenstein and taken up by Bourdieu, Taylor, and Varela is to look to our embodied practices as that which carries our understanding of how to follow a rule.

As we move to embodied understanding, we do not leave framing, formulation, representation, or justification behind.[12] Rather, we are shifting our focus to what is primary and persistent in our dealings. In our everyday goings-on, humans act in immediacy to their situation. "Our lived world is so ready-at-hand that we have no deliberateness about what it is and how we inhabit it."[13] We are able to get from place to place without planning, able to navigate a conversation without thinking of where to stand, able to walk in a way that projects our sense of ourselves without conscious thought, able to respond in sport to the play which erupts upon us without stopping to strategize. In these examples, the body moves and carries out the understanding. The body "does not represent what it performs, it does not memorize the past, it *enacts* the past, bringing it back to life."[14] These actions are taken without explicit reflection or formulation. They are embodied, first and foremost.

In this perspective, the body takes on a role of far greater importance than in the view of humans as disengaged observers. The body is "not just the executant of the goals we frame, nor just the locus of causal factors shaping our representations."[15] Instead, bodily presence shapes our very

---

9. Taylor, "To Follow a Rule," 165.

10. Taylor, "To Follow a Rule," 166.

11. Wittgenstein, *Philosophical Investigations*, §217, 85.

12. Varela, *Ethical Know-How*, 5–6. Taylor, "To Follow a Rule," 170.

13. Varela, *Ethical Know-How*, 9.

14. Bourdieu, *The Logic of Practice*, 73. Bourdieu's mention of the past illustrates his position that practices are historical and social; they are learned through experience of situations and passed down from generation to generation.

15. Taylor, "To Follow a Rule," 170.

perceptions of a situation. In this approach, reality is "perceiver-dependent, not because the perceiver 'constructs' it as he or she pleases, but because what *counts* as a relevant world is inseparable from the structure of the perceiver."[16] Additionally, the body is the site of our understanding; the way my body moves or takes a stance is the demonstration of my understanding.[17] That I turn right before the road sign signals that I understand the sign. That I move to my left to field the ball and then throw to first base indicates that I understand the game of baseball.

What enables this embodied understanding is a background understanding or habitus. A habitus is a

> system of durable, transposable dispositions, structured structures predisposed to function as structuring structures, that is, as principles which generate and organize practices and representations that can be objectively adapted to their outcomes without presupposing a conscious aiming at ends or an express mastery of the operations necessary in order to attain them.[18]

Bourdieu's definition is dense, compressing crucial components of habitus into one sentence. First, a habitus is a disposition, a stance toward the world. Such a view stands in continuity with Martin Heidegger's position that humans' primary stance toward the world is one of care, rather than one of disengaged neutrality.[19] A habitus, as a system of dispositions, is an overall stance of concern toward the world. This system is durable and transposable, persisting from event to event and adapting to a variety of interactions. Its status as transposable can be seen when, for whatever reason, a temporary sign takes the place of a regularly constructed street sign. Even though its form may be new to us (paper, a different color), we are still able to understand it and act accordingly. In the realm of sport, the game is playable in a professionally maintained arena and in a small-town alleyways.

---

16. Varela, *Ethical Know-How*, 13. I am slowly building toward the application of these views on wisdom. However, here we can note that this "perceiver-dependent reality" distances this approach from empiricism. In this, I agree with Michael Fox in rejecting empiricism as an adequate understanding of wisdom, even though we differ on our counter-proposals. Fox, "The Epistemology of the Book of Proverbs," 670–74. Fox advocates a view consistent with the coherence theory of truth which foregrounds propositions, even as he acknowledges the need for a "sense for what is harmonious—the moral equivalent of a musical ear." Fox, "The Epistemology of the Book of Proverbs," 675, 677.

17. Taylor, "To Follow a Rule," 171.

18. Bourdieu, *The Logic of Practice*, 54.

19. Heidegger, *Being and Time*, 180.

A Contemporary Conception of Wisdom

In addition to its dispositional and transposable nature, Bourdieu asserts that a habitus arises from one's history (personal and collective) and works to shapes one's interaction in a given situation: "The *habitus*, a product of history, produces individual and collective practices—more history—in accordance with schemes generated by history."[20] One is trained in a habitus by one's community and personal experiences. This habitus conditions the interaction, opening up and constraining possibilities of action; certain features "show up" for the agent and others do not, the effect of which circumscribes possible avenues of action.[21]

An important facet of a habitus is its social nature. It is not monological, the property and sole operation of one person. Rather, to be effective it must be shared. Conversations work as partners act in common rhythm with one another. Gift giving requires both the giver and the recipient to share a common sense of what is going on for the gift to have meaning. The road sign only works if everyone shares the understanding of the rules of the road. The importance of a common understanding is even the case when encounters are not face-to-face.

> In a different form [background understanding] can also constitute a political or religious movement, whose members may be widely scattered, but who are animated together by a sense of common purpose—such as linked the students in Tienanmen Square and their colleagues back on the campus and, indeed, a great part of the population of Beijing.[22]

A habitus is a socially shared, often unarticulated, understanding embodied in practices. It is socially shared and inculcated by society. Now, contrary to a game, in which one chooses to participate in a quasi-contract, social life lacks a choice; "one does not embark on the game [of social life] by a conscious act, one is born into the game, with the game; and the relation of investment . . . is made more total and unconditional by the fact that it is unaware of what it is."[23] In addition to the absence of choice in much of life, everyday experience has a paucity of formulated rules when compared to a

---

20. Bourdieu, *The Logic of Practice*, 54. Emphasis original. David Ford writes, "Wisdom is immersed in history and at the same time oriented towards its fulfillment." Ford, *Christian Wisdom*, 16.

21. Varela, *Ethical Know-How*, 13. This point is also made by Heidegger, *Being and Time*, 138–39. See Hubert L. Dreyfus' helpful discussion in *Being-in-the-World*, 189–91.

22. Taylor, "To Follow a Rule," 172.

23. Bourdieu, *The Logic of Practice*, 67.

game. Sports come with a rule book; but, as many parents have discovered to their dismay, there is no rule book for raising children.[24]

In addition to its enabling function, a habitus also functions to evaluate actions taken, determining their success or failure. An action "makes sense" retrospectively if it produces an outcome in harmony with the operative habitus. In the example of a game, my action "makes sense" if the game continues. If, instead of throwing the baseball to first base for the out, I turn and throw it to the spectators, the game stops and questions arise ("why did you do that?"). For the road sign, my right turn "makes sense" if I, and everyone else, can continue driving without interruption. If I turn left, I am likely to get into an accident, at which point I will be asked to account for my actions.[25] The further determination of an action as "good" (not just sensible) also involves the community.[26]

> One of the fundamental effects of the harmony between practical sense and objectified meaning (*sens*) is the production of a common-sense world, whose immediate self-evidence is accompanied by the objectivity provided by consensus on the meaning of practices and the world, in other words the harmonization of the agents' experiences and the constant reinforcement each of them receives from expression—individual or collective (in festivals, for example), improvised or programmed (commonplaces, sayings)—of similar or identical experiences.[27]

The community provides the criteria for determining an action's goodness in its reinforcing expressions. These expressions ingrain a sense of hoped-for outcomes, along with those to be avoided.[28] The ultimate proof of my ac-

---

24. "There is no scientific formula for bringing up children or coping with suffering, trauma or death." Ford, *Christian Wisdom*, 1–2. There *are* many self-help books full of parenting tips. However, they do not function in the same way as rule books for sport or driving. Parenting books are much closer to "wisdom sayings." I will address the relationship between articulated wisdom and habitus later on.

25. These examples point toward the role of articulations, which I will address in a moment. We should also note that an explanation may be required even if I do not get in an accident. A police officer, a passenger in the car, or someone whom I regale with my daring adventure later will ask for some account of why I did not obey the sign.

26. We can imagine scenarios in which our actions make sense but they were the wrong choice; "I get why you did it, but it didn't work out."

27. Bourdieu, *The Logic of Practice*, 58.

28. Through "modes of deferment and presentation, the subtlest nuances of social position, of the sources of prestige, and hence of what is valuable and good, are encoded." Taylor, "To Follow a Rule," 179.

A Contemporary Conception of Wisdom

tions' goodness is in a change in my social standing. If I play the game well, my teammates hold me in high esteem (even if we do not win), and give me high-fives, or accolades, and generally move around me in a "good" way. If I drive well, I avoid the embarrassment of traffic tickets or car accidents which lead to social shame or at least awkwardness when I volunteer to drive. Even those actions taken without observers are evaluated in the light of these social reinforcements. I feel like a morally noble person, which shapes my body posture and the way I project myself in social space.[29] Or I am ashamed of my choices because I have learned that this is not in accordance with the desired outcomes of the habitus. Consequently, I take a different stance when in company.

To summarize my argument to this point, human beings act in accordance with an ingrained habitus which enables and constrains possibilities within a given moment as well as evaluates the choices of the agent. The preceding discussion impacts our understanding of wisdom, moving it away from a predominantly cognitive function dependent on mental representations to a practical sense. Wisdom is the capacity of one to enact practices in a given context which consistently yield "good" results as determined by the appropriate habitus. It is the life analogy to a player's "feel for the game."[30]

Within a game, this "feel" is "the almost miraculous encounter between the *habitus* and a field, between incorporated history [the *habitus*] and an objectified history [the practice enacted], which makes possible the near-perfect anticipation of the future inscribed in all the concrete configurations on the pitch or board."[31] The feel is not something which can be attained by force of will alone. The will is important as a commitment to the game, "but only by birth or by a slow process of co-option and initiation which is equivalent to a second birth" does one attain it. The same could be said for wisdom.[32] Wisdom is a characteristic of a person whose enacted practices in given situations leads us to ascribe to them a practical sense for what to do in order to achieve future beneficial outcomes in those situations. A wise person consistently performs well, as ascertained against

---

29. Bourdieu notes "that most of the words that refer to bodily postures evoke virtues and states of mind." Bourdieu, *The Logic of Practice*, 70.

30. Bourdieu, *The Logic of Practice*, 66.

31. Bourdieu, *The Logic of Practice*, 66.

32. As noted above, one's participation in life is not a result of choice in the same way as participation in a game.

the background of a certain habitus. While some people may seem to have wisdom "from birth," for most it takes time.[33] It is for this reason that wisdom is often anecdotally associated with age.

Becoming wise requires time under the tutelage of those who are wise. Tutelage toward wisdom can be overtly didactic but its primary form is arguably embodied co-ordination between two individuals working toward a new shared habitus. This requires commitment which is itself an enacted practice taken on the basis of a prior-formed habitus. One desires to be wise because of the socially formed standards of good, and therefore one moves in that direction by sitting themselves alongside the wise teacher. Most often, though not always, these moves toward a tutor are spontaneous because they occur without reflection, as the above discussion has attempted to show with most enacted practices.

As previously noted, this approach acknowledges that human beings are not silent actors; humans speak. The position I am advocating interprets speech in its capacity as an action. With our words, we act. Speech-act theory offers analyzes statements according to three categories: a locution (statement), illocution (the syntactical force of a statement), and perlocution (the result of the statement, its effect on the audience). The perlocutionary force of speech relies on a social context for its effectiveness. This context is the habitus, which influences which speech options are available as appropriate and evaluates options taken. In other words, speech occurs in many practices; embodied knowing is present in all practices. As such, speech is a species of the broader genus of practice-enacted-within-a-habitus.

There are times at which reflection does occur in which agents frame representations as to the "rules of the game," formulating a reason or recalling a saying to justify an action or guide a decision. Within the approach outlined above, the formulation is not the same as, nor is it determinative of, the practice.[34] The formulation is an attempt to generalize and make timeless what is primarily contextual and temporal. My navigational

---

33. Bourdieu, *The Logic of Practice*, 68. By birth, Bourdieu is referring to "native membership," that is, one who begins their life in relation to the particular habitus and is thus formed from the earliest moments. Earlier in his arguments, he writes, "Early experiences have a particular weight because the *habitus* tends to ensure its own constancy." Bourdieu, *The Logic of Practice*, 60. Early inculcation through guided practices provides the baseline for all future formation. With regards to wisdom, this would seem to be a product of "good upbringing," whatever that means against the backdrop of a given habitus.

34. We regularly act without formulation.

know-how in my neighborhood is dependent on where I am in the community (contextual) and changes as I move through the streets (temporal); not every street or house "shows up" for me at once. If I were to formulate this know-how in a map, it is an attempt to produce the entire neighborhood at one moment, in which the main street is always seen in relation to the smaller alleyways. Thus the formulation (map) is not the same as the practice (navigational sense), as it alters through a different stance toward contextuality and temporality. In this way the formulation can be seen to lack the ability to totally account for the practice. For example, in gift-giving there is a proper time for giving a gift and it is accompanied by a sense of uncertainty as one awaits the reaction of the recipient.[35] The lack of context and timing in a formulation, such as "always give a gift to those of higher social standing," does not communicate these nuances.

Even though formulations are not equivalent to the practice,[36] they do make positive contributions. A statement that can be deemed wise or good is itself an enacted practice understood against a habitus. A legislative body may enact a law for application to the community. The formulation is dependent on prior practices; either as a formulation of "what we have always done" or as a formulation of "what we should do" in a situation envisaged but not yet existing (as in the case of laws regulating an emerging technology). In the former case it is easy to see that the articulation is drawing on practice. In the latter case, the foreseen situation can only be understood, only make sense, against the existing habitus carried in present practices. The community may read or hear this formulated law and deem it "good" as a way of guiding its members to the proper application of the right practice in the right way. Moreover, formulations offer a chance to critique existing practice. It opens "a possibility of criticism and reformulation that is essential to human rationality."[37] By bringing the articulation to speech, the practice becomes something for the community to evaluate. In a more immediate case, in the moment of decision, a formulation brought to mind can help to clarify what is at stake for the agent.[38] The language

---

35. Taylor, "To Follow a Rule," 177.

36. Bourdieu and Taylor use negative language to assess this relation of articulation to practice: "error," Bourdieu, *The Logic of Practice*, 81; "distort," Taylor, "To Follow a Rule," 176. I am trying to view the relation more holistically and will attempt to show that in a dialectical relationship, articulation and practice inform one another.

37. MacIntyre, "Review of Charles Taylor, *Philosophical Arguments*," 96.

38. Taylor, *The Language Animal*, 137. As I read Taylor, whether intentional or not, this later position reflects an integration of MacIntyre's critique.

brings into focus an otherwise inchoate sense of conflict, and therefore shapes the conflict in its particular way. With this being said, there is always more than one articulation (saying, rule, norm) available by which to understand a situation. Additionally, rules do not interpret themselves; they are only understood within a particular habitus; "without a sense of what [the rules] are about, and an affinity to their spirit, they remain dead letters or become a travesty in practice. This sense and this affinity can only exist where they do in our unformulated, embodied understanding [that is, habitus]."[39] Furthermore, it is only by enacting the rule that we understand it and thereby show its meaning. Formulations can be helpful for providing clarity in a situation as to what is at stake, but the at-stake-ness[40] is circumscribed by a habitus. Through their use in bringing clarity to the community and providing an opportunity for critique, formulations exist in a dialectical relationship with practices, even as the habitus and enacted practices remain primary in our dealings.

What then is Christian wisdom? This project is one in which I am seeking to hear, within a Christian frame of reference, a word from a biblical book concerned with the topic of wisdom. Given the preceding discussion, Christian wisdom is the capacity for one to make decisions deemed "good" when understood against a Christianly formed habitus. A Christian habitus is one shaped by the expressions of Christian life: the liturgy, prayers (formal and informal), songs, spiritual disciplines, Scripture, theology of the church, and family and communal life. These enactments inculcate in the participant a set of concerns for the world, a way of "intending" the world.[41] As above, the embodied enactments are crucial; they are aided by formulations but not dependent on them.[42] This Christian habitus is learned through practices alongside others who are considered "wise" in its ways. The practices together operate to form a distinct telos, or end, by which individual practices are judged. This telos, as a judgment of goodness, is witnessed to in the social realm, just as with the driving or game-playing examples above; the embodiment reacts in a way indicating

---

39. Taylor, "To Follow a Rule," 179. The inscribing of a rule "erupts" the relation between speech and its perlocution-enabling context; it must be re-integrated into a habitus for it to have meaning. See Ricoeur, "What Is a Text?," 121.

40. I fear I am reading too much Heidegger with a construction like this!

41. Smith, *Desiring the Kingdom*, 70.

42. For one such reading of the church's liturgies, see Wolterstorff, *The God We Worship*. For the role of doctrine in this approach, see Lindbeck, *The Nature of Doctrine*.

the success or failure of the enactment.[43] To state the Christian telos briefly, with all the accompanying caveats of formulations vis-à-vis habitus, it is to love God with all of one's being and to love one's neighbor as yourself (cf. Matt 22:37–40).

Considering the Book of Proverbs and Wisdom as Embodied Know-How

The above discussion has articulated an understanding of wisdom as embodied know-how through interaction with contemporary philosophical resources. Stuart Weeks, out of a close study of the nature of wisdom as presented in Proverbs 1–9 in its ancient context, arrives at several conclusions that match well with the previously outlined position.[44] It is worthwhile to note them here, prior to applying the understanding arising from the contemporary frame to the text.

Earlier, I cited Weeks study in relation to the form and content of instructional material in the ancient Near East.[45] In particular, Weeks notes that there seems to be no fixed form or content in the genre, outside of the feature of a father passing down teaching to his son. Instead of relying upon an unsubstantiated fixed form, Weeks exhorts scholars to "assess instructions primarily within their own cultural contexts" (102). For Proverbs 1–9, this context is Israel's faith. Proverbs 3 provides the father's summary of what constitutes instruction, and the chapter's vocabulary is reminiscent of the language of the Law, particularly (though not exclusively) found in Deuteronomy and Jeremiah (96–102).

According to Weeks' analysis, the view presented by Proverbs 1–9 was of people having to choose to become wise, through instruction, rather than wisdom or folly being inherent at birth. From the choice to become wise by submitting to instruction, one was promised wisdom, which is "best translated as 'know-how', and the term can be applied to a variety of technical skills. When used in a general way, it indicates knowledge of how to survive and prosper in the world: it is the 'know-how' of living" (106). The social and cosmic order provided the way to evaluate this success (107–8).

---

43. In this understanding, the enactments of a non-Christian could also be considered wise within a Christian frame of reference.

44. Weeks, *Instruction and Imagery in Proverbs 1–9*, 96–127. References to Weeks' work will be indicated in parenthetical citations for the next few pages.

45. See the discussion of the historical context of Proverbs 1–9 in chapter 2.

Education in wisdom was formative, in that, in a context of competing "voices," an individual could mature from simple to wise (108) through a process of internalizing the Law (112–13). Weeks argues that Law and wisdom are brought into close relationship in the text; wisdom is "the condition achieved by those who have internalized the Law" (113).[46]

Like the approach to wisdom drawn from contemporary philosophical resources, Weeks's reading articulates wisdom as know-how, related to surviving and prospering in the world. It is a sense formed through certain practices outlined in instruction. And its success is related to the broader social environment. Weeks' reminder of the need to contextualize research appropriately in ancient instructional material can be applied, *mutatis mutandis*, to the present discussion as well. His work helpfully challenges the above discussion to be contextualized in the particulars of the text and a community. However, the particular context of this writing of this book is the twenty-first-century Western milieu. As such, the perspective on wisdom outlined in the first portion of this chapter is also a work of contextualization. That resources exist to aid a renewed understanding of wisdom as know-how in the contemporary frame means that there are helpful bridges on offer in order to embody the kind of life Proverbs 1–9 portrays. Therefore, the discussion now turns to reading Proverbs 1–9 in light of wisdom as embodied know-how, and then to an articulation of how Proverbs 8 might be rendered in a life today.

An approach to wisdom that foregrounds it as embodied leads to a number of implications regarding the book of Proverbs.[47] I name two here and will briefly consider each of them in turn. First, it offers one way of accounting for the presence of both imperative and indicative pedagogy in the prologue of Proverbs (chs. 1–9). Second, the importance of the fear of

---

46. In a later chapter surveying the influence of Proverbs 1–9 in later Jewish texts, Weeks argues "When such a variety of texts pick up the figure of Wisdom and associate her with the Law, it is manifestly simpler to deduce that they all understood this association to be implied in their common source, than to propose that they influenced each other or independently succumbed to some outlined influence." Weeks, *Instruction and Imagery in Proverbs 1–9*, 168.

47. I am not alone in considering Proverbs, and the way of wisdom, to be about more than the literary formulations. See Murphy, "Wisdom—Theses and Hypotheses," 39; Morgan, *Wisdom in the Old Testament Traditions*, 22; Hill, *Wisdom's Many Faces*, 4. Each of these three posits wisdom as a way of life or worldview. My treatment here is distinct from theirs, even as I agree that wisdom as presented in Scripture is more than the words of the text.

A Contemporary Conception of Wisdom

the LORD as the keynote of Proverbs "shows up" as pointing to a disposition, a habitus.

Bernd Schipper highlights imperative instruction and indicative instruction as two pedagogies in the book of Proverbs.[48] The imperative focuses on the formulations of wisdom; these are the "do this" and "do not do this" proverbs (cf. Prov 4:24). This form is often, though not exclusively, associated with discipline (מוּסָר) and correction (תּוֹכַחַת, cf. Prov 5:12). In contrast, the indicative treats the student as the subject and wisdom as the object (cf. Prov 2:1–5). Schipper argues the goal of this form is "rational understanding and insight."[49] These passages consider the nature of wisdom rather than wise sayings themselves. Schipper relates these two pedagogies to the two stages of wisdom learning: "In one case, wisdom students are given the foundations of sapiential knowledge through direct commands, while in the other, advanced wisdom students are provided with a deeper level of sapiential education through indicative discourse."[50] Michael Fox, reflecting on the imperative commands in Proverbs 1–9, concludes "the teachings do not seem all that difficult."[51] Rather, in his view, the commands point to a higher aim of the book's instruction, which is wisdom as a moral disposition.[52]

Within the embodied understanding of wisdom stated above, these two forms relate to the dynamic of formulations (imperative) and practical sense (indicative). The imperative formulations describe practices to enact which have traditionally demonstrated wisdom. They are practices for the beginner to start on the path of developing wisdom, that capacity to consistently enact practices so that one succeeds in a given situation. These practices are enacted under the tutelage of one who has gone before; in the book this person functions as the "father." That, per Fox, the imperatives do not ask for much is a feature of practical pedagogy: "The cunning of pedagogic reason lies precisely in the fact that it manages to extort what is essential

---

48. Schipper, *Proverbs 1–15*, 28.
49. Schipper, *Proverbs 1–15*, 28.
50. Schipper, *Proverbs 1–15*, 29.
51. Fox, *Proverbs 1–9*, 347.
52. Fox, *Proverbs 1–9*, 348. Earlier, I noted that Fox's conception of wisdom is as a cognitive activity, a perspective which is distinct from the one I am offering in this chapter. Nevertheless, that Fox states that the higher aim of the book is moral disposition alerts us to the fact that his conception may not be entirely cognitive, unless his sense of one's moral compass is itself also heavily reliant upon cognition.

while seeming to demand the insignificant."[53] The practices move the body in certain ways within a given social sphere, embodying a way of life. Practices are not ends in themselves; they rely on a background to make sense as well as the additional capacity (practical sense) to know when to enact which practice in a particular manner. The indicative instruction in Proverbs could be understood to gesture toward this broader context requisite for the imperatives to "work."

In addition to offering one angle of vision on the two pedagogies of the book, an approach to wisdom which foregrounds its nature as embodied in practices understood within a habitus shapes our understanding of the keynote of Proverbs: "The fear of the LORD is the beginning of wisdom" (Prov 9:10; cf. 1:7; 15:33). This statement grounds the particular understanding of wisdom presented by the book of Proverbs. The keynote states the foundation is attitudinal and dispositional; developing wisdom requires the proper orientation of one's desires.[54] Within the viewpoint of Proverbs, the right orientation of desires is properly expressed through fear of the LORD. It is this orientation which makes possible the acquisition and advancement of wisdom.[55]

Within this approach to wisdom, the fear of the LORD functions as a habitus, a system of dispositions which enables and evaluates the enactment of practices. The fear of the LORD can be manifested in relation to numerous topics with varying implications; creation, the divine, the Torah, worship, etc. Significantly, fear is a dispositional term; what counts is the way one *relates*.[56] The habitus, as a system of dispositions, is what enables practices to "make sense." The keynote would then be asserting the need for this background habitus before any of the aphorisms or teachings will be seen as valuable or be put to "good" use. An additional feature of a habitus noted above is that it is formed over time rather than acquired in a moment. If the fear of the LORD is understood as a habitus, then Proverbs 1:28–31 can be taken to mean that the wicked who previously rejected this system of dispositions cannot hope to call it up in the moment of crisis. Even if one were to adopt this phrase qua doctrine or formulation in the heat of the moment, it would only make sense against the background of a habitus and

---

53. Bourdieu, *The Logic of Practice*, 69.

54. Fox, *Proverbs 1–9*, 348.

55. "The fear of God is the sphere within which wisdom is possible and can be realized, the precondition for both wisdom and ethical behavior." Fox, *Proverbs 1–9*, 69.

56. Proverbs 8:13 defines the fear of the LORD negatively, again in dispositional terms.

A Contemporary Conception of Wisdom

when enacted in a practice; mere oracular enunciation does not constitute the fear of the LORD. Interpreting the fear of the LORD as a habitus thus offers one way to make sense of its function in the book of Proverbs.

Reading Proverbs 8 through the Heuristic of Wisdom as Embodied Know-How

Proverbs 8 presents a view of the world in which the voice of wisdom addresses us; "Does not Wisdom call?" (Prov 8:1) is a rhetorical question which expresses the conviction that she does indeed call. In the world in front of Proverbs 8, human beings are addressed consistently and pervasively by the voice of Wisdom. As surveyed above, the dominant pre-understanding of the secular age presents a challenge to understanding this address, by complicating our understanding of this voice. A disenchanted world is one in which meanings are not understood to inhere in "things," all meaning is humanly given.[57] We may be tempted to respond in such a way that does not take seriously one of the two worlds of this encounter (Prov 8 and our own): either the text is just wrong, there are no more "spirits" in the world, any "spirit" or "voice" is just in the head, therefore we should ignore this feature of the text; or our "world" is wrong, this voice is there and we need to accept it. Neither of these approaches would accomplish the goal of reading the text as I have outlined, which is transformation of self in front of the text. In these two false trails we leave with our pre-understandings unaltered by the power of the text.

The conception of wisdom as embodied know-how offers a fruitful path beyond this impasse. Within this understanding, the call takes on a hermeneutical function; it is a feature of a habitus formed by the text which then opens up a way of experiencing the world. Understanding this voice as a hermeneutic takes seriously both the content of Proverbs 8 as well as its broader context in Proverbs 1–9. These introductory chapters of the book of Proverbs seek to give the reader an interpretive framework for the remainder of the book (chs. 10–31) and, by extension, for the whole of life. As stated above, the indicative sections of Proverbs 1–9, which includes Proverbs 8, "gesture" toward the need for a background understanding, a

---

57. Again, it is important to recall that Taylor is describing conditions of belief, not formulated beliefs themselves. Even if one affirms meaning as given by God, the context of so many other options for life presses one for the realization that *they* believe this to be so, while others do not. This recognition shapes even a belief in God-given meaning.

habitus, in order to appropriate both the imperative teachings of the prologue and the proverbs proper. Proverbs 8, as the longest use of personified Wisdom, is an extended section calling for the reader to recognize the importance of this habitus and appealing for them to be formed in it.

A hermeneutical understanding of the appeal of Wisdom takes seriously the content of Proverbs 8. The chapter opens with its rhetorical question, asserting the presence of Wisdom's call (Prov 8:1). It continues by declaring that this call is found in the everyday experiences of life (Prov 8:2-3). The call of Wisdom is ubiquitous. A hermeneutical framework understands this as a feature of a habitus. There can be no experience in which there is no background operating. Rather, the habitus constitutes the experience by "showing" certain features and providing options by which the perceiver can navigate the particular encounter.[58] The call invites and enables the reader to perceive a possibility present in each encounter, appealing to those who are aware of themselves as malleable moral agents seeking to become like Wisdom in character.

Over time, and with "practice," agents can develop "practical sense" or "wisdom" by which they repeatedly and reliably enact choices that result in positive results. These results are evaluated as positive within the constraints of the socially shared habitus.[59] Wisdom's self-evaluations in Proverbs 8, along with her promised rewards to those who heed her, can be taken to address the formative capacity of practice within her habitus. Her own virtues speak to the qualities of this habitus, qualities in which a follower can hope to be formed. Her speech (Prov 8:6-9), her character (Prov 8:13), and her capacities (Prov 8:14-16) are exemplary of what following her can give. She is the model for a life formed by the habitus of Wisdom; following her shapes one to have a similar character and capacities.[60] These features of Wisdom and the formation she offers can be taken as the shaping function of practices within a certain habitus. Being trained

---

58. Bourdieu, *The Logic of Practice*, 55.

59. Bourdieu, *The Logic of Practice*, 58.

60. Fox notes Wisdom's role as an exemplar in his comments on verse 12, "Wisdom is describing herself in terms of a wise human being, and an attribute of the wise is that they can gain or 'find' knowledge." Fox, *Proverbs 1-9*, 272. Aletti also comments on formative function such that, while no embodiment of Woman Wisdom comparable to the adulterous as Woman Folly is provided by the book, the book ends with the Woman of Worth in Proverbs 31. After a long apprenticeship to wisdom, the student is able to identify the manifestation of Wisdom in the world. Aletti, "Séduction et parole en Proverbes I-IX," 144.

A Contemporary Conception of Wisdom

up in the habitus of Wisdom opens up certain options which are otherwise unavailable. One can then develop a capacity to "choose well" such that the results are evaluated in the qualitative terms of Wisdom's speech. This approach can also be applied to Proverbs 8's relationship to Proverbs 10–31. The qualities mentioned through Proverbs 8 give evaluative terms by which the reader can then understand their own choices; thereby proving a hermeneutic for applying the aphorisms of chapters 10–31.

The social nature of a habitus also provides an account for the place of wealth in Wisdom's promises. Even though she says that she is to be preferred over wealth (cf. Prov 8:10–11, 19), Wisdom does still hint that her followers may indeed gain material wealth (Prov 8:18, 21). Making choices heralded by a community as good raises one's reputation and can lead to increased financial opportunities and rewards. This is not automatic, as it depends on the formation of those with means within the community. If those with wealth do not share the habitus of Wisdom, they will not value those formed by her. Concomitantly, if those who do value her do not have means, they have nothing to share. Understanding Wisdom as habitus thus opens up a way to hear both the promise of wealth and the qualification to that promise present in Proverbs 8.

A distinct feature of the poem is its universal audience (Prov 8:4), including those deemed unable to answer Wisdom's call (Prov 8:5, cf. 1:20–33). The formative nature of a habitus provides at least one way to understand this tension. One is formed in a habitus no matter who one is. As such, depending on one's formation, the option to heed the call represented by Wisdom, to adopt her habitus, may not "show up" for a given person. However, from another perspective, no one is outside the possibility of moving toward a new habitus, developing it in concert with the tradition of practices it hands down. There is no way to predict whether someone would be open.[61] Historically speaking, the tension within the text could stem from observations behind it; namely that some deemed "callow" do respond and take correction while the vast majority do not. Aside from its historical background, understanding Wisdom qua habitus opens up a way to read this tension holistically, including both the "yes" (Prov 8:4) and the "no" (Prov 1:20–33). Proverbs 8 contains the "yes," the affirmation of Wisdom's universal appeal. The appeal can be understood hermeneutically, that is, as describing the kind of stance toward others enabled by the habitus. The terms used for the audience are ethnically neutral (בְּנֵי אָדָם, אִישִׁים, Prov

---

61. Bourdieu, *The Logic of Practice*, 56.

Wisdom in the World

8:4). As mentioned above, verse 5 includes those of dubious moral quality (כְּסִילִים, פְּתָיִם). That Wisdom addresses these groups, who exist outside the normal circumscribed perimeters of a wise, moral Israelite, shapes the perceptions of those formed in her habitus. The reader is invited to see them as addressed by the same voice which addresses them. They are thereby portrayed as malleable moral agents just like the reader.

Proverbs 8 provides qualitative vocabulary by which the reader can "see" and assess practices. It also shapes the reader's understanding of others by opening up a stance toward those who are not wise, nor Israelites. This latter move is what I would like to call a subjectifying one; it makes the "other" a subject rather than an object. A subjectifying stance is a distinct feature of the habitus depicted by Proverbs 8. The audience of Wisdom is one junction at which this can be seen. The virtues of Wisdom are another. Wisdom abhors those qualities which would separate one from others and allow them to take advantage of them (cf. Prov 8:13), while she extols virtues which move one toward others (Prov 8:20). Within this stance, Wisdom's appeal to power can also be understood. In verses 14–16, Wisdom speaks of enabling good and effective rule, the chief marker of which is justice (צֶדֶק, 8:15b). The kind of rule which Wisdom enables is one which promotes social order.[62] This particular view of power is one which is not for one's own benefit, but for the benefit of others.[63] Wisdom's reference to rulers is not restrictive but as an example; what she says of rulers is to be applied to all readers.[64] Readers are invited to see whatever power they may have and to apply it in a way that benefits others. Other people thereby "show up" within this habitus in a particular way.

Verses 22–31, with their appeal to the Wisdom's perduring presence through time, can also be understood as recommending a subjectifying stance. As I address in more depth in my next chapter, one way to understand Wisdom's persistence through time is that she has spoken to others in the past. The reader is not the first to hear Wisdom's call. As such, those who have gone before become "persons of interest," people to whom the reader is to relate in order to discover, hear, and follow Wisdom. Additionally, verses 27–29 speak of the Lord's work to put limits within the

---

62. Schipper, *Proverbs 1–15*, 303.

63. The opposite is found in the offerings of the adulterous woman, which effectually destroy the community. Aletti, "Séduction et parole en Proverbes I–IX," 139.

64. Plöger, *Sprüche Salomos*, 90.

created order, using language reminiscent of divine decrees.[65] The world of inanimate objects is thus construed as the site of the LORD's activity and the reader is invited to relate to it not only as an object of study, but as bearing witness to and participating in the LORD's ongoing work.

The final portion of Proverbs 8 casts the pursuit of Wisdom in terms of intimacy.[66] While not unique among Proverbs in doing so, the terminology here is strikingly erotic. How can a reader appropriate this erotic personified presence within a secular age and an understanding of Wisdom as a habitus? The work of Nicholas Lash, particularly in which he interacts with Martin Buber's *I and Thou*, provides a helpful way to appropriate not only the message of verses 32–36, but of the entire poem.[67] Buber outlines two basic stances toward the world, I-it and I-you.[68] Buber speaks of these as two modes of being in the world; one experiences the world as objects and things (I-it) and the other relates to it as "the world of relation."[69] Though presented in counterpoint, these are not to be understood as two competing options. The stance toward the world as an object arises from the fact that we relate; that to which we relate calls upon us to be understood, be it a person, an institution, or a rock.[70] At issue is whether one remains in this objectifying stance. The calling to be human is, having taken the world (people, trees, granite rocks) in this way, to take up again the stance of relating. The latter stance is one of love, in which those partners of our encounters can surprise us, shape us, challenge us, etc. It is admittedly a risky stance, as it requires of us a basic trust in the other.[71] To do this is difficult in a world dominated by objectification; what is required is a community of love.[72] To not adopt this stance, and to remain in the I-it world,

---

65. Schipper, *Proverbs 1–15*, 311–12.

66. Fox, *Proverbs 1–9*, 290.

67. Lash, *Easter in Ordinary*. Lash recapitulates many of the main arguments of his book in two particularly helpful essays; "On What Kinds of Things There Are" and "Creation, Courtesy and Contemplation." Martin Buber, *I and Thou*. Lash's interaction with Buber is helpful for two reasons. First, he responsibly appropriates Buber within a Christian frame of reference (which I share). Second, he makes his arguments acknowledging the complexity of our current "world" in a way not unlike my attempted interaction with Charles Taylor.

68. Buber, *I and Thou*, 53.

69. Lash, *Easter in Ordinary*, 187.

70. Buber, *I and Thou*, 73–75. Lash, *Easter in Ordinary*, 191.

71. Lash, *Easter in Ordinary*, 192–93.

72. Lash, *Easter in Ordinary*, 194–95.

is to turn away from the distinctly human, that is, to turn toward death.[73] While I make no contention that this particular understanding was present at the time of the writing of Proverbs 8, Buber via Lash offers a way of appropriating the intimate and consequential call of Wisdom, and the need to maintain one's devotion to her, in a secular age.

While I have just acknowledged that this particular understanding may not have been present at the book's originating moments, it is a view that is not alien to the content of Proverbs. Arndt Meinhold observes that the particular character of faith in Proverbs is a two-sided combination of love of God and love of neighbor: "Das Besondere des JHWH-Glaubens kommt in Sprüchebuch vor allem dadurch zum Ausdruck, daß die unauflösliche Zweiseitigkeit der Frömmigkeit—hin zu JHWH und gleichzeitig hin zum Mitmenschen, und zwar besonders in Form von Barmherzigkeit und Recht gegenüber den Bedürftigen."[74] Meinhold points to chapters 2 and 3 of the book as exemplifying this special theology. Stuart Weeks also explores this, in particular arguing that chapter 3 represents a summary of proper instruction. Chapter 3 verses 1–10 focus on honoring the Lord and verses 21–35 relate to proper behavior toward human beings.[75] In between these two sections stands 3:11–20, which relates wisdom and instruction with the Lord God. One way to read the linkage between love of God and of human beings is in something like the subjectifying mode I advocate above, in which one takes up the risky stance of love toward the other as a means by which one encounters and honors God in the world.

The intimate appeal of Lady Wisdom can be heard as a call to subjectify the world; approaching other human beings, the tradition, the decrees of God, and the inanimate world in order to relate rather than dominate. This is a particular disposition toward all things, a habitus, engendered by the particular content of Proverbs 8 and the device of personification at work throughout. Within the book of Proverbs, this stance toward the world offers a habitus in which the shorter aphorisms make sense and can be enacted successfully. The nature of Proverbs' project as described in Proverbs 1:1–7 is to shape a student to live life successfully (vv. 2–4) and to give them a sense for the world (vv. 5–6), both grounded in the fear of the Lord (verse 7). This keynote of the book highlights the way one relates

---

73. Lash, *Easter in Ordinary*, 193. Lash quotes another work of Buber's, in which Buber characterizes Israel's choice as between community and perishing "in an icy death."

74. Meinhold, *Die Sprüche*, 39.

75. Weeks, *Instruction and Imagery in Proverbs 1–9*, 100.

A Contemporary Conception of Wisdom

to the Lord God of Israel as paramount in the pursuit of wisdom. The general proverbs of the book touch on a plethora of life's spheres, giving the impression that wisdom has to deal with all of life. According to this reading, Proverbs 8 indicates a subjectifying mode of being-in-the-world by which a student is enabled to see, act, and reflect in such a way that they are successfully relating to the Lord in every encounter. It couches the application of the proverbs of chapters 10–31 in a relational mode rather than a mechanistic mode. The success of a particular practice offered by an individual proverb is dependent on relationship. This contrasts with reading the proverbs in a "pull the lever" kind of way, as if they guaranteed their own outcome.

This reading of Proverbs 8 takes seriously both the world in front of the text and the world of a secular age. The portrait offered by the text of a persistent and profitable call of Wisdom is heard as a habitus, operative in every arena of life, in which the reader can be formed as they submit to the practices outlined in the book of Proverbs. This reading acknowledges the nature of a disenchanted secular age without ignoring the call as presented in the text. The reading also challenges aspects of the dominant pre-understanding of the secular age; particularly instrumental objectification which is so deleterious to relationships, both human relations and relations with the created world.

9

Three First Attempts at a Renewed Christian Reading of Proverbs 8

As exposited in a previous chapter, the work of Paul Ricoeur and Charles Taylor enjoined upon the reader the task of appropriating the world in front of the text. Appropriation is a dialectical movement between the text's projected world and the lived world of the reader. Charles Taylor's work, *A Secular Age*, aids readers situated in the twenty-first-century Western milieu in understanding their world. This world is complicated and multi-faceted. It follows from this that the move of appropriation will be varied.

In this final portion of the book, I seek to illustrate moves which appropriate the world of Proverbs 8 and integrate it with differing aspects of a Christian life in the twenty-first century. In the chapter immediately preceding this one, I approached the subject matter of Proverbs via contemporary reflection on the nature of human involvement in the world. Thus, I began from the contemporary frame and then approached Proverbs 8. In these next essays, the text is the primary focus. The first essay articulates an existential understanding of the world in front of Proverbs 8. After this, and taking cues from the history of interpretation surveyed in section 2, I seek to integrate the chapter, particularly verses 22–31, with Christian reflection upon the doctrine of God's Trinity. The final appropriating reading seeks a two-testament understanding by integrating Proverbs 8 and the theme of light in John's Gospel.

It is conceivable that these selected readings could be ordered differently. I have chosen to proceed with that which interacts most closely with the whole chapter of Proverbs 8 (an existential reading of the world projected by the entirety of the chapter), and then that which focuses more on one sub-section of the chapter (verses 22–31 in relation to the doctrine of God's Trinity), and end with a reflection whose main work is devoted to John's Gospel, which is then brought into relationship with Proverbs 8.

An Existentially Oriented Reading of Proverbs 8

In what follows, I will attempt to articulate one reading of the mode of being-in-the-world proposed by Proverbs 8 for Christian readers. The challenge here is to state this world without distortion of the text, even as I do so using language drawn from my own context and tradition. Working to understand the text in its literary and historical contexts allows the text its own integrity and produces some safeguards against overriding its meaning. Therefore, my previous work is not left behind, but carried into this exercise. First, I will set out the distinct contribution of Proverbs 8 to a world and then I will broaden the scope to include the prologue of the book of Proverbs (chapters 1–9).

The Distinct Contribution of Proverbs 8

As a text Proverbs 8 opens up a multi-faceted world constituted by certain features that in turn offer a new mode of existing in the world. This world is persistently and pervasively filled with the inviting presence of a personal voice in the world, a voice that is profitable for our hearing. Accordingly, we are offered a mode of being in the world that is open to this voice and its offerings in each moment of our lives.

The above articulation stems from integrating the results of reading the text in its literary context. I will review those results below as I draw out a potential articulation of the world in front of the text. The review is intended to illustrate and ensure that this sense of the world is indeed grounded in the text of Proverbs 8. Proverbs 8:1–3 focus on the location in time and space of the call (קרא) of Wisdom. The rhetorical nature of the opening question of the chapter, "Does not Wisdom call?" assumes that Wisdom is indeed calling persistently.[1] Readers need not object to this assertion because it may not agree with our experience. Rather, our present task is to suspend our critique and disbelief and allow the text to construct its world. At a later point, objections and critique can be registered in order to sharpen an appropriation of the passage. The world in front of the text is

---

1. Schipper, *Proverbs 1–15*, 294.

pervaded by a voice, Wisdom, who is calling not only to those who know her voice via the Old Testament, but all people. By using the terms אִישִׁים and בְּנֵי אָדָם, verses 4 and 5 specify the audience as ethically undifferentiated humanity.[2] The locations given for this call communicate to us an "ongoing, typical occurrence," one not truly confined by a specific location but found throughout the city, the inhabited world, and the cosmos.[3] So even though we do not inhabit the originating context of these words they open up a horizon in which even we modern readers are addressed.[4]

Even though Proverbs 8 can be characterized as Wisdom's self-recommendation, it is nevertheless an invitation to the hearer of the voice to pay attention to her.[5] The poem's "grand celebration of Wisdom . . . all leads to the practical conclusion that it is good to seek and obey her."[6] In Proverbs 8:4–11 Wisdom calls (אֶקְרָא, v 4) and commands (הָבִינוּ, twice in v. 5; שִׁמְעוּ, v. 6; קְחוּ, v. 10) the reader with the aim of establishing a relationship. The invitation includes descriptions of Wisdom's value which increase the allure of heeding this invitation. Wisdom has the capacity to give the discerning power necessary to succeed in life (עָרְמָה) to those who lack it (פְּתָאִים), and sense (לֵב) to those who would otherwise reject the profitable voice calling to them (8:5) (כְּסִילִים). However, we are not to think that Wisdom's appeal is to our mercenary desires: Wisdom's words are heralded as morally pure (cf. vv. 6–8). Wisdom appeals and exhorts, giving us the impression that she wants the hearer to come to her; her invitation is neither neutral nor disinterested. Correspondingly, her call is not to a disinterested audience, but one presumed to operate on desires. It is those who do not want to be פֶּתִי or כְּסִילִים, as well as those who value her moral virtues, who will respond to her. Her allure to one's deep seated orientation is redolent of the motto of Proverbs, "the fear of the LORD is the beginning of knowledge" (1:7a). The

---

2. Perdue, *Proverbs*, 141; Whybray, *Proverbs*, 122.

3. Fox, *Proverbs 1–9*, 267.

4. We should note that this sort of explicit openness in the words of the text is not necessary for understanding the text as open to us as well. Ricoeur writes, "If the meaning of a text is open to anyone who can read, then it is the omni-temporality of meaning which opens it to unknown readers; and the historicity of reading is the counterpart of this specific omni-temporality. From the moment that the text escapes from its author and from his situation, it also escapes from its original audience. Hence it can procure new readers for itself." Ricoeur, "Appropriation," 154.

5. Cf. Fox; Whybray, *Proverbs*, 119.

6. Fox, *Proverbs 1–9*, 289.

motto states an attitudinal prerequisite to growth and Wisdom's invitation appeals to that attitude.⁷

The world before the text here is one in which the readers are morally interested agents. The invitation travels to the center of our desires, our grander visions of the good life. Within this appeal, Wisdom's invites her audience to be formed along the lines of her virtue. Her self-descriptions offer themselves as a mold according to which the student will be shaped.⁸ She is offering to be our teacher, not primarily of our heads but of our hearts/guts.⁹ To inhabit the world in this way would be to attend to our desires and working definitions of virtue and vice as the site of Wisdom's call.

Both the second (vv. 4–11) and third (vv. 12–22) sections of Proverbs 8 cast Wisdom as profitable to the hearer. Verse 5 states that Wisdom will give shrewdness (ערמה) and sense (לב) to the hearer. Obtaining these characteristics would presumably transform one from a פֶּתִי and כְּסִילִים to be like one who understands (מֵבִין) and finds knowledge (מֹצְאֵי דָעַת) (v. 9).¹⁰ More personally, those who love Wisdom are rewarded with her own love (v. 17). That which is pursued with one's whole being responds in kind.¹¹ Even though the poem is keen to emphasize Wisdom's gifts as superior to material gain, material rewards are still counted among her benefits (v. 18). William McKane notes that the wealth she offers is nuanced in verse 18 such that it is understood not as "meretricious or speculative wealth; it is located in a framework of values and is an ingredient of a way of life which bestows *gravitas* and social wholeness."¹² Given the purpose of the whole book to offer wisdom to the reader, these various personal benefits offer us a picture of what attaining wisdom looks like. Once again, this appeals to the desires of the reader.

---

7. Fox, *Proverbs 1–9*, 103.

8. Schipper, *Proverbs 1–15*, 299. I want to be careful not to disregard knowledge as part of Wisdom's pedagogy. She certainly speaks of knowledge (דעת) (cf. 8:10,12). However, given the logic of her appeal, it seems better to foreground desires and intentions rather than data or other cognitively construed characterizations of her education.

9. Cf. Prov 4:20–27 and its "sapiential teaching on the body" which focuses on the heart as the driver of human behavior. Schipper, *Proverbs 1–15*, 184.

10. Schipper, *Proverbs 1–15*, 299.

11. Fox, keeping with his understanding of wisdom as a cognitive faculty, likens this to the sense of reciprocal response from the subject matter one is studying. Fox, *Proverbs 1–9*, 276.

12. McKane, *Proverbs*, 350.

Wisdom in the World

While certainly personally beneficial, it is noteworthy how Wisdom's gifts are a boon to the whole community. The quote from McKane above already points in this direction as the wealth offered by Wisdom bestows honor on the community. The capacities delineated in verse 14 are "the faculties of statecraft, wielded by effective rulers to achieve their goals."[13] As attributes desired for rule, they are intended to bless the whole society. The following verses (vv. 15–16) reinforce this impression with references to royalty and rule; justice (צֶדֶק) stands out as the defining mark of these rulers who are led by Wisdom. The connection to the portrait of the ideal king in Isaiah 11:2 further underscores the idea that these features are intended to benefit the many rather than only the individual. With this being said, the focus on rulers is not intended to restrict Wisdom's reach. Rather, rulers illustrate the kind of success she brings to those who listen to her. "Was den Fürsten, insofern sie Liebhaber der Weisheit sind, gelingt in ihrem guten Regiment, verheißt die Weisheit mutatis mutandis allen ihren Liebhabern."[14] Each hearer is offered the chance to bring effective and beneficial order to their own domain of influence.

These verses continue to fill out the picture of the world in front of the text. Heeding this voice of Wisdom, which is pervasively and persistently calling to each person, bring benefits to the listener. They become one who understands, obtains their hearts desire, and receives the love of Wisdom. These benefits shape their character as well as bring moral virtue and effective action to the community. As such, readers are challenged to conceive of themselves as malleable in character, and to evaluate their desire to bless those around them. To be in this way is to be open to transformation, to each moment as having potential to shape one in character in a beneficial way.

The fourth section of the chapter, verses 22–31, makes a different move. In my reading of the world in front of the text, these verses function within the poem to speak to the priority and persistence of Wisdom in creation, underscoring her benefit. The structure of this section communicates a connection from the Lord God of Israel at the dawn of His creative work to the voice presently addressing the children of humanity (בני אדם). Verse 22 begins with the Tetragrammaton and verse 31 ends with בני אדם, the same phrase used for Wisdom's audience in verse 4. Thus, the poem

---

13. Fox, *Proverbs 1–9*, 273.
14. Plöger, *Sprüche Salomos*, 90.

is structured from the LORD to the audience of her address.[15] The initial verses of this section emphasize Wisdom's temporal precedence over all other works in creation through its plurality of temporal clauses.[16] From the very beginning of creation, Wisdom has been intimately familiar with the LORD's way, that is, His "divine pattern of creative acts."[17] When God issues His divine decrees (חקק), Wisdom was there (שָׁם אָנִי), beside Him faithfully (אָמוֹן). And now, she is not only His delight, but she herself delights in the children of humanity. The flow of the passage moves from the very dawn of time to the present day. Throughout each portion of this movement before (vv. 22–26), during (vv. 27–29), and after creation (vv. 30–31), Wisdom perdures.[18] "Wisdom in these verses reflects a resistance to that which does not endure—that is, a resistance to mortality."[19] Wisdom has been continually and without deviation present to the LORD God and His ways; the description of her constancy at the LORD's side is not left in the past but remains true in the present. Therefore, Wisdom is a trustworthy guide for her listeners/lovers in the way that leads to life (cf. v. 35).

The space opened up before the text by verses 22–31 is one of remarkable depth.[20] The voice calling to the reader echoes back through the eons to the dawn of time. The voice has a pedigree established in God's own creative pattern of action. The mode of being-in-the-world opened up for the reader is one grounded in time and space. That she has been calling to others, daily delighting in the children of humanity (בני אדם), suggests that others have heard the call and, perhaps, followed it, which would enjoin upon the reader curiosity toward this way as lived by others. The singular voice of Wisdom unites the apparent plurality of those responding to this voice.[21] Her delight has led many scholars to see in Wisdom a childlikeness. If so, this may offer a further nuance of a stance in the world which is like

---

15. Collett, *Figural Reading and the Old Testament*, 99. Collett argues that the movement from the LORD to Adam frames all time.

16. As noted in chapter 2, the translation of קנה in Prov 8:22 is far from simple, with ardent advocates for each of the three notable possibilities ("create," "beget," "acquire"). My preference is the translate the verbs "brought forth." Additionally, I understand that the primary aim of the text is to raise Wisdom's profile in the eyes of the reader.

17. Murphy, *Proverbs*, 50.

18. Weeks, "The Context and Meaning of Proverbs 8:30a."

19. Collett, *Figural Reading and the Old Testament*, 99.

20. Given the section's focus on the waters and the depths (vv. 27–29), the pun is intended.

21. Camp, *Wisdom and the Feminine in the Book of Proverbs*, 216.

an infant who is inherently dependent and open to what the parents have to offer.²²

In the final section of Proverbs 8, verses 32–36, the voice recurs to explicit invitation. Verse 32 frame Wisdom's invitation to the current moment, the "now" (עַתָּה). The reader is labeled among her children (בָּנִים) and therefore one of her addressees (cf. v. 4).²³ The section both promises benefit to the listener and calls for persistence on the part of student. Verses 33 and 34 focus on the need for the listener to match Wisdom's faithfulness to the LORD; just as she is daily (יוֹם יוֹם, v. 30) by His side, so the student must watch daily (יוֹם יוֹם, v. 34) at Wisdom's door as part of accepting her discipline (verse 33). Doing so renders one blessed (אַשְׁרֵי, verse 32, 34), finding life and favor from the LORD (verse 35). The language of verse 34 is erotic in that it pictures "a lover waiting to catch a glimpse of an influential lady, mistress of the house or palace."²⁴ The ongoing nature of watching at Wisdom's door renders the finding of wisdom (מצא, verse 35) as an ongoing, dynamic activity. Additionally, verse 35 links Wisdom to the LORD, such that her gifts are accompanied by His favor. Moreover, the decision placed before the reader is consequential. There are only two options for the reader, each with starkly different outcomes. Either the reader loves Wisdom and finds life (vv. 34–35), or they hate her and experience harm (חֹמֵס נַפְשׁוֹ) on the way to death (מָוֶת, verse 36).²⁵ Within verses 32–36, hatred of Wisdom means neglecting or rejecting her discipline (verse 33). In the broader scope of the book, this stance is reflective fools (אֱוִילִים), whose "Deep-seated attitudes, rather than lack of raw intelligence, prevent them from gaining Wisdom" (cf. Prov 1:7).²⁶

The final invitation reinforces many of the preceding facets of the world in front of the text. Wisdom appeals to the desires of the reader.²⁷ The voice speaking to the listener can be heard at the point of their longings. For those who are attracted to her offer, she calls for complete and consummate devotion. The only other option is to hate her. The clarity and seriousness

---

22. See David Ford's discussion of wisdom in Luke 10:21–24 in *Christian Wisdom*, 20–25, esp. 24.

23. Schipper, *Proverbs 1–15*, 288.

24. Fox, *Proverbs 1–9*, 290.

25. Baumann, *Die Weisheitsgestalt in Proverbien 1–9*, 290. L. Boström, *The God of the Sages*, 149–50.

26. Fox, *Proverbs 1–9*, 68.

27. "The attraction of Wisdom is erotic in its power, and the wise pursue her as ardently as a lover does his beloved." Fox, *Proverbs 1–9*, 290.

Three Attempts at a Christian Reading of Proverbs 8

of the decision raises the stakes of this projected world. In each moment, Wisdom calls one to choose between life or death; there is no third alternative. Fox clarifies the language of verse 36 as not "speaking of moral sins but describing a personal, 'emotional' relationship: love and devotion versus offensiveness and hatred."[28] When we consider the text projecting a world in front of it, we can perhaps take the scare quotes off of Fox's "emotional"; the mode-of-being into which the reader is invited includes the emotions, as certainly the reward of life and favor include the recipient's emotions. Finally, this section draws together Wisdom and the LORD such that heeding this voice is linked to heeding to the LORD; it has the tenor of the divine.

To summarize the world in front of the text presented within the confines of the chapter, Proverbs 8 projects a world in which a voice, tinged with the tone of the divine is persistently appealing to the longings of every person. It is a voice that offers to form their character to that of the voice for the benefit of themselves and their community. The voice has a depth in time and space; it speaks in the manner of tradition. The possibility opened up by the text is heeding the voice, which involves the listener in a complete commitment of submitting each moment to the discipline and way of Wisdom. To be in this world is to be addressed as a moral agent at the level of one's longings and to respond by relating to the world personally, to the benefit of self and others, walking in paths similar to those who have gone before.

Prior to moving beyond chapter 8 to the book and then broader canon, it is beneficial to reflect on the metaphorical device of personification which runs throughout the chapter. Both Claudia Camp and Michael Fox address the function of personification, offering various conclusions as to its effect.[29] Lennart Boström interprets the personification of wisdom as "a literary and moral counterbalance to Lady Folly," and goes on to warn, "one should be extremely careful not to inject too much theological content into what may well be a purely literary phenomenon."[30] One can certainly take note of Boström's warning, and still, given the view of language and the text's capacity to project a world surveyed above, seek to address how the metaphor adds to the meaning of the text. Within the context of Proverbs 8, one function to consider is personification's capacity to personalize what

---

28. Fox, *Proverbs 1–9*, 291.

29. Camp, *Wisdom and the Feminine in the Book of Proverbs*, 209–22. Fox, *Proverbs 1–9*, 293.

30. L. Boström, *The God of the Sages*, 58.

would otherwise be abstract.³¹ As a species of metaphor, personification works to identify a meaning that is new; it is not simply to associate one set of attributes of one thing to another.³² Charles Taylor asserts that, through "metaphoric attribution, the phenomenon swims into our ken along with the attribution. It comes to light in the tension between the two foci, A and B."³³ Metaphor is creative, bringing discovery and invention together. This creative use of metaphor can stem from "cases where we feel a sense that there's something new to be said. This may be at first inchoate; we are groping for something, we know not quite what. And then we coin a new expression which resolves this tension."³⁴ The creative metaphor not only includes a description of some sort, but it is also accompanied by vividness.³⁵ Thus, the personification of wisdom as a woman can be understood to highlight the manner in which one encounters wisdom, in a personal way.

We could speculate on proposed schemes of the literary development of the book of Proverbs through the lens of "groping" to articulate something inchoate. Michael Fox suggests that the father-son dialogues in Proverbs 1–9 were written by a single author, while the passages which contain personified wisdom ("interludes") stem from different hands in response to the lectures. "Given the diverse authorship of at least some of the interludes, along with the resonances of the lectures in the interludes, we can picture the process of growth as a series of insertions by scribes learning from and building on them."³⁶ Why would these scribes respond with personification? W. F. Albright³⁷ and C. Bauer-Kayatz³⁸ have pointed to ANE precedence for personifying a deity or abstract concept in texts.

---

31. Camp, *Wisdom and the Feminine in the Book of Proverbs*, 213.

32. See Ricoeur, "Metaphor and the Central Problem of Hermeneutics," 133–34.

33. Taylor, *The Language Animal*, 146.

34. Taylor, *The Language Animal*, 137.

35. Taylor uses the example of "the chairman ploughed through the discussion," "I might have said: 'the chair was rushing us, he was ignoring our desire to discuss the issues more thoroughly', and the like. But the metaphorical attribution brings all this and more out in a more vivid form. It brings out the determined, the ruthless insensitivity with which he drove (another metaphor) the meeting, by invoking the ploughman, who is (rightly in this case) intent merely on digging the furrow, sweeping all obstacles in his path." Taylor, *The Language Animal*, 139.

36. Fox, *Proverbs 1–9*, 328.

37. Albright, "The Goddess of Life and Wisdom," 285–86.

38. Bauer-Kayatz, *Studien zu Proverbian 1–9*, 93–119.

Three Attempts at a Christian Reading of Proverbs 8

However, this does not fully account for adopting personification within the tradition. Whybray remarks upon the differences between the Egyptian literature and personified wisdom:

> the fundamental principle of *maat*, though personified and even deified in Egyptian religion, is never referred to in a way which offers a parallel with the figure of wisdom; and where the word *seboyet*, "instruction," which is the nearest equivalent to "wisdom," is never any other than a common noun. Egyptian literature entirely lacks any personified abstract quality which could have given rise to the figure of wisdom.[39]

He likewise casts doubt upon a Caananite background on the basis that this theory, argued in particular by W. F. Albright, appears to rests on weak evidence.[40] Nevertheless, Whybray supports the idea that at least some features of personified Wisdom are drawn from outside of Israel.[41] However, we are drawn back to Otto Plöger's important question, "warum sich die Weisheit in Israel solcher Anleihen bediente?"[42]

Taylor suggests one possible answer to Plöger: without the device of personification, a lacuna was sensed within the community of tradents in the presentation of wisdom.[43] Perhaps encounters with Egyptian or Canaanite personifications provided a spark, which then illuminated through its tensive relations something necessary for the construal of wisdom for future generations. One facet of that "something" was that in the attempt to walk that path of wisdom, one needed to account for a personal element, which personification supplied.[44] Theologically, this sense may have derived from a discomfort with the otherwise mechanistic presentation of reality present in the father-son dialogues.[45] The personification of Wisdom

---

39. Whybray, *Wisdom in Proverbs*, 78.
40. Whybray, *Wisdom in Proverbs*, 84–87.
41. Whybray, *Wisdom in Proverbs*, 82, 87.
42. Plöger, *Sprüche Salomos*, 97.
43. Similarly, Whybray states "The very fact that the additions were made indicates that those who made them considered the discourses to be unsatisfactory, or at least in some way inadequate, yet believed that, properly interpreted, they contained valuable teaching." Whybray, *Wisdom in Proverbs*, 92–93.
44. My comment here is redolent of, but different from, that of Don Collett, who states that in the poem, we are dealing with a "who" rather than a "what." Collett, "A Place to Stand," 177. At this stage in my argument, personified Wisdom remains a literary device. At a later point, I will address how this interacts with the doctrine of God.
45. Whybray, *Wisdom in Proverbs*, 93.

introduces a lively, active presence into the economy into which the book forms the reader.

Proverbs 8 in the Context of Proverbs 1–9

Attending to the world in front of the text includes the world as presented by the broader whole, which in this case means the book of Proverbs and, more distantly, the canonical books of the Old and New Testaments. The constraints of any book are such that I can only gesture toward suggested connections with other OT texts. Below, I will offer an exploration of similar New Testament dynamics, thereby moving towards a two-testament witness to life lived before the Triune God.

Up to this point, I have attempted to stay within the bounds of Proverbs 8. I have construed an existential proposal of chapter 8 as being in the world as a moral agent, open to the consequential personal invitation of Wisdom at the level of one's desires that one may be shaped to the benefit of self and community. As soon as we broaden our scope to include Proverbs 1–9 we are met with the fact that Wisdom is not the only voice that addresses the reader. The voice of the father and of Woman Folly address the reader too; the former offering a harmonious though not identical invitation, the latter a contrasting but no less consequential appeal.

The voice of the father is similar to that of personified Wisdom. In Proverbs 8:1–3, the third person speech introducing Wisdom reads easily as the voice of the father, even if it is not so explicitly identified. Reading these verses as spoken by the father links the agendas of the two speakers, regardless of their redactional history.[46] Like Wisdom, the father adjures the son to commit his ways to following the path of Wisdom (cf. Prov 2:1–5; 3:1–2). The path of attaining wisdom, according to the father, is arduous and requires endurance.[47] Nevertheless, the path promises rewards; some

---

46. Fox argues that the father-son dialogues preceded the personified Wisdom passages ("interludes"). These latter passages were created in response to the dialogues. If we accept this re-construction it supports reading the third person introduction in 8:1–3 as the father's voice. See Fox, *Proverbs 1–9*, 324–29. Schipper has a much more complex proposal for the formation of the book. He details multiple stages in which various authors/redactors struggle over how Wisdom should be conceived in relation to the Lord and Torah. See Schipper, *Proverbs 1–15*, 47–60. So conceived, the various passages are understood less as complementing one another and more as correcting or redirecting those which were chronologically prior.

47. Fox, *Proverbs 1–9*, 131–132.

Three Attempts at a Christian Reading of Proverbs 8

material (Prov 3:10), others not (Prov 3:35). According to the father, learning wisdom is not only an intellectual exercise, but also a moral one (cf. Prov 2:20–22). Even deeper than individual acts, that into which the father invites the son is "not only knowing but also *desiring* to do what is right."[48] The appeal, as with chapter 8, is directed towards the desires of the reader/hearer. Without the proper configuration of desires, the knowledge component of the father's pedagogy is moot. However, with the proper desire expressed through perseverance, the learner can be assured that they will find wisdom (cf. Prov 2:1–15). The confidence in success in the quest for wisdom, properly pursued, is akin to Wisdom's promise in Proverbs 8 that "I love those loving me, and the one who looks for me diligently will find me" (v. 17). Wisdom assures her audience that she will meet them on their path; the father promises that those who seek wisdom will find it.

While there are similarities between Wisdom and the father, there are differences as well. First, the two voices relate themselves to the reader/hearer in distinct ways. The father places himself alongside his son as at one time a learner: "When I was a son to my father—tender, the only child of my mother (וְיָחִיד לִפְנֵי אִמִּי)—then he taught me and he said to me, 'Let your heart grasp my words; guard my commandments that you may live'" (Prov 4:3–4, my translation). The father, as another personal voice in the book, identifies with the seeker. Wisdom identifies with what is sought (cf. Prov 8:35). A second difference between these two voices is their relationship with the LORD. The father speaks of wisdom as given by God (cf. Prov 2:6); Wisdom speaks of herself as intimate with the LORD God, such that finding her grants one favor with the LORD (Prov 8:22–31, 35). Additionally, the two voices offer different accounts of the more immediate location of wisdom. The father's directs the reader to his own words which are contained within the book.[49] We are invited to understand the shorter sayings to follow in chapters 10–31 to be additional instantiations of the father's teaching. In contrast, Wisdom points beyond the words of the book. Her general audience (Prov 8:4–5) and her claim that foreign rulers rule by Wisdom (Prov 8:16) supports the understanding that Wisdom is more

---

48. Fox, *Proverbs 1–9*, 133. Emphasis original.

49. Murphy, *Proverbs*, 15. Murphy asserts that these commandments are not the Torah. While that may be the case in the immediate context of Proverbs, connecting the commandments of the father to those of the Torah is sensible when we consider the broader witness of the whole canon of the OT. Fox's description of the father's commandments ("Don't rob; don't kill; don't commit adultery; be honest; trust God") is redolent of Deuteronomy and the Ten Commandments. Fox, *Proverbs 1–9*, 347.

than that which is contained in Proverbs, even if those words are a faithful path to her. A fourth difference can be seen in that the father speaks one-to-one, whereas Wisdom cries out and is available to all.[50] Finally, these two relate to the fear of the LORD in different ways. The father extols the fear of the LORD as vital to attaining wisdom (cf. Prov 1:7, 9:10). He promises that following his teaching will culminate with the fear of the LORD: "Then you will understand the fear of the LORD, and you will find the knowledge of God" (Prov 2:5).[51] While the father points toward the fear of the LORD, Wisdom herself seemingly fears the LORD (Prov 8:13). If we abide by the adage that Wisdom can give what she possesses, then following her shapes one in this fear.

The voices of the father and of Wisdom are not identical and consequently one should not subsume the other.[52] They work in concert with one another. The setting of the father's voice is pedagogical; we hear this voice in those places in which we expect to be taught. Wisdom's voice is out "in the streets" (Prov 8:2–3); her setting is the practical experience of attempting to abide by the father's instructions: "while the [father] remains (presumably) in the classroom, [Wisdom] descends into the arena and offers a challenge to evil where it is to be found."[53] That her voice is directly reported in the text, the father's domain, similarly highlights the complementarity of the two. Finally, Wisdom is greater than the father; the claims she makes vis-à-vis the LORD and all wise teaching grants her a ubiquitous presence offering magnanimous rewards.

We seek to understand the proposed world of Proverbs 8 in concert with the voice of the father present throughout Proverbs 1–9. Proverbs 8 offered us a mode of being as a moral agent, addressed by a personal voice throughout the everyday interactions of one's life at the level of our desires. The voice of the father ties this voice closer to the experience of others who

---

50. Dell, *The Book of Proverbs in Social and Theological Context*, 101.

51. Schipper notes a distinction between Proverbs 1:7, in which the fear of the LORD is the prerequisite to wisdom, and Proverbs 2:5, in which it is the result of wisdom. These are "diametrically opposed" to one another. Proverbs 1 offered the final redaction in which the concept of imperative instruction as the necessary for success in life took precedence over passages which emphasized Wisdom apart from imperative pedagogy. Schipper, *Proverbs 1–15*, 58. I should note here that, contra Schipper, I do not consider 1:7 and 2:5 to be "diametrically opposed." Rather, they are complimentary in important ways that speak to the lifelong process of formation in wisdom.

52. Fox, *Proverbs 1–9*, 359.

53. Whybray, *Wisdom in Proverbs*, 77.

have gone before. The stance offered is not contradictory to experience and tradition. Rather, tradition is complementary to this invitation, even as it is not identical to it. From the father's emphasis on the book of Proverbs, we understand that the tradition can be accessed in the text, while the personal voice of Wisdom calls us through and beyond the text. Within the contemporary conception of wisdom laid out in the last chapter, the father represents articulations, while Wisdom gestures toward the habitus behind the articulations.

Over against the concordant voice of the father stands the voice of Woman Folly (אֵשֶׁת כְּסִילוּת).[54] While she is only explicitly named in the final chapter of the prologue (9:13), Woman Folly functions as a unified presentation of the strange/foreign woman warned against in the preceding chapters.[55] She represents all foolishness[56] and, therefore, she serves as a symbol which incorporates all that opposes wisdom, even those passages which do not speak in a feminine voice.[57]

The origin of this contrasting figure has been a matter of study among scholars. Gustav Boström views the "strange woman" as representing the threat of a foreign sexual cult in the world behind the text of Proverbs.[58] Christl Maier rejects Boström's thesis; "Boströms Hauptargument hat keinen Anhalt am Text."[59] Maier asserts that the "strange woman" in the text represents both a typical figure whom a student of the book might encounter and something more.[60] The "something more" is the threat to community cohesion represented by adultery. "Die Warnung vor der ‚fremden Frau' ist als Versuch der Etablierung einer gesellschaftlichen Norm zu beschreiben ... Die Texte plädieren für eine Bewahrung der Ehegemeinschaft, die für Frauen eine exklusive sexuelle Beziehung zu einem Mann bedeutet,

---

54. Different titles are given to this opposing figure through Proverbs 1–9. She is referred to as a "strange woman" (אִשָּׁה זָרָה, 2:16; 5:3, 10, 20; 7:5) or the "foreigner/stranger" (נָכְרִיָּה, 2:16; 5:10, 20; 6:24; 7:5). Only Proverbs 9:13 uses the title אֵשֶׁת כְּסִילוּת.

55. "Chap. 9 suggests a symbolic identification of Woman Stranger with Woman Folly, and this figure is opposed to Wisdom." Murphy, *Proverbs*, 282. I accept Murphy's reading and will therefore use "Woman Folly" to refer to the figure variously presented throughout Proverbs 1–9.

56. Fox, *Proverbs 1–9*, 300.

57. Such as the invitation of "sinners" (חַטָּאִים) in Proverbs 1:10ff.

58. Boström, *Proverbiastudien*, 103–55.

59. Maier, *Die 'fremde Frau' in Proverbien 1–9*, 255–56.

60. Maier, *Die 'fremde Frau' in Proverbien 1–9*, 258.

als Voraussetzung für eine intakte Familie."[61] Both of these scholars focus on the sexual nature of this opposing figure. However, Stuart Weeks' study places this figure in the context of her opposition to Wisdom, and seeks to allow this structural feature drive the understanding of the figure. He asks, "Why . . . is the character consistently described as 'strange' or 'foreign', rather than simply as an adulteress, and why is there so much emphasis on her speech rather than her marital status?"[62] Through attention to the literary context of Proverbs, as well as post-exilic books of the Old Testament (which Weeks takes to be contemporaneous with Proverbs 1–9), Weeks asserts "for the original readers, her name conjures up associations with the seduction of Jews into apostasy, and the association is reinforced by the further reference to smooth speech as her principal characteristic."[63] Weeks' position is to be preferred, as it provides an understanding that centers on how the received text portrays the strange woman, which does not foreground adultery but the danger of straying from the path held out by the father and Wisdom, a path that is consistently brought into relation with faithfulness to the LORD God of Israel.

In various ways throughout chapters 1–9, Woman Folly is presented as an opposing figure to Wisdom. The tool that Folly uses in order to seduce the youth of the book is speech.[64] The words of Woman Folly are described as smooth (חלק) (Prov 2:16; 5:3; 6:24; 7:5, 21), a term that "takes on the meaning 'to flatter,' such as by (false) prophets who do not speak the truth but instead say flattering things."[65] Within the book of Proverbs, speech characterized as חלק only leads to evil (cf. Prov 26:28; 28:23; 29:5). Outside of the book, Psalm 5:9-10 [Heb. 8-9] places smooth talk as a characteristic of the death-bound wicked, contrasted with God's way of righteousness (צְדָקָה) and His upright path (הַיְשַׁר[66] לְפָנַי דַּרְכֶּךָ). Proverbs 8 describes Wisdom's words as righteous (צֶדֶק) (v. 8) and upright (יְשָׁרִים) (v. 9). Thus in this most frequent characterization of Folly, her smooth talk, she stands in opposition to Wisdom (and the LORD). Folly is unfaithful to her love (2:17a),

---

61. Maier, *Die 'fremde Frau' in Proverbien 1–9*, 267.

62. Weeks, *Instruction and Imagery in Proverbs 1–9*, 87.

63. Weeks, *Instruction and Imagery in Proverbs 1–9*, 141–42.

64. Aletti insightfully observes that the focus of Folly's seduction is not her beauty but her words. "Séduction et parole en Proverbes I–IX," 129.

65. Schipper, *Proverbs 1–15*, 116. Dell explains the image of lips dripping honey as denoting Folly's speech as insincere. Dell, *The Book of Proverbs in Social and Theological Context*, 41.

66. Qere. The Kethib is הוֹשַׁר.

Three Attempts at a Christian Reading of Proverbs 8

her God (2:17b), and her husband (7:19); Wisdom is faithful to love those who love her (8:17) and to her God (8:30). The paths of Folly lead to death (2:18–19; 5:5–6; 7:27; 9:18) whereas Wisdom's path leads to life (8:35). Proverbs 7:9 imaginatively paints Folly's appearance "in the twilight, in the evening, at the time of night and darkness." While Wisdom's address is not explicitly said to be during the day, her very public location and call to all people suggests so.[67] In addition to these comparisons of content, the structure of the book sets up a contrast between the characters. Proverbs 8, the longest speech of Wisdom, follows after the longest meditation on Woman Folly, in chapter 7.[68]

Even with these distinctions, the two women are also presented in similar tones. Indeed, as Aletti notes, the vocabulary associated with Folly seems deliberately ambiguous; much of this vocabulary is shared with the teaching of the father and of Wisdom.[69] The most noticeable example of the similarity between Folly and Wisdom is found in Proverbs 9, in which both women issue invitations using the exact same words: מִי־פֶתִי יָסֻר הֵנָּה (9:4a, 16a). Proverbs 5:3 claims that Folly's lips drip honey (נֹפֶת תִּטֹּפְנָה), an erotic image.[70] Wisdom is also presented in erotic terms, such as in Proverbs 8:34.[71] Additionally, just as the student is able to embrace (חבק) the bosom of the foreign woman (5:20), so he is able to embrace Wisdom (4:8). Woman Folly seems exceedingly eager for the attention of the student, is desperate for them.[72] Wisdom also *"wants* human attention. That is why she is furious when men ignore her"; she goes into the busiest places to issue her invitation, which is addressed to all kinds of people.[73] Wisdom, according to 8:1–3, calls out in every place, amidst the everyday business of life; she "plunges into the midst of this hustle and bustle to reach people where *they* are."[74] Folly is also presented as ubiquitous; "Now in the street,[75]

---

67. Fox, *Proverbs 1–9*, 265.

68. Chapter 8 "has no doubt been placed here in order to present Wisdom as the alternative to the 'loose woman' of the preceding Instructions and the woman of 7:6–23." Whybray, *Proverbs*, 120.

69. Aletti, "Séduction et parole en Proverbes I–IX," 132.

70. Schipper, *Proverbs 1–15*, 200.

71. Fox, *Proverbs 1–9*, 290.

72. Fox suggests eagerness is implied by the use of ארב in 7:12. Fox, *Proverbs 1–9*, 253.

73. Fox, *Proverbs 1–9*, 357. Emphasis original.

74. Fox, *Proverbs 1–9*, 267. Emphasis original.

75. The root translated here as "street" (חוּץ) also appears in 8:26, in Wisdom's proclamation that she was present when the Lord created the first of the חוּצוֹת.

now in the squares, and beside[76] every corner, she lies in wait" (7:12). Her presence is marked by her loudness (הֹמִיָּה, 7:11; 9:13). The very streets in which Wisdom cries out are described as loud, using the same root: בְּרֹאשׁ הֹמִיּוֹת תִּקְרָא (1:21a). Wisdom and Folly vie in overlapping locations with similar invitations, both appealing to the desires of their audience.

Proverbs 1–9 presents Wisdom and Woman Folly in competition with one another for the attentions of the reader/hearer. In each moment, one is allured by, on the one hand, Wisdom aided by tradition and, on the other, Folly. Each of these voices is experienced in one's desires and the choice between them is weighty. However, their speech and description is so similar that one cannot detect the difference between them merely by content. Aletti connects this with the strategy of the book.[77] Ultimately the book is concerned what kind of person one wants to be. Proverbs has a preferred telos for the reader; the book aims to persuade the reader/hearer to follow Wisdom/the father. Weeks, who takes up Aletti's work, observes that the purpose of the ambiguity and overlap between Folly and Wisdom "is apparently to emphasize that the problem presented by the bad characters [Folly, sinners, etc.] is not that of the temptation to do wrong so much as the recognition of what *is* wrong: they force their hearers to discern true speech from false speech. . . . What [the students of the book] require is an informed, intelligent understanding of the situation and the consequences."[78] The voices of the father and Wisdom provide a positive picture of the formational results of heeding them. In contrast, Folly's invitations focus solely on the immediate fruit (cf. Prov 7:18). She never promises long-term formation;[79] it is the father's role to describe the deadly outcome of her path (cf. 2:18–19; 5:5–6; 6:32; 7:22–23, 26–27).[80]

These three voices are framed together in the introduction and conclusion to the prologue of Proverbs (chs. 1 and 9). In chapter 1, after the prefatory verses (vv. 1–7), the father speaks. In his speech, he quotes the words of sinners (חַטָּאִים, v. 10). The sinners' speech (vv. 11–14) is reminiscent of the

---

76. While Wisdom is אֶצְלוֹ אָמוֹן ("constantly by His side"), Folly is אֵצֶל כָּל־פִּנָּה תֶאֱרֹב ("beside every corner, she lies in wait").

77. Aletti, "Séduction et parole en Proverbes I–IX," 133.

78. Weeks, *Instruction and Imagery in Proverbs 1–9*, 81–82.

79. According to Aletti, Folly calls into question the consequence declared by other portions of the book vis-à-vis adultery. "Séduction et parole en Proverbes I–IX," 135–36.

80. Weeks, *Instruction and Imagery in Proverbs 1–9*, 80. Van Leeuwen interprets this as framing the invitation of Folly for the safety of the reader/hearer. See van Leeuwen, "Liminality and Worldview in Proverbs 1–9," 127.

Three Attempts at a Christian Reading of Proverbs 8

insalubrious invitation of the adulterous woman, for whom Woman Folly stands as a unifying figure.[81] The chapter is completed with Wisdom's first speech, in which she warns her public audience of the dire consequences of ignoring her (vv. 22–33). These three voices work together to introduce the reader/hearer to a hazardous world in which they will be tempted by conflicting voices. To attain the lofty goals of the book (cf. vv. 1–7), the reader must hear (שְׁמַע) and not forsake (אַל־תִּטֹּשׁ) the teaching (תּוֹרַת) of their elders[82] (v. 8). Absolute commitment is necessary because they will be enticed (פתה) by other voices, here introduced as "sinners" (חַטָּאִים, v. 10). The way of these sinners is a way leading to evil and death (vv. 15–19). To the voices of the elders and the sinners is added the voice of Wisdom, whose admonitory address to the פְּתָיִם the reader overhears (vv. 22–27). At verse 28, Wisdom shifts from directly addressing those who have rejected her to reflecting on their fate.[83] This turn invites the reader to reflect on their own stance in light of the whole chapter. The first audience mentioned in chapter 1 are the inexperienced (פְּתָאיִם, v. 4), and at the end Wisdom speaks of the fate of those inexperienced (פְּתָיִם, v. 22) who refuse to listen to her. The פְּתָאיִם are those for whom there is still hope; they can still turn and listen.[84] Thus, the chapter uses all three voices to introduce the need for an open stance toward what the book has to offer.

From an existential perspective, this opening chapter affirms the sense gained by hearing the three voices in the following chapters. The path of the student toward wisdom is fraught. To be open to wisdom sets one in a life-or-death situation. Chapter 1 emphasizes the dire consequences of ignoring Wisdom, forsaking the tradition, and walking the path of sinners.[85] It is a negative portrait, designed to prod the addressee toward tradition and the voice of Wisdom.[86] The portrait works by showing what kind of person

---

81. Schipper, *Proverbs 1–15*, 76.

82. I use this term to include both father and mother mentioned in verse 8. While "parents" would also work, I take the meaning of the titles as not restricted to biological relationship.

83. Murphy, *Proverbs*, 11.

84. Longman, *Proverbs*, 97.

85. "Wisdom demands a basic stance toward wisdom itself: a loving openness to wisdom's message, whether this is sweet or harsh, alongside a dread of the consequences of rejecting it.... Other interludes will emphasize the right stance; this one seeks to scare us away from the wrong one." Fox, *Proverbs 1–9*, 105.

86. Schipper, *Proverbs 1–15*, 85.

Wisdom in the World

ignores wisdom and appeals to the audience's desires: "you do not want to be like that, do you?"

At the other end of the prologue Wisdom, Folly, and the tradition are presented as a triptych.[87] Wisdom and Folly issue their invitations using strikingly similar language (vv. 1–6, 13–18). In between these two figures the voice of tradition speaks (vv. 7–12).[88] These verses speak in generalizations, reminiscent of the father's instruction in the prologue and anticipating the aphorisms of chapters 10–31.[89] Within this voice of the tradition, verse 11 stands out as marked by a first person pronoun (כִּי־בִי), which is more like Wisdom's speech than the father's. One way of accounting for this is text-critical, emending the first person pronoun to a third person feminine. Another option is to read it as evidence of the intimate connection between tradition and the voice of Wisdom, or even the voice of the LORD.[90]

The concluding chapter and its world places the reader at a crossroads. On two competing heights (מְרֹמֵי קָרֶת, vv. 3, 14) stand the houses of Wisdom and Folly. Which will the reader choose? Aiding the reader is the tradition, which is itself infused with the voice of Wisdom (v. 11), who meets the reader at the intersection.[91] The conclusion confirms the portrait painted by chapters 1–9; the path of wisdom is one of choices of great consequence, its decision point is the here and now. The triptych urges the student to enter into the following aphoristic proverbs seeking to enter the house of

---

87. Waltke and Schipper present the contrasting speeches of Wisdom and Folly as a diptych. However, neither of them integrates verses 7–12 into this presentation. Waltke categorizes these verses as instruction without relating this to the voice of the father in the book. Waltke, *The Book of Proverbs*, 430. Schipper is influenced by understanding verses 7–12 as later additions. He characterizes them as an interlude without integrating this into a re-characterization of the structure as a triptych. See his *Proverbs 1–15*, 321, 331.

88. Fox (*Proverbs 1–9*, 306, 317) and Schipper (*Proverbs 1–15*, 321) both understand these verses to be later additions added to the book at various times of its latter stages of development. Fox goes so far as to address 7–11 after verse 33, and then verse 12 after an intervening excursus. Regardless of its pre-history, my aim is to understand the verses in the final presentation of the text.

89. Schipper, *Proverbs 1–15*, 321.

90. Verse 10 references the LORD through the divine Name (יְהוָה) and another title for God (קְדֹשִׁים). These are possible antecedents for the speaker in verse 11, even as they resonate more with Wisdom-speech in the prologue. This is another case of ambiguity and suggestive overlap between the LORD and Wisdom, which I will address more fully in the next portion of this chapter on Wisdom and Nicene Trinitarian theology.

91. Wisdom sends out her maidens (v. 3), whereas Folly only sits in her doorway (v. 14).

Wisdom, and not Folly. The words themselves will guide them, as one who identifies as a פֶּתִי (vv. 4, 16), into a relationship with Wisdom (חָכְמוֹת, v. 1).[92]

Conclusion

The above attempt to present an integrating world in front of Proverbs 1–9 illuminates the distinct contribution of Proverbs 8. Proverbs 8 is a sustained appeal by the voice of Wisdom, specifying her audience, benefits, and bona fides. Wisdom in Proverbs 1 focuses on the consequences of ignoring her. In Proverbs 9, she offers a final appeal on the basis of the preceding chapters. Proverbs 8 articulates the gains of heeding Wisdom, a point which the father also makes by speaking about wisdom. The length of chapter 8's first person speech stresses the personal nature of her invitation. The chapter's exposition of Wisdom's benefits along with its depiction of her persistence through time in all of creation with the children of humanity (בני אדם) and the LORD are unique contributions to the book. Without Proverbs 8, the voice of Wisdom would be an underdeveloped persona, sounding only a note of judgment (chap. 1), which would make for a weak counter to the sensuous invitation of Folly (chaps. 7 and 9).[93] Being-in-the-world in this mode would be a somber affair, based on the terror of punishment. With Proverbs 8, the voice one hears in the world becomes personal, persistent, and profitable. She is cast as a reality independent of the words of the book of Proverbs and someone worthy of attention. Proverbs 8 dramatically shifts the mode of being-in-the-world to a joyful pursuit of moral formation in relationship with something best understood as personal.

A Possible Trinitarian Reading of Proverbs 8

In our survey of the history of interpretation, a frequent topic in the study of Proverbs 8 was the relationship between the figure of Wisdom and the LORD God proclaimed by the scriptures. Within the Christian tradition, this relationship featured centrally in the debates over the nature of the second person of the Trinity in the fourth century A.D. In what follows, I offer

---

92. Schipper, *Proverbs 1–15*, 323. In this way, the world in front of Proverbs 1–9 shapes one's entry into Proverbs 10–31. It is beyond the scope of my current project to develop this further.

93. Wisdom's speech, in chapter 8, "differs from chapter one in its more uniformly persuasive and positive tone." L. Boström, *The God of the Sages*, 149.

a second attempt for a renewed Christian reading by addressing Proverbs 8's interaction with Nicene Trinitarian theology. My approach begins with the facets of the text that press the issue upon a contemporary Christian reader, particularly when read in light of the history of interpretation. I will then provide a brief survey of some representative modern interpreters and their reading of the relationship between personified Wisdom and the Lord. Next, I will explicate a regulative understanding of speech of God, and particularly the doctrine of God's trinity. Finally, I will return to the text and bring together this understanding of the Trinity and the world before the text of Proverbs 8.

Text and Interpretation

The issue of the relationship between personified Wisdom as witnessed to by Proverbs 8 and the Lord God of Israel calls for the attention of the reader on the basis of two sources. First, the text itself can be read to generate these questions.[94] Second, the history of interpretation, particularly in the intertestamental period and the Nicene period, presses upon readers to attend to this issue.

The Relationship between Wisdom and the Lord in the Text of Proverbs 8

The semantics of the poem in chapter 8 bears witness to a relationship of some sort between the Lord of Israel and personified Wisdom. In verse 13, we can infer that Wisdom claims to have יִרְאַת יְהוָה, attesting to a stance before the Lord. Verses 22–31 make strong claims of connection. Verse 22 states יְהוָה קָנָנִי, Wisdom being the object of the verb. Even though the meaning of the phrase is debated, it unequivocally establishes some kind of association between personified Wisdom and the Lord. Verses 23–25 continue to expand on this through declarations by Wisdom that she was נִסַּכְתִּי (verse 23) and חוֹלָלְתִּי (twice, verse 24 and 25).[95] The passive nature of these

---

94. By this wording, I acknowledge that there are other ways to read the text of Proverbs 8 which do not draw the interest or attention of the reader to Wisdom's relationship with the Lord.

95. In the earlier analysis of Proverbs 8, I translated the chapter in order to offer a reading of it in its literary context. My aim in this paragraph is to establish that the text raises the issue of the relationship between personified Wisdom and the Lord. By not translating these verses here, I intend to focus on the issue itself before weighing in on the particular kind of relationship to which they bear witness.

verbs draws on the Lord as the antecedent; God was behind these actions, even as the manner of the Lord's involvement is a matter of debate. In verses 27–29, Wisdom is present while the Lord establishes (כון) the world; amidst the creative acts mentioned, Wisdom declares שָׁם אָנִי (verse 27a). Verses 30–31 state that Wisdom continues to be associated with the Lord. In verse 30, she is declared to be beside Him (אֶצְלוֹ) as אָמוֹן and is daily His delight (following the LXX, ἐνευφραίνετο).⁹⁶ In the concluding section of the chapter, Wisdom declares that those who find her obtain favor from the Lord (verse 33b). The prevalence of these claims understandably leads to reflection as to the nature of this relationship. Widening our scope to the remainder of Proverbs 1–9, one other text is brought into our consideration. Proverbs 3:19 is often marked as bearing witness to in miniature to what Proverbs 8 (esp. vv. 22–31) does in an expanded format.⁹⁷

The Relationship in the History of Interpretation

The words of Proverbs 8 indicate some kind of relationship between personified Wisdom and the Lord. With this being said, it need not be the case that readers are drawn to this relationship as a major point of interest.⁹⁸ However, alongside the text the history of interpretation encourages attention to the nature of Wisdom's relationship to the Lord. Beginning with the literature of the intertestamental period, the tradition of interpretation develops the statements of Proverbs 8 in various ways.⁹⁹

The book of Sirach is the earliest extant document to make use of Proverbs 8.¹⁰⁰ In Sirach 24:9, Wisdom speaks in the first person. She claims to have been created (ἔκτισέν) by God (v. 9). Unlike the presentation in Proverbs 8, in Sirach 24 Wisdom does not claim any connection to God's

---

96. That a text critical question needs to be answered here, just to say what is in the text, illustrates the dialectical rather than sequential relationship between text and interpretation.

97. Alan Lenzi offers one take on how these two texts are related from a compositional perspective, "Proverbs 8:22–31," 687–714.

98. Ryan O'Dowd's commentary focuses on more practical implications of how this passage contributes to an understanding of wisdom. He spends less time on explicating how Wisdom may be related to the Lord of Israel. O'Dowd, *Proverbs*, 155–56.

99. Otto Plöger identifies both continuity and discontinuity in the Nachleben of personified Wisdom. Plöger, *Sprüche Salomos*, 98. We need not force the varieties within this material into a consistent schema of development.

100. Loader, *Proverbs 1–9*, 368.

creative acts. However, Wisdom journeys through many of the same locations which are in view in Proverbs 8:24-29.[101] Wisdom is commanded by the LORD to dwell in the sanctuary in Jerusalem (vv. 10-11) and is identified with the Torah (v. 23). Sirach's development of personified Wisdom ties together Wisdom's coming from the mouth of God (ἐγὼ ἀπὸ στόματος ὑψίστου ἐξῆλθον [Sir 24:3], cf. Prov 2:6) with the Torah. In this construal, "Wisdom is closely associated with God but distinct from him."[102] However, this identification should not be wholly understood as the written word. Sirach 24:3 ends by stating that Wisdom ὡς ὁμίχλη κατεκάλυψα γῆν; it is hard to imagine the written Torah doing this, even as it faithfully contains wisdom. As such, Sirach's presentation of Wisdom foregrounds its relation to Torah; Wisdom as something outside of the text remains, albeit in the background.

The Wisdom of Solomon is another text that draws on the imagery and language of Proverbs 8 and personifies Wisdom. Wisdom of Solomon 7:22 speaks of Wisdom as the πάντων τεχνῖτις, an appellation that appears to be an interpretation of אָמוֹן in Proverbs 8:30. The author of the Wisdom of Solomon goes on to describe Wisdom as intimately related to God:

> ἀτμὶς γάρ ἐστιν τῆς τοῦ θεοῦ δυνάμεως
>   καὶ ἀπόρροια τῆς τοῦ παντοκράτορος δόξης εἰλικρινής
>   διὰ τοῦτο οὐδὲν μεμιαμμένον εἰς αὐτὴν παρεμπίπτει.
> ἀπαύγασμα γάρ ἐστιν φωτὸς ἀϊδίου
>   καὶ ἔσοπτρον ἀκηλίδωτον τῆς τοῦ θεοῦ ἐνεργείας
>   καὶ εἰκὼν τῆς ἀγαθότητος αὐτοῦ (Wis 7:25-26)

> For she is a breath of God's power
>   and a pure emanation of the glory of Almighty God
>   for no impurity goes into her
> For she is a reflection of eternal light
>   and a spotless mirror of God's works
>   and an image of His goodness.

Wisdom here is closely related to God as an emanation.[103] According to Wisdom 8:3-4, Wisdom lives with God and is "one initiated in the knowledge of God and one who chooses his works" (Wis 8:4). In chapter 9 of the book, the author prays for God to send forth Wisdom to guide him in his

---

101. Loader, *Proverbs 1-9*, 368.
102. Loader, *Proverbs 1-9*, 368.
103. See translation and commentary of Winston, *The Wisdom of Solomon*, 184-90.

works as king and judge of the people (cf. Wis 9:7–10). This book, then, treats personified Wisdom in a more personal and cosmic way, treating her as an active agent in the world, closely related to, and yet distinct from, the Lord. Although personal Wisdom aids the recipient in following the commandments (cf. Wis 9:9), the identification between Wisdom and Torah is much less than in Ben Sira.[104]

The patristic era offers another significant point of interest, as it explicitly engages with Proverbs 8 in relation to Christian theology.[105] In his *Dialogue with Trypho*, Justin Martyr quotes from Proverbs 8, including the LXX's additional words previous to verse 22, as evidence of an eternally begotten Son attested to in Israel's Scriptures (*Dial.* 1.61). Specifically, he argues from this text that "Μαρτυρήσει δέ μοι ὁ λόγος τῆς σοφίας, αὐτὸς ὢν οὗτος ὁ θεὸς ἀπὸ τοῦ πατρὸς τῶν ὅλων γεννηθείς, καὶ λόγος καὶ σοφία καὶ δύναμις καὶ δόξα τοῦ γεννήσαντος ὑπάρχων." Justin's focus, befitting his aim in the *Dialogue*, is the establishment of a certain kind of relationship that coheres with the early church's worship and witness. In Proverbs 8, he reads the relationship between Wisdom and the Lord in a way that Wisdom is a personal figure, a cosmic agent, not unlike the interpretation in the Wisdom of Solomon, albeit here in an explicitly Christian framework.

Justin provides an early data point for explicitly Christian theology. There are many others who follow after him. For the purposes of this section, the debate leading up to and surrounding the Council of Nicaea are of most interest. We have already surveyed Athanasius' interpretation of Proverbs 8.[106] Justin Martyr, Athanasius, and even Arius read the relation between Wisdom and the Lord of Israel ontologically; referring to a personal being in relation to the essence of God. As was true with Justin's goals for his *Dialogue*, in these later writers Wisdom as Torah is subsumed under the category of the Son as the Word. The precedent for such a move was set in John 1, and this chapter exerted its influence on the readings of the early church.

---

104. Other interactions can be found in *Genesis Rabbah* and Philo of Alexandria. However, these are not addressed in this book.

105. It is very likely that the history of interpretation of Proverbs 8 in the pre-Christian era, witnessed to by the Wisdom of Ben Sira and the Wisdom of Solomon, influenced the early Christian usage of the passage.

106. See chapter 4 above.

Representative Contemporary Understandings of the Relationship between the LORD and Wisdom

In recent years, scholars have articulated various views on the connection between personified Wisdom and the LORD. A central point of contention is how Wisdom relates to the being of the LORD God of Israel. From these studies a spectrum of positions emerges. At one point on the spectrum are those who argue that personified Wisdom is presented as one in being with Israel's LORD, coherent in principle with a position represented by the Nicene-Constantinopolitan creed regarding the nature of God. At another point are those who conclude that personified Wisdom is a subordinate agent present in creation, often through recourse to the ancient Near Eastern context. Another prominent position interprets Wisdom as an attribute of the LORD.

The Brazos commentary on Proverbs by Daniel Treier and a monograph by Don C. Collett[107] represent contemporary arguments for Wisdom as one in being with the LORD of Israel, coherent with the Nicene Creed's theology regarding the relationship between the Father and the Son. Both ground their conclusions in the compatibility of the text to Nicene theology, as opposed to the text as read against the history of ideas or literature. In Treier's view, the poem's structure and vocabulary provide a presentation parallel to the New Testament's teaching of Christ and can therefore be read in a way consistent with the Nicene Creed. The chapter "gives every appearance of trying to convey Wisdom's distinctiveness, not her fit within creaturely categories."[108] She offers an invitation for divine self-revelation through personal relationship with her on the basis of her own origins, which are mysteriously connected with God's life. In a way parallel to Philippians 2, the path offered by Proverbs 8 "requires *both* divine condescension *and* human form for us to attain."[109] Continuing, Treier writes, "Jesus Christ therefore does not finally complicate the interpretation of Prov. 8 but presents instead the resolution of a mystery latent in the text, though not always clearly recognized."[110] Treier's approach is one that reads Proverbs

---

107. Collett, *Figural Reading and the Old Testament*.
108. Treier, *Proverbs and Ecclesiastes*, 49.
109. Treier, *Proverbs and Ecclesiastes*, 51.
110. Treier, *Proverbs and Ecclesiastes*, 51.

8 as open to a Christological teaching conducive to Nicene theology when read within a Christian frame of reference.[111]

Don Collett's treatment of the passage argues that Proverbs 8 supports a distinction of persons within the ontology of Israel's LORD.[112] His position is that Proverbs 8 is a case study that supports a view that the Old Testament is "fully capable of providing the church with a place to stand and offer her christo-trinitarian claims."[113] As strongly as he states this position, he also recognizes that reading Scripture requires some presuppositions, which enable certain kinds of readings.[114] His book begins by advocating one such presupposition, namely that the "structuring of time in creation provides the basis for the logic of the relation between word (*verbum*) and thing (*res*) intrinsic to figural reading and for figural ways of ordering time."[115] The *verbum-res* dynamic shapes Collett's understanding of metaphor, not as "mere ornament" but as referential and therefore constructive for dogma; that is, metaphors are not be cast aside but read as disclosive for the church's beliefs.[116]

Collett's argument focuses primarily on the meaning of אָמוֹן in Proverbs 8:30 and the use of architectural metaphors in the chapter. He comes to the poem with an understanding that its distinct contribution to Proverbs 1–9 is "to specify the *origin* and *relationship* of Wisdom to the LORD."[117] Collett argues against a view of Wisdom in Proverbs 8 as an attribute of Israel's LORD on the basis of the distinction that is sustained between the LORD and Wisdom throughout Proverbs 8, as well as throughout the prologue chapters of 1–9. Instead, he reads the structure of the poem and the word אָמוֹן as attributing to Wisdom an active agency: evidence for which

---

111. Treier allows for other readings when he writes, "It is not appropriate for Christian theologians to tell Jewish readers how they ought to read Old Testament texts as *their* scriptures." Treier, *Proverbs and Ecclesiastes*, 49.

112. Collett, *Figural Reading and the Old Testament*, 102.

113. Collett, *Figural Reading and the Old Testament*, 97.

114. Collett, *Figural Reading and the Old Testament*, 51.

115. Collett, *Figural Reading and the Old Testament*, 17. This word-thing relationship is grounded in the two creation accounts of Genesis 1:1—2:3 and 2:4–25.

116. Collett, *Figural Reading and the Old Tesatment*, 99–101. Collett does not interact with Paul Ricoeur's understanding of metaphor which, like his own, views metaphor as more than ornamental. Unlike Collett, Ricoeur's view of its ontological force is more akin to Heidegger in that metaphor refers non-ostensively and projects a possible mode of being-in-the-world before the reader. See Ricoeur, "Metaphor and the Central Problem of Hermeneutics," 138–43.

117. Collett, *Figural Reading and the Old Testament*, 89. Emphasis original.

he see in Wisdom's house-building in Proverbs 9:1.[118] Additionally, that Wisdom speaks in the first person and (distinct from Proverbs 3:19) is the object of God's action (cf. Prov 8:22) casts her as an agent.[119] Additionally, Collett calls attention to Wisdom's persistence through time; she is there before, during, and after creation. These features of the poem are read as placing Wisdom alongside Israel's LORD. If, according to Collett, allowance is made for the "monotheism" of the Old Testament to be defined by how the text presents God, then the "scriptures disclose [the LORD's] identity in a manner that reveals the unique character of his oneness, a peculiar form of monotheism capable of supporting distinction of persons within that oneness, as Proverbs 8:22–31 teaches and the early church confessed."[120]

Both Daniel Treier and Don Collett understand the relationship between Wisdom and the LORD to be coherent with the early Christian church's confession of the triune nature of God. In different ways, both acknowledge that this reading is done within the church's confessional frame of reference. The other positions advanced in recent scholarly treatments of this issue do so apart from explicit theological commitments, instead reading the passage with the world of ancient Israel in view. Two of the more prominent options among these scholars have already been encountered in section 2's survey of the history of interpretation. As noted in the survey of Otto Plöger and Michael Fox, Wisdom is understood to be a subordinated created being. Tremper Longman illustrated a second prominent option, by which Wisdom is understood to be an attribute of Israel's LORD.

What Do We Mean by God?

Prior to further study and engagement with the question of the relationship between Wisdom and the LORD, my pre-understanding of the referent of the words "God" and "LORD" merits brief comment. The reasons for this are similar to those given in my previous writing on a contemporary conception of wisdom. Without my own pre-understanding, I would not be

---

118. Collett, *Figural Reading and the Old Testament*, 91. Collett writes, "The interplay between the images of creation and house is commonly found in ancient Near Eastern portrayals of cosmic creation as house-building, and an active rendering of *ʾāmôn* as 'architect' or 'artisan' allows this figural and contextual linkage to emerge by presenting Wisdom as an architect of creation in 8:30, followed by Wisdom as house-building in 9:1."

119. Collett, *Figural Reading and the Old Testament*, 95–96.

120. Collett, *Figural Reading and the Old Testament*, 102.

equipped to make a foray into the relationship between Wisdom and God, even in an historically descriptive fashion, as I have to have some conception by which to understand these figures. Additionally, by foregrounding my operating assumptions the reader is made aware of and can better evaluate my argument.[121]

While there are many ways of handling the commitments involved in Nicene Christianity and their impact on one's reading of the text, here I will follow a regulative or cultural-linguistic approach to the issue. "The function of church doctrines that becomes most prominent in this perspective is their use, not as expressive symbols or as truth claims, but as communally authoritative rules of discourse, attitude, and action."[122] Doctrines, such as the doctrine of God's Trinity expressed in the Nicene-Constantinopolitan Creed, are one facet of Christianity's "language." Along with other expressions, such as liturgy and hymnody, the language of a religious faith works as a "medium that shapes the entirety of life and thought."[123] This could also be characterized as a hermeneutical understanding of religious faith potentially functioning to open up certain experiences and in turn being interpreted and adjusted as a result of those experiences.[124]

Nicholas Lash offers an explanation of the Christian doctrine of God's Trinity within a regulative understanding of doctrine.[125] Lash states theologically the case for this approach: "even if the 'nature' of God is unknown to us, because we cannot understand God, cannot *grasp* him in concept or image, cannot render his mystery comprehensible, we may perhaps, nevertheless, in relation to him, living in his presence and responding to his address, successfully *refer* to God, make true mention of him."[126] The function of doctrine, including the Nicene trinitarian doctrine of God, is to ensure true reference to God rather than true description of God. More specific to the Nicene Creed, its use is to "make a second-order claim to the effect that whatever is to be said of the Father is to be said of the Son, save only

---

121. Bultmann, "Is Exegesis without Presuppositions Possible?," 194–200.

122. Lindbeck, *The Nature of Doctrine*, 18.

123. Lindbeck, *The Nature of Doctrine*, 33.

124. Within this view, the "external features" of a religion are primary; the inner experiences of the individual are shaped by and derived from them, "rather than [the external features being] an expression or thematization of a preexisting self or of preconceptual experience." Lindbeck, *The Nature of Doctrine*, 34. There is clear synergy here with Pierre Bourdieu's conception of a habitus, with which I interacted in a previous chapter.

125. Lash, *Easter in Ordinary*, 257–85.

126. Lash, *Easter in Ordinary*, 257–58.

that the Father alone is Father and the Son alone is Son."[127] These claims are "identity-sustaining rules of discourse and behavior governing Christian uses of the word 'God'" so that the church can faithfully form people to perceive and respond to the mystery of God handed down through the ages of the church.[128]

Lash moves from these more abstract considerations to the impact made by the doctrine of God's Trinity. This doctrine

> serves, at one and the same time, to indicate where God is to be found and—by denying, at each point, that what we find there is to be simply identified with God—to prevent us from getting stuck in one-sidedness, for the effect of such one-sidedness (or exclusiveness) is always in one way or another to make us misidentify some feature of the world with God, and this (however unwittingly and guiltlessly entered into) is idolatry.[129]

In Lash's approach, the Christian doctrine of God includes both affirmation and denial. God is to be found in all life, every sphere of activity, and every manifestation of beauty. This is the implication of the teaching of God as present Spirit. And yet, there is an absolute difference between God and the world. God is not an object in the universe; in the Christian "language game" the word "God" refers to no "thing," visible or invisible. This is the implication of God as Father, creator of heaven and earth, and therefore not among the created things. The third aspect of the doctrine of God's Trinity is the Word, or Son of God, whereby God addresses the creation. Without this, the doctrine of God would be a static and unresolvable paradox of God-everywhere and God-not-here. However, Christians believe that this God who is present ("Spirit") and yet nowhere contained ("Father") also appears and addresses, most particularly in the person of Jesus Christ ("Son"). The historically particular appearance and address of God in Christ leads to the belief that God is a God who always speaks, addresses, and appears. That God appears and addresses redeems for the Christian a use for the word "God" in Christian speech and conduct.[130]

The use of this doctrine is referential rather than descriptive; it regulates the Christian's experience of God. It does so by a movement of constant self-correction "for each of the three principle modes of our propensity to

---

127. Lash, *Easter in Ordinary*, 259.
128. Lash, *Easter in Ordinary*, 260.
129. Lash, *Easter in Ordinary*, 267.
130. Lash, *Easter in Ordinary*, 269.

Three Attempts at a Christian Reading of Proverbs 8

freeze the form of relation with God into an object or imagined possessed description of the divine nature."[131] Within this perichoretic movement, Christians engage the world. They do so shaped (and being shaped, as the process of being this kind of person is never-ending) to expect the address of God, for God is present in the creation and yet not confined by nor contained within it. The doctrine of God's Trinity forms the believer to trust that the mystery by whom they are addressed is truly God while avoiding freezing God in that mode of address or location.[132]

Lash's exposition can appear to be in tension with the church's preference for personal language for the three-ness of God's Trinity: Father, Son, and Spirit. To understand the Trinity in terms of presence, absence, and address seems to lack these personal markers. On this, Lash writes,

> We address God as "you," and speak of God as "him," rather than as "it," not because God is "a person" (which he certainly is not, for he is not *an* anything), but because our Christian experience of the manner of God's action requires us to acknowledge ourselves to be not merely produced but addressed, not merely made but loved, and speaking and loving are *personal* characteristics.[133]

In other words, the personal nature of the Christian experience of God makes appropriate the use of personal pronouns. Moreover, that all three (Father, Son, and Spirit) are conceived of in personal terms communicates that the believer's "experience of the mystery of God is truly experience of God *himself*."[134] Thus, the doctrine of God's Trinity is not primarily adding more information about God's nature, but shaping the lived mode of being of a Christian such that believers are formed to encounter the mystery of God in a certain way, and to be confident in the veracity and fullness of that encounter.[135]

Lash offers one perspective on how the doctrine of God's Trinity, expressed within the Nicene Creed, can be understood to operate regulatively

---

131. Nicholas Lash, "When Did the Theologians Lose Interest?," 135.

132. Lash, *Easter in Ordinary*, 279.

133. Lash, *Easter in Ordinary*, 276. Emphasis original. On page 278, Lash refers to Augustine, *De Trinitate*, book 7, chapter 4 as an historical precedent for his position.

134. Lash, *Easter in Ordinary*, 279. Emphasis original.

135. While this view may be distinct when compared with contemporary usage, it may not be so in relation to the world out of which the book of Proverbs arose. Boström notes that, within the context of the ancient Near East, "personal God" should not be understood as an anthropomorphic description, but as describing the kind of relationship that existed between a god and human. L. Boström, *The God of the Sages*, 194.

in line with George Lindbeck's proposals. Turning back to Proverbs with this understanding of God, a fresh path is opened for understanding the relationship between personified Wisdom and the LORD.

The Trinitarian Dynamics of the World in Front of Proverbs 8

Above, I argued that the world before the text of Proverbs 8 offers a mode of being in the world as one addressed, at the level of one's desires, by a personal, persistent, and consequential voice. At that point in my argument, the relationship between this voice of Wisdom and the LORD was assumed. Now I have the opportunity to expand upon and argue for this assumption. In the world before the text of Proverbs 8, the relationship between the LORD and the voice of Wisdom is analogous to a mode of life shaped by the Trinitarian understanding of God outlined above. This position is supported by the world of the text features of Proverbs 8 as well as the interaction between this chapter and the nature of order in Proverbs 10–31.

In Proverbs, Wisdom calls out (cf. Prov 1:20; 8:4; 9:4). The textual voice of her speech invites the reader into the world in front of the text in which they conceive of themselves as addressed. A feature of the personification of Wisdom, in addition to its role in dramatization and unification, is the personalization of her call. The reader is invited to tune their ear to a voice that has a personal tone. Readers can seek to discern the voice of Wisdom in the voice of people around them. The text provides a hermeneutic for entering into conversations; the person is called to metaphorically "lean in" to these conversations in order to parse whether and how they are invited to walk in the way of Wisdom. Within this dynamic, the reader seeks a personal voice behind, under, and/or through the voice of their interlocutor. This overlaps with a mode of being shaped by the doctrine of God's Trinity. In such a life, one understands oneself to be addressed by the Son, whose address and invitation are to be construed personally, spoken in love (cf. Prov 8:17).

The perduring nature of Wisdom, existing as she has from the initiating moment of creation to the present day (vv. 22–31), also shares an orientation with the doctrine of God's Trinity. As written elsewhere, that Wisdom has been present throughout all time opens the reader to the wisdom of others through tradition. She is now and always has been "laughing in the world, His earth, and [her] delight is in the sons of Adam" (Prov 8:31, my translation). As such, the reader is invited to consider that others

Three Attempts at a Christian Reading of Proverbs 8

have heard her and heeded her call. The reader is shaped in studiousness toward tradition. A similar inclination is noted by Rowan Williams regarding the concept of revelation considered within a Trinitarian framework; "'revelation' is a concept which emerges from a questioning attention to our present life in the light of a particular past—a past seen as 'generative.'"[136] Drawing on the work of Williams, Lash writes on the doctrine of God the "Word": "words were borrowed from elsewhere (words such as 'theos' and 'deus') to serve as tokens of reference for that holy mystery in relation to which the people sought to live, and to the 'address' and 'presence' of which initiative was ascribed."[137] In other words, the tradition of meditation on the nature of God funds present thought and experience. Both a life shaped by the world before the text of Proverbs 8 and the Nicene "identity-sustaining rules of discourse and behavior"[138] share a deference to and dependence upon those who have gone before.

The above two considerations can be adopted apart from one's stance regarding Wisdom's relationship to the LORD of Israel. Proverbs 8's presentation exhibits tension and ambiguity; there exists a similar tension in Proverbs 10–31, which resonates with the affirmation and denial present within the doctrine of God's Trinity. In Proverbs 1–9 two features can be observed regarding the presentation of Wisdom vis-à-vis the LORD. On the one hand, Wisdom speaks and acts in a way reminiscent of Israel's LORD. Baumann observes that Wisdom "ist ein himmlisches, also transzendentes Wesen. Ihre Rede hat an zahlreichen Stellen Parallelen zu JHWH-Reden; sie spricht mit einer Vollmacht, die der JHWHs nahekommt. Diese Aspekte weisen sie als eine göttliche Gestalt aus."[139] Wisdom's offer of love and life are made with only tangential reference to the LORD (cf. Prov 8:17, 35–36). Her call for devotion to her parallels the LORD's call to dedicate one's time to the Torah, God's words (compare Prov 8:34 and Ps 1:2).[140] On the other hand, a distinction between Wisdom and the LORD is maintained throughout Proverbs 8.[141] Although named tangentially, the LORD is still cited as the source of favor and life in Proverbs 8:35. It can be argued that Wisdom fears the LORD (Prov 8:13). Her presence through time is pictured alongside (

---

136. Williams, "Trinity and Revelation," 199.
137. Lash, *Easter in Ordinary*, 270.
138. Lash, *Easter in Ordinary*, 271.
139. Baumann, *Die Weisheitsgestalt in Proverbien 1–9*, 312.
140. Baumann, *Die Weisheitsgestalt in Proverbien 1–9*, 312–13.
141. Collett, *Figural Reading and the Old Testament*, 88.

Wisdom in the World

אֶצְלוֹ) the Lord God (Prov 8:30). These features make most sense if Wisdom and the LORD are understood as distinct figures. How is one to understand the presentation of personified Wisdom in light of this tension?

On the surface it would be understandable to conclude that Proverbs 8 is written to clarify the nature of the relationship between the LORD and Wisdom.[142] However, the very terms which might at first appear to clarify actually mystify:

> Einer expliziten Verhältnisbestimmung der Weisheit zu JHWH entziehen sich die Reden der Weisheitsgestalt jedoch: In Prov 8,22–31—dem Text, der sich einer Verhältnisbestimmung am meisten annähert—wird die Erschaffung der Weisheitsgestalt durch JHWH mittels dreier Verben zum Ausdruck gebracht, die sich in ihrer Bedeutung nicht eindeutig festlegen lassen . . . Eine derartige Anhäufung uneindeutiger Termini wird kein Zufall sein.[143]

The ambiguity of these terms does not necessarily mean that definitions cannot be arrived at with a moderate amount of certainty. It does, however, open the door to consider what effect this ambiguity may have on an interpretation which includes considerations of the world in front of the text. In such an approach, that one possible definition of terms or conception of Wisdom's role in the whole poem can be countered by another bears a resemblance to the dynamics of the doctrine of God's Trinity explicated above.[144] That Wisdom at one point seems very much to be the LORD of Israel in the "dress" of personification and then at another point is clearly differentiated from the LORD, is redolent of the "unceasing dialectically corrective movement"[145] of experience shaped by Trinitarian theology.

This dynamic can be observed outside of the confines of Proverbs 8 and its debated terms. Since at least the twentieth century, Wisdom has been related to a concept world order. Von Rad argued that Wisdom was "der aus der Schöpfung ergehenden Stimme der Urordnung."[146] Even as his

---

142. See, for example, Lenzi, "Proverbs 8:22–31: Three Perspectives on Its Composition," 714.

143. Baumann, *Die Weisheitsgestalt in Proverbien 1–9*, 312.

144. "The undecidability of the meaning of W/wisdom . . . is present in the texts themselves, where wisdom flows from one overlapping meaning to another and back again, meandering over a territory marked by the diverse lexical meanings assigned to the very same word when it appears in different contexts." Carole Fontaine, *Smooth Words*, 2–3.

145. Lash, *Easter in Ordinary*, 271.

146. Von Rad, *Weisheit in Israel*, 213.

Three Attempts at a Christian Reading of Proverbs 8

position has been criticized for going beyond the terms of the text,[147] the book of Proverbs does in some sense depend on a reliable order in the world for the logic of its promises. Citing Proverbs 10:3 and 15:25, James Loader writes "Jahwe wiederholt vorgestellt wird als der, der den normalen Gang der Ordnung durchsetzt, der also hinter der Ordnung steht."[148] The Lord's role as the guarantor of order is a necessary theological component to the act-consequence nexus often observed in Proverbs.[149] The Proverbs upon which Loader draws are sayings which explicitly make this connection. Even in those sayings in Proverbs 10–31 where it is not so clearly stated, the frame provided by Proverbs 1–9, and the larger context of Old Testament faith provide a background which reinforces an understanding of divine sanction for the act-consequence nexus.

With this being said, Proverbs also acknowledges that the Lord is the negative limit of order.[150] The order proclaimed and assumed by many of the Proverbs and their deed-consequence nexus is not such that the Lord of Israel is bound mechanistically and stripped of freedom. Loader cites Proverbs 10:22, 16:1, 33, and 19:21 as points at which a distance is set up between human action and their results. Thus, while some texts affirm the divinely sanctioned order, others deny the order its own independence and assert it as only guaranteed by the Lord. The saying and whatever practice it may encourage should not be understood to contain the divine order in themselves.

Proverbs contains within its collection certain verses that set these two paradoxical positions side by side. Proverbs 22:2 and 29:13 offer examples of the paradox in the topic of poverty and wealth. Despite the strong teaching of right actions bringing right results, it is not the case that the poor are to be blamed for their poverty. Rather, they are to be recipients of mercy within the community (cf. Prov 14:21; 28:27). The basis for these appeals to mercy is theological; the Lord God made both poor and rich. Broadening his view from the issues of poverty to order, Loader paraphrases: "Ordnung und Aporie begegnen einander; Jahwe hat sie alle gemacht."[151]

The broader dynamic at work around the concept of order in Proverbs 10–31 calls upon the reader to take a similar stance toward the world that is

---

147. Baumann, *Die Weisheitsgestalt in Proverbien 1–9*, 287–88.
148. Loader, "Lebensgestaltung als weisheitliche Lebensverantwortung," 725.
149. Loader, "Lebensgestaltung als weisheitliche Lebensverantwortung," 726.
150. Loader, "Lebensgestaltung als weisheitliche Lebensverantwortung," 726–28.
151. Loader, "Lebensgestaltung als weisheitliche Lebensverantwortung," 731.

found in Proverbs 1–9 vis-à-vis Wisdom in the world. In both cases, order and Wisdom are claimed to be present in the world; "Does not Wisdom cry out?" (Prov 8:1). And yet Wisdom, like the divinely sanctioned order, is not to be presumed upon. If one waits to call on Wisdom until the day of calamity, their cries will be met with mockery (Prov 1:26–27). As such, Wisdom is not a "thing" waiting inertly for one to use as needed. Rather, it takes on the dynamics of a personal relationship. Just as the balancing between order and aporia calls for mercy, so the particular way in which Wisdom is in the world enjoins upon the student a humble stance of relating to her through others. The conjunction of Proverbs 1–9 with Proverbs 10–31 sets these two dynamics side-by-side and, as I have argued above, mutually reinforce each other.

Furthermore, the kind of stance in the world called for by Wisdom in Proverbs 1–9 and order/aporia in Proverbs 10–31 resonates with that called for by the Christian doctrine of God's Trinity. As outlined above, within this framework, Christians are to affirm God's presence without presuming upon it, for God is transcendent as well as immanent. Within this paradox, the Word of God shapes one's stance as a divine address in, over, and through creation such that the believer "leans in" to hear and respond to God's mysterious and personal call.

Conclusion

Earlier I cited Hans-Georg Gadamer's assertion that reading takes place within a *wirkungsgeschichtliches Bewusstsein*.[152] The argument above has sought to acknowledge and embrace the historically influenced nature of interpretation. While one can, through acknowledgment, objectify their pre-understandings, some form of them is always operative in interpretation. That the history of interpretation has shaped how one interacts with a text is one aspect of reading as *wirkungsgeschichtliches*. Above, I have acknowledged my adherence to Nicene Christianity and my attempt to receive the passage within that faith tradition. Following on the position outlined by Nicholas Lash, my allegiance to this tradition shapes experience in a determinative way, as a habitus for reading.

Having acknowledged this, what I have attempted to show above is that Proverbs 8 is a text wherein this *regula lectionis*[153] operates in a different

---

152. Gadamer, *Truth and Method*, 312. Emphasis original.
153. I am here modulating on the role of the *regula fidei* in Christian reading.

way. The text projects a coherent mode of being-in-the-world analogous to that of the Nicene Creed. As such, it is not just that the world of the text is received by one seeking to live in the world projected by the Nicene Creed. Rather, the text links to the Creed in a first-order rather than a second-order way. The text offers an affirmation or exegetical authorization for the creed-generated stance. As a result, Proverbs 8, apart from its role in the history of Christian theology, is an appropriate place to turn to in order to understand, ground, and shape a Trinitarian mode of being-in-the-world. Even as I have argued that there is coherence between the Creed and Proverbs 8, I hope to have illustrated that the Creed does not pre-determine the meaning of this text. Rather, the Creed opened up an avenue of questions, which in turn deepened an appropriation of the text and the Creed.

My reading comes to a conclusion similar to Dan Treier and Don Collett in that I understand Proverbs 8 to be coherent with Nicene Trinitarian theology. However, the path that I have followed is different, as it has proceeded on a different understanding of coherence, one that has sought resonance between the mode-of-being projected by the text and the regulative framing provided by the Creed. My conclusion regarding the relationship between personified Wisdom and the LORD of Israel is that, read within a Nicene framework, Wisdom participates in the LORD, faithfully bringing the divine invitation into the life of the believer, thereby offering them a hermeneutic for experiencing life in the world. Wisdom is the voice of God, the divine invitation, which offers a pathway to formation, a formation that is found in attention to the voice. However, as an experience within creation, this voice does not fully contain the uncontainable LORD, who is nevertheless omnipresent throughout the created order.

Gadamer, et al, "secularize" ruled reading so that all interpretative activity is understood as influenced by prior commitments of the reader.

Wisdom and the Johannine Witness

In this last section of the book my third attempt at a renewed Christian reading seeks a two-testament witness to the reality of God as heard through Proverbs 8. To be sure, it is artificial to separate the New Testament witness from the trinitarian discussion of the previous section. However, this is a pragmatic decision to enable better reflection both on Proverbs 8 in itself and as mediated via John's Gospel.

In his 1992 book, *Biblical Theology of the Old and New Testaments*, Brevard Childs argued that the goal of canonical reading of Christian Scripture is to press to the subject matter within and underlying Scripture. "The dialogical move of biblical theological reflection which is being suggested is from the partial grasp of fragmentary reality found in both testaments to the full reality which the Christian church confesses to have found in Jesus Christ, in the combined witness of the two testaments."[154] The enterprise suggested is an explicitly Christian one as the instrument of reflection is the two testament canon of the Christian church. Childs asserts that each testament possess a "partial grasp of fragmentary reality"; he does not comment further on what makes the witness of each testament fragmentary. Theologically, the nature of God is such that all speech is, to some degree, figurative, non-equivocal, and therefore fragmentary. Even so, the language of the Bible is recognized within the Christian tradition as being foundational for the church's understanding of God. Therefore, it is best to understand Childs' point as relating to the complementary nature of the witness of the two testaments, rather than a demotion of the language of the Bible to same plane as all speech. The two testaments are witnesses, whose two accounts undergird the church's claims regarding God.[155]

Up to this point, this study has engaged with the Old Testament witness. Through attention to the three worlds of the text, we have read Proverbs 8 as inviting the reader into a certain mode of being-in-the-world which is attentive to the personal voice of God in all of creation. In order to be fully Christian interpretation of the subject matter, we now turn to the New Testament and its discrete witness. Our hope is not that this will correct, override, or in any way supersede the Old Testament witness. Rather, the aim is that attending to New Testament dynamics will provide for us an additional partial witness to God. Taken together with the Old Testament's

---

154. Childs, *Biblical Theology of the Old and New Testaments*, 85.
155. Schneiders, *The Revelatory Text*, 132–38.

partial witness we would have a canonical, whole-Bible witness to a particular facet of life lived in relation to the Holy Mystery of God.

Due to the restraints of space, we will confine our focus on the New Testament to one particular theme in one particular book: the role of light in the Gospel of John.

The Dynamics of Light in the Gospel of John

Indicators for Relating Wisdom and Light

The relationship between Word and Wisdom is commonly remarked upon in commentaries on John 1.[156] However, R. W. L. Moberly points out the conceptual similarities between wisdom in Proverbs 8 and light in the Fourth Gospel.[157]

> The notion in Proverbs 8 that wisdom is actively present in the world, taking the initiative to engage people and seek a positive response from them, is replicated in the Gospel of John, where the Word, who is the divine agent of creation in the mode of Wisdom, is "the true light [*phos*] that shines on [*photozei*] on everyone" and "became flesh and lived among us" (John 1:9, 14 AT).[158]

Moberly's focus, which I share, is on dynamics, how this concept operates and "moves" in the text. As with Wisdom, light pervades creation and is available to all people (John 1:9a) and yet comes to encounter and confront people in distinct, decision-inducing moments (John 1:9b–11; 3:19–21). If these initial indicators are granted, I propose to explore how light operates in the Gospel of John with the aim to set this alongside Proverbs 8's presentation.

Light in the Gospel of John

The symbol of light features prominently in the Gospel of John. It is introduced in the theme-setting prologue of the Gospel and it is developed through the book into a metaphor interpreting the ministry of Jesus. By attending to this metaphorical association, my focus in the following

---

156. See Haenchen, *John*, 138–40; Beasley-Murray, *John*, 9.
157. Moberly, *The God of the Old Testament*, 42–45.
158. Moberly, *The God of the Old Testament*, 43.

paragraphs will be to investigate how this relationship opens up a possible understanding for one's life in the world.

In the prologue, light is introduced in relation to the eternal Word (λόγος) of God. The Logos existed with God in eternity; "in the Logos was life, and that life was the light of humanity" (John 1:4). In this statement, light, life, and Logos are all associated with one another. Indeed, they are linked "so powerfully that the cluster dominates the symbolic system of the entire narrative."[159] This linkage is stated tersely at this point; no expansion is given. Even so, the reader is already implicitly drawn into a key contention of John's Gospel: true life and sight are had only in relation to the Logos of God, Jesus Christ. In anticipation of the narrative to follow, the life brought into being through the agency of the Logos was the light of all humanity (my paraphrase of verses 3–4; cf. John 3:16).[160] This light shines on all humanity, not solely on a portion of it.[161]

On the heels of the relating of Logos, life, and light comes a foreshadowing of the conflict narrated in 1:5. "And the light shines in the darkness, and the darkness did not overcome[162] it." Here the antithesis of light is introduced, alluding to the hostility which the Logos will face. The light-life of the Logos is not the only option presented in the Gospel; there are other possibilities. However, nowhere in the Gospel will these be accorded a status on par with the light-life offered in the Logos. Scholars have noted the strange grammar of this verse: the verb φαίνει in verse 5a is present tense while the verb κατέλαβεν in the second half of the verse is in the aorist tense.[163] On a symbolic level, this verse acknowledges the presence of darkness and evil in the world as real while also subordinating it to the stronger opposition of the light.[164] As the narrative unfolds, darkness moves to

---

159. Culpepper, *Anatomy of the Fourth Gospel*, 190.

160. David Ford remarks that logos draws on both the Scriptures of Israel (the Word of God) and the Hellenistic milieu (logos as ordering principle). Ford, *The Gospel of John*, 29–30.

161. Beasley-Murray notes that John 1:9b could also be understood as relating the light to all people: "The expression 'all who come into the world' was common among Jews to denote everyone." Beasley-Murray, *John*, 12.

162. That κατέλαβεν can mean either "overcome" or "understand" alludes to the important role insight and faith have in the narrative of John.

163. Haenchen, *John 1*, 114.

164. Ford, *The Gospel of John*, 33–35 engages in this sort of symbolic reading, as does Estes, "Dualism or Paradox?," 112–13. Moberly notes that, as Proverbs does not account for the origins of folly, neither does John speak to question of how darkness came to be in this world created by the Word. Moberly, *The God of the Old Testament*, 45.

engulf the Light of the Incarnate Word[165] but he is shown to conquer it through the resurrection.

John 1 continues by introducing a witness to the light, John the Baptist.[166] In the fifth chapter, this assessment of John will be repeated. John is not the light, but a witness to it (John 1:6–8); John was a burning and shining lamp, but Jesus is greater (John 5:35–36). The lamp is subordinate to the light, as a particular instance of bringing light; it is not the light itself.[167] These passages emphasize the role of a witness (μαρτυρία) to the light to point away from themselves in order that all might believe in the light.[168] Significantly, this initial mention of a witness is balanced at the other end of the Gospel of John, with the written Gospel presenting itself as a witness (21:24) in order that others might believe (20:31). These verses ascribe an important but relativized role to both the living and written witnesses. They bear witness to the reality of the light; its character, presence, and truth. Within the context of the prologue, we might understand this as one facet of the light's "shining" in the darkness. And yet, their importance is relativized as they serve to point others to the light; they themselves are not the reality.[169] This guards against an idolatry of persons or texts. Additionally, John 1:6–8 inform the reader that the proper response to the light is to believe (πιστεύω), a point that will be developed through the Gospel narrative. John uses this verb "close to one hundred time, almost three times as often as in the Synoptics combined."[170] John's usage of πιστεύω communicates a concern for an "active, relational trust in Jesus Christ" over a more cognitive understanding.[171]

In John 3, light is brought into greater association with the ministry of Jesus and its use in the context adds greater power to the symbol. The imagery is already hinted at in the timing of Nicodemus' visit. He comes to visit Jesus at night, a time of darkness. In their conversation, Jesus speaks to him

---

165. There is perhaps a linkage here to cosmic darkness in the dramatic statement of the onset of night in John 13:30.

166. In the world behind the text there is some reason to believe that the Prologue moves to disallow too high of a view of John the Baptist. Beasley-Murray, *John*, 12.

167. Culpepper, *Anatomy of the Fourth Gospel*, 191.

168. The noun μαρτυρίαν occurs once in verse 7 and the verb μαρτυρήσῃ appears twice, once in verses 7 and once in verse 8. Their proximity to one another has an emphatic effect.

169. Köstenberger, *John*, 33.

170. Köstenberger, *John*, 34.

171. Köstenberger, *John*, 34.

Wisdom in the World

of his mission in the world. John 3:16 offers a "confessional summary of the Gospel."[172] There is some debate regarding where to end the speech of Jesus, at verse 15 or as extending through verse 21. On the basis of terminology, structure, and grammar, Lightfoot, Bultmann, and Köstenberger, among others, agree that John 3:16–21 should be understood as a later exposition by the author of the gospel account.[173] Nevertheless, there is no clear distinction in the text between these words and those preceding. Brown, who argues against separating verses 16–21 from that which precedes it, writes, "Of course the evangelist has been at work in this discourse, but his work is not of the type that begins at a particular verse. All Jesus' words come to us through the channels of the evangelist's understanding and rethinking, but the Gospel presents Jesus as speaking and not the evangelist."[174] In considering the world behind the text, it is beyond doubt that the words of Jesus have been mediated through the witness of the church. This calls us back to Schneiders' discussion regarding the New Testament's character is a witness to the proclaimed Jesus through the medium of the historical Jesus.[175] When we turn to the world of the text, the lack of a clear textual marker between verses 15 and 16 invites the reader to take these words on equal authority to those of Jesus.

The words of John 3:16–21 make salvation the central mission of the Son. Even so, there is judgment and condemnation as a result of his mission (vv. 17–18). The light metaphor is introduced to explicate how this can be so, specifically through light's illuminative power.

> And this is the judgment [κρίσις]: that the light has come into the world, and humanity [ἄνθρωποι] loved the darkness rather than the light because their works were evil. For everyone who practices wickedness hates the light and does not come to [πρὸς] the light, lest his works be called to account [ἐλεγχθῇ]. But whoever does what is true comes to the light, so that it might be made manifest [φανερωθῇ] that his works have been carried out in God. (John 3:19–21)

"Light is not only the revelation of the *logos*; it reveals the nature of all who come in contact with it, and the judgment upon each person is determined

---

172. Beasley-Murray, *John*, 51.

173. Lightfoot, *St. John's Gospel*, 118; Bultmann, *The Gospel of John*, 153 n.1; Köstenberger, *John*, 114.

174. Brown, *The Gospel According to John*, 149.

175. Schneiders, *The Revelatory Text*, 102.

Three Attempts at a Christian Reading of Proverbs 8

by his or her response to it."[176] Light now is not just about "seeing" but also about being seen. It exposes one, bringing about a decisive moment of judgment (*krisis*); "by their attitude to Him [Jesus], and to His works and words, they pass judgment on themselves, a judgment either of acquittal or of condemnation."[177] Christ's coming into the world reveals that the deeds of some are evil and others are not. R. W. L. Moberly points out that the encounter with the Light "is intrinsically moral . . . to embrace good rather than evil."[178] However, rather than being moralistic, within the broader context it is faith which defines one as good or evil. In this, we are given a way of reading future interactions with Jesus in the Gospel as of ultimate significance; the readers are now informed that one's reaction to Jesus exposes them for who they already are and has eternal consequences.[179]

In John 8, the association between the light and Jesus come to a climax in Jesus' declaration that he is "the light of the world" (John 8:12). This statement incorporates the symbol of light into a metaphorical utterance about Jesus, drawing in what has been said before about light into a new understanding of Jesus. His statement makes explicit that Jesus is the light spoken of in the prologue; he is the Logos in whom humanity has the light of life. Building on the encounter with Nicodemus, it is one's encounter with Jesus which is determinative and decisive for their salvation. Those who respond favorably find life; they have the light of life. Those who do not respond favorably to Jesus walk in darkness, loving wickedness more than the light. Up to this point the light has been understood as generally available (John 1), as characteristic of Jesus' mission (John 3), and transmissible through testimony (John 5). However, no parameters had been given for discerning light shining in the darkness in and amongst one's experiences of the world. Now, "John 8 lays down the basic guideline for [the] process of discernment: that the primary emphasis is on the 'I am' of Jesus."[180]

John 9 offers an extended narrative which expands upon what it means to encounter Jesus as the light. While many scholars conclude that John

---

176. Culpepper, *Anatomy of the Fourth Gospel*, 191.

177. Lightfoot, *St. John's Gospel*, 114.

178. Moberly, *The God of the Old Testament*, 44.

179. In the context of John 3, it is curious that Nicodemus' response to this speech of Jesus is not recorded, and we are left without an evaluation of him until the end of the gospel, when we read that he took part in the respectful burial of Jesus (cf. John 19:39).

180. Ford, *The Gospel of John*, 181.

9:4–5 is a later insertion,[181] John 9:4–5 links the story with the developing symbol of light in the gospel thus far. In John 9, Jesus encounters a man who is born blind, a description which picks up on much of the gospel's symbolic tapestry up to this point. The repetition that he was blind from birth (John 9:1, 2) is reminiscent of the conversation with Nicodemus (John 3). Additionally, redolent of chapter 8, one who is blind is walking in darkness, unable to see the light. In John 9, Jesus heals the man's eyesight so that he can see. This sets off a narrative which expands "further the symbolic value of light and . . . [provides] an index to the value of various characters."[182] Crucial for the overall purpose of the Gospel of John, once he is healed the man does not initially "see" Jesus; his sight is restored to him when he obeys Jesus' command, and when he returns from the pool the text implies that Jesus is gone.[183] From this point on, the man's sight takes on significance greater than mere physical, ocular vision: "Sight becomes insight into the identity of Jesus, a willingness to believe, and finally faith."[184] The man becomes a witness to Jesus, the light of the world, through his testimony before the Pharisees. He is granted the light of life in his ability to believe in Jesus (cf. John 17:3). Conversely, the Pharisees, who are physically able to see, move "to ignorance (which is exposed by irony), rejection of Jesus and the man who has accepted him, and finally the sentence of blindness."[185] At the end of the narrative, Jesus' words recall John 3 and its teaching on judgment, thereby offering a sort of *inclusio* to the light language earlier in the chapter.

Both the man born blind and Nicodemus offer examples of gradual growth toward faith in Jesus in the Gospel of John. The Pharisees and other Jewish leadership exemplify the opposite, but equally gradual, decline toward rejection of Jesus. The gradual nature of these changes in response to Jesus nuances the otherwise sharp contrast offered in the book between

---

181. Cf. Bultmann, *The Gospel of John*, 330.

182. Culpepper, *Anatomy of the Fourth Gospel*, 191.

183. The reader will later be told that this whole gospel is written so that the reader would believe, as well as contain a benediction on those who have not seen and yet believed. John's Gospel therefore becomes a witness, a way of encountering Jesus, activating an encounter with the Light whereby one must decide to love the Light or hate it. That this man, who is an archetype for a believing witness, does not see Jesus physically at first, and yet is willing to believe and bear witness no matter the cost, is exemplary for the believing community.

184. Culpepper, *Anatomy of the Fourth Gospel*, 191.

185. Culpepper, *Anatomy of the Fourth Gospel*, 192.

Three Attempts at a Christian Reading of Proverbs 8

"love and hatred, life and death, light and darkness, truth and falsehood."[186] These contrasts can lead one to think John offers a dualistic, sectarian vision of the world; the narrative, however, shows otherwise, when read in the light of the Prologue.

Next, in John 12, Jesus' hour is inaugurated when a group of Greeks desire to see Jesus. Again, for those who have read the gospel up to this point and have been inducted into its symbolic tapestry, the desire for sight is a request for more than a visual impression. Rather, one is seeking to believe in Jesus. Immediately, Jesus begins to speak of death; his own via the parable of the grain of wheat (John 12:24), and then for any who follow him (vv. 25–26). He then speaks of the judgment of this world, recalling John 3.

Bultmann notes that no direct answer is given to Greeks in the passage; instead they disappear from the narrative.[187] He concludes that, as elsewhere, the text has been fragmented and some form of response has dropped out. However, without any indication as to what this might have been, he reservedly moves forward to interpret the text as it stands in the final form.[188] In that context, he interprets the Greeks as seeking the historical Jesus, but this is the wrong kind of request. For Jesus to be the Lord of all the nations, he must first go through his death and resurrection. This leads Bultmann to the conclusion that "The question at issue is not all the attaining of a direct historical 'contemporaneity;' the important thing rather is to gain a relationship to the exalted Lord."[189] Such a relationship is mediated through the apostles (Philip and Andrew), which reminds the reader of the role of the witness to the light recorded in John 1:7, and which the gospel account itself will claim to be (John 20:31). The substance of the mediated relationship is the Risen Lord; as John 20:29 will clarify, there is no diminishment because of historical distance.

In John 12:35–36, the crowd is admonished to walk in the light while one has the light.[190] Verse 44 reads as a logical continuation from verse 36,

---

186. Lightfoot, *St. John's Gospel*, 118.

187. Bultmann, *The Gospel of John*, 420–21, 423.

188. "Accordingly we shall so proceed in the interpretation that follows [assuming that 12:23–33 form some sort of response to the Greeks]. Nevertheless we must realise that in so doing we are simply following the train of thought of the discourse; for the suspicion cannot be suppressed that between v. 22 and v. 23 a whole piece has fallen out." Bultmann, *The Gospel of John*, 420–21.

189. Bultmann, *The Gospel of John*, 424.

190. Culpepper, *Anatomy of the Fourth Gospel*, 192. Culpepper interprets these words as implicitly directed to the reader. While this position seemingly goes against the grain

as it develops the theme of following with belief, sight, and light (vv. 44–46).[191] However, in between these verses comes 36b–43, which state that Jesus departed and hid himself from the crowd. In this ordering, the section interprets what it means to walk in the light (cf. vv. 35–36a) as believing on the basis of the signs which Jesus has done (v. 37). Disappointingly, many did not believe in Jesus (v. 37), which the Gospel understands through the words of Isaiah. The crowds of those who did not believe had been confronted with the light, the revelation of Jesus' character through the testimony of his works, but they loved darkness more than the light. Some did believe but were afraid to confess their faith. Such faith does not measure up, for it is a similar lack of true love; "for they loved the glory that comes from man more than the glory that comes from God" (12:43).[192]

In the ordering of the final form, in which Jesus has removed himself from the crowds, it is startling to read of Jesus crying out his words in verse 44: why is he crying out in private?[193] Perhaps this is a subtle rebuke against those who keep their faith quiet, introducing an evaluative summary of Jesus' ministry and the need for a proper response. Verses 44 through 50 clarify that how one responds to Jesus is the same as one's response to the Father.[194] In verse 46, the reader is reminded of the prologue, as Jesus states "I have come into the world as light." This was the Word who was with God and is God, in whom is life, the light of humanity, the true light coming into the world, belief in which qualifies one to be children of God. As the Gospel transitions from Jesus' public ministry which has included his deeds and his words, these verses offer an interpretation of that ministry and an appeal for belief on the part of the reader.

John 13 transitions to Jesus' private meal with his disciples followed by his prayer, arrest, trial, condemnation, crucifixion, and resurrection. In contrast with the Synoptics, Jesus' teaching of his disciples is concentrated on this one night; "it is of symbolic significance that the scene takes place at

---

of the immediate context, it is nevertheless congruent with the overall goal of the gospel (John 20:30–31).

191. Bultmann offers an alternative understanding, in which 12:34–36 follow after 12:44–50. *The Gospel of John*, 342.

192. Both John 3:19b and John 12:43 speak of loving something of humanity more than that which is from God: "καὶ ἠγάπησαν οἱ ἄνθρωποι μᾶλλον τὸ σκότος ἢ τὸ φῶς" / "ἠγάπησαν γὰρ τὴν δόξαν τῶν ἀνθρώπων μᾶλλον ἤπερ τὴν δόξαν τοῦ θεοῦ." Through subtle textual resonances such as this, the text continues to develop and unite its themes.

193. David Ford also raises this issue. *The Gospel of John*, 248.

194. Whitacre, *John*, 324.

night."[195] Although φῶς does not occur in this latter portion of the Gospel,[196] these chapters continue to draw upon the symbolic tapestry into which "light" has been woven. The text continues to allude to the struggle between light and darkness: once Judas leaves the table of the Last Supper, John dramatically records that "it was night" (John 13:30b); when the soldiers come to arrest Jesus, they are carrying "lanterns and torches," which are for those who walk in darkness (cf. John 18:3).[197] Many characters interact with Jesus, which reveals their character and allows them an opportunity to believe or to be condemned by their unbelief. However, none of them believe; neither Annas, nor Caiaphas, nor Peter, nor Pilate. Particular attention is paid to the conversation with Pilate, who is confronted by the truth (John 18:38 cf. 1:14, 17; 3:21). One inducted to the symbolism of the Gospel can readily interpret this encounter as one with the Light.[198]

Pilate, a gentile, is a counter-example to the Greeks of John 12; unlike them, his faith is not willing to be made public, and it wilts due to fear of the Jews (John 19:12–13 cf. 12:42–43). The narrative records him making various attempts to prevaricate in his judgment of Jesus; he does not directly responds to Jesus' claim of his mission to bring truth, instead he replies "What is truth?" (18:38); he tries to get the crowds to make the decision for him by allowing a political prisoner to go free, only to have it backfire on him as the crowd chooses Barabbas (18:39–40); and finally he determines to flog Jesus in order to then release him, only to have the crowd pressure him more (19:1–16a).[199] Once again, the Gospel records a gradual change, this time in rejection of Jesus.

On the other side of the crucifixion, in the early morning, Mary Magdalene, Peter, the unnamed disciple, the disciples, and Thomas all follow the example of the man born blind by moving gradually toward full belief in Jesus. Each of these passages is described with vocabulary associated with light and sight. Peter, the unnamed disciple, Mary, and Thomas all encounter Jesus in the dark (John 20:1, 19). Peter and the unnamed disciple see and believe (John 20:8). Mary Magdalene sees Jesus (20:14) and then

195. Bultmann, *The Gospel of John*, 458.
196. Köstenberger, *John*, 250n.2.
197. Culpepper, *Anatomy of the Fourth Gospel*, 192.
198. With John 18:37, "Pilate himself is put on the spot through this statement; he is asked whether he is willing to listen to the voice of the Revealer, and he must show whether he 'is of the truth.'" Bultmann, *The Gospel of John*, 655.
199. Bultmann is particularly attentive to these as attempts to escape the judgment moment of a decision regarding Jesus. *The Gospel of John*, 655–58.

WISDOM IN THE WORLD

declares her sight of him to the other disciples (John 20:18). The disciples see the Lord and are glad (20:20). Thomas demands to see the marks in Jesus' body; indeed, his whole faith is made to rest on sight of his wounds (John 20:25b). In each of these circumstances, sight is physical. However, Jesus' words in response to Thomas move the reader from desiring physical sight to the kind of insight which the Gospel, in its symbolic development, has called for (John 20:29). These words suggest "that if seeing is believing, as it was for Thomas, believing is also seeing. What matters is the relationship established by faith. But this faith is not a vague or general feeling, nor is it merely an intellectual assent to a position. It is openness and acceptance and trust directed toward God in Jesus."[200]

John 21, while perhaps a later addition to the Gospel,[201] offers an illustration of what disciples should expect in "walking in the light" of faith in Jesus Christ as the Word of God.[202] The text alerts us to this in its opening statement that Jesus "revealed [ἐφανέρωσεν] himself in this way [οὕτως]" (John 21:1). Seven disciples are in Galilee for an undisclosed purpose.[203] Their encounter with Jesus takes place during the mundane activity of fishing. "The primary concern is with the person of Jesus, his self-revelation, and his freedom to be present, to speak, to serve, and to love. *It is presence within ordinary life, with its necessities of working and eating.*"[204] It is in this way (οὕτως), in the sphere of everyday life, that the Lord revealed himself, bringing light into the darkness of their life (cf. v. 4). That Jesus appears here, and the text does not relate to the reader his departure, speaks of Jesus' freedom "to appear or not, but he is always present as God is present."[205] After a fruitless night of fishing, Jesus addresses the disciples from the shore. He calls them "children" (παιδία) and commands them to put their nets

---

200. Whitacre, *John*, 486.

201. In addition to the strong indication that chapter 20:31 formed the conclusion of the book, Lightfoot notices that John 21 makes reference "to the Lord's 'coming' in a sense which is absent from the earlier chapters." Nevertheless, he concludes that it has been added to the chapter in order to agree with the other Gospel accounts that the principal manifestation of the Risen Lord was in Galilee (cf. Matt 28:16–20; Mark 14:28; 16:7). *St. John's Gospel*, 338, 341.

202. Ford, *The Gospel of John*, 416.

203. At least in the Gospel of John the purpose is not disclosed. Mark's Gospel records Jesus telling his disciples to meet him in Galilee (Mark 14:28; 16:7). Whitacre, *John*, 489.

204. Ford, *The Gospel of John*, 418. Emphasis original.

205. Ford, *The Gospel of John*, 417. As will be discussed shortly, the ubiquity of the Light is parallel to that of Wisdom in Proverbs 8:1–3.

down on a particular side of the boat (vv. 5–6). The command stem from insight into the workings of the natural world: their barren nets become too full to haul in. Wisdom leading to a successful venture follows from obeying Jesus' commands.[206] Through this, the Lord is recognized for who he is. In the logic of the Gospel of John, this then functions as another sign whereby Jesus is shown to be the Son; it is the light whereby Jesus and the disciples are more fully known.

The Dynamics of Light in the Gospel of John

The Gospel of John draws the symbol of light from the reader's everyday experience into the particular world of witness to Jesus Christ narrated within its pages. Through the Gospel, light is deployed to symbolize encountering the Son of God in a decisive way. This encounter is revelatory both of the nature of Jesus and the character of the person so engaged. A positive response leads one to experience the fullness of life; the true life that is found in relation to Jesus as the Logos, the only Son of the Father (John 1:4, cf. 10:10). A negative response reveals one as already condemned, actively loving darkness and wicked deeds more than the true life brought into the world by the Logos.

Although the various scenes in the Gospel no doubt have a deeper meaning, the settings of these encounters are part of the everyday routine of life. A wedding is the setting for the first of Jesus' signs (John 2:1–11); the (unfortunately) normal rhythm of the temple court with its vendors is the site for the second (John 2:13–25). A woman drawing water at a well (John 4), a pool where the invalid seek healing (John 5:1–18), a countryside (John 6:1–15), a lake (John 6:16–21), and the city streets of Jerusalem (John 9) are all mundane places. And yet, they are the sites of encounter with the Light of the World. John 21 offers a post-resurrection encounter with Jesus, once again in a run-of-the-mill location.

For the reader who responds in faith to the Jesus of the Gospel of John, every location becomes pregnant with a possible encounter with Jesus, an opportunity for a sign to respond to in order to grow in faith or be revealed as a lover of darkness. The everyday has the potential of becoming a moment of *krisis* spoken of in John 3:19. The Gospel of John is written so that

---

206. While the vocabulary varies, there is conceptual overlap here with Wisdom addressing the audience as children. Proverbs uses the language of child (παιδίον, cf. Prov 4:1 LXX), as well as son (υἱός, cf. Prov 8:4,31). In John 21, the Risen Lord addresses the disciples as children (παιδία).

the reader might believe that Jesus is the Son of God, the Logos in whom there is life and light, which has come into the world, and is the true light of all humanity (cf. John 20:30–31; 1:1–18). That light is so ubiquitous in human life, and so central to humanity's rhythm of life, makes it a fitting symbol for an encounter with Jesus in the everyday. The belief called for by the Gospel is not only in the historical person of Jesus and claims about him, but a belief about the world in which the believer lives and moves and has their being. This belief is one which reshapes all of life into a possible encounter with the Risen Lord. The incumbent stance for the believer is one of openness to the presence of God in the world, as made manifest (φανερόω) in Jesus Christ.

Conclusion

Walter Moberly notes that the "deep similarities between Proverbs 8 and John's Gospel are more at the level of conceptualities than of terminology or imagery."[207] Those looking for the latter kind of linkage focus more on exploring the connection between λογος and חכמה. The analysis above has sought to map the dynamics of Light in the Fourth Gospel and how it is interwoven with the rich symbolism of that Gospel. The way Light is deployed and related to Jesus shared many similarities to the interpretation of Proverbs 8 detailed earlier in this study.

Moberly offers a concise summary of these similarities: "the agent of God's creation, Wisdom or Word, remains active within creation, no less now than then. This dimension of reality engages people and seeks a life-giving response from them."[208] Proverbs 8 begins with a description of Wisdom's ubiquity (vv. 1–3) and the universality of her audience (vv. 4–5). The Light of the World is also present in creation (John 1:1–4) and shines on people without qualification as to ethnicity or moral qualification (1:4,9; 3:16–21). Both Wisdom in Proverbs 8 and Jesus in the Gospel of John offer life and the favor of God to those who respond positively (Prov 8:35; John 1:4,9; 12:44–50). This elevates the stakes of response; when confronted with Wisdom/Word one is brought into a decisive moment of judgment (*krisis*). Hearing these two witnesses together links the moral and spiritual spheres of life. The good person, the wise person, is the one who responds to Jesus in faith. Likewise, they who respond in faith are drawn into a life

---

207. Moberly, *The God of the Old Testament*, 45.
208. Moberly, *The God of the Old Testament*, 45.

of Wisdom, in which following Jesus shapes how one approaches speech, money, and all of the other topics of Proverbs. That the Word was the agent of all creation reinforces this connection (John 1:1–4).

Having acknowledged these similarities, each testament offers a distinct witness to the subject matter of Scripture. Each must be heard in its integrity to shape our understanding of God and our sense of living life in His presence.[209] The distinct contribution of Proverbs 8 is its emphasis on the generality of God's presence and address. The God who made the world remains active in addressing its inhabitants through the created order. Alternatively, Light in John is focused on the particular person of Jesus Christ. At stake in Proverbs is one's temporal "success" and the formation of one's character (8:12–21, cf. 1:1–7). In John, one's eternal status hangs in the balance in the encounter with the Light (3:16–21). Now these need not be strongly bifurcated; it is certainly possible to coordinate these arenas of life. However, the distinct witness of each "fills out" different facets of life before the LORD God.

Listening to both testaments yields a view of reality in which God is present, seeking a life-giving relationship with all of His creatures. The LORD is not far off. This LORD took on flesh and dwelt among us, but prior to and after this incarnate life, His presence remains. Both Wisdom and Word are present and appeal to those who have ears to hear and eyes to see. David Ford's comment on the Gospel of John could be equally applied to Wisdom in Proverbs 8: "The Gospel is written to draw people into this ongoing drama of love that follows Jesus into darkness, in the confidence that love, not darkness, will have the last word."[210] The response sought in both is an openness to encountering Him in the everyday arenas of life. Both acknowledge that this openness is not automatic; folly and darkness are both present in the world.[211] And yet, as one is open, the promise is that Wisdom will speak, the Light will shine, and the people of God will meet their LORD within the created order and be guided in following in the way that brings life.

---

209. Childs, *Biblical Theology of the Old and New Testaments*, 85.
210. Ford, *The Gospel of John*, 34.
211. Moberly, *The God of the Old Testament*, 45.

10

Conclusion

IN THIS BOOK, I set out to read Proverbs 8 as Christian Scripture, in light of its literary context in an ancient collection, its history of interpretation, and as a word for the people of God today. The first section laid the groundwork for what followed. The first chapter introduced a methodology which respected the many facets of reading the Bible as Christian Scripture. In such a reading, the text as an historical document, as an enduring literary classic, and as a revelatory witness to God all must receive attention in order to honor the nature of the Bible as Scripture. The second chapter explored the text as an ancient piece of poetry, and used grammatical and literary tools to produce a foundation for further enquiry.

The second section recognized that the reading of texts takes place in traditions. Hans-Georg Gadamer's concept of *wirkungsgeschichtliches Bewußtsein* was introduced as the means by which to grapple with the nature of such embedded reading. Gadamer helps to illuminate how tradition is an aid, rather than an obstacle, to reading. Following on this, I surveyed a selective history of the interpretation of Proverbs 8, distinguishing between pre-modern and modern, and between secular and confessional readings. A key difference between these was the sense of immediacy between the text and the reader which pre-modern readings displayed, contrasted with the sense of distance displayed by modern takes on the passage. Even those writing from within the Christian tradition for the sake of that tradition had this distance, although the four which I surveyed displayed varying approaches to reading the text for faith within the modern frame. One result of this survey of interpretation was an appreciation for the depth of meaning which Proverbs 8 can generate.

Conclusion

Section three focused on reading the text as Christian Scripture in light of both the history of interpretation and the insights of modern biblical scholarship. I engaged two thinkers who are significant figures in their own fields, Paul Ricoeur and Charles Taylor, and who offer the opportunity to re-think certain facets of biblical study. Their work opens up the nature of texts and language as expressive of a greater reality which must be engaged dialogically by a participant. Reading the Bible as Scripture takes up their work while also offering a distinct set of commitments for such a dialogical reading strategy. I then outlined a contemporary conception of wisdom, offered as a heuristic tool by which to engage in a fuller dialogue with Proverbs 8. From there, I engaged in three first-attempts at a renewed reading of Proverbs 8 as Christian Scripture. These three took up the text in three different dialogues, in relation to three distinct fields of Christian life. The first sought to relate the text to a mode of being-in-the-world which distorted neither the text nor the nature of living in a secular age. The second brought Proverbs 8 into dialogue with Nicene Trinitarian theology, specifically through a dialogue between the worlds projected by the text and the doctrine of God's Trinity. The third attempt related Proverbs 8 to the theme of light in the Gospel of John in order to produce a two-testament witness to the reality of God, the world, and human nature.

While I hope that this study has advanced the conversation around reading Proverbs 8 as Christian Scripture, I recognize that more work is necessary. One avenue for further study is how the three first-attempts I have offered relate to one another. Is there a way to further synthesize these three dialogues into one coherent sense of the text's witness to God, the world, and human life? Or, are these necessarily distinct dialogues? Additionally, reading the text in different contexts would surely shape the nature of the study. For example, I focused on the nature of the secular age as disenchanted in the existential reading of Proverbs 8. Another reader might think another facet of the contemporary social imaginary is more relevant to this conversation. Another might read the text in a non-Western context, thereby making Taylor's analysis less applicable.

I began the book with an eye toward two goals. The first was exploring how an ancient document which has been gathered into the canonical Christian Bible could be read and taken up as the Word of the Lord for the people of God today. The second was to illustrate how one could appreciatively and critically honor the insights modern biblical scholarship in the endeavor to read the Bible as Christian Scripture for today. In the end, it is for the readers to decide how successful I have been.

Bibliography

Albright, William Foxwell. "The Goddess of Life and Wisdom." *The American Journal of Semitic Languages and Literatures* 36 (1920) 258–94.

Aletti, J. N. "Séduction et parole en Proverbes I–IX." *Vetus Testamentum* 27 (1977) 129–44.

Athanasius of Alexandria. *Contra Arianos II*. In *Nicene and Post-Nicene Fathers*, edited by Philip Schaff and Henry Wace, 348–94. Translated by J. H. Newman. 14 vols. Second Series. Peabody, MA: Hendrickson, 1994.

Ayres, Lewis. *Nicaea and Its Legacy: An Approach to Fourth-Century Trinitarian Theology*. Oxford: Oxford University Press, 2004.

Baehr, Peter. "Purity and Danger in the Modern University." *Sociology* 48 (2011) 297–300.

Bartholomew, Craig G. *Introducing Biblical Hermeneutics: A Comprehensive Framework for Hearing God in Scripture*. Grand Rapids: Baker, 2015.

Barton, John. *A History of the Bible: The Story of the World's Most Influential Book*. New York: Viking, 2019.

Baumann, Gerlinde. *Die Weisheitsgestalt in Proverbien 1–9: Traditionsgeschichtliche und theologische Studien*. Tübingen: Mohr-Siebeck, 1996.

Bauer-Kayatz, Christa. *Einführung in die alttestamentliche Weisheit*. Biblische Studien 55. Neukirchen-Vluyn: Neukirchener Verlag, 1969.

———. *Studien zu Proverbian 1–9*. WMANT 22. Neukirchen-Vluyn: Neukirchener Verlag, 1966.

Beasley-Murray, George R. *John*. 2nd ed. Word Biblical Commentary 36. Nashville, TN: Thomas Nelson, 1999.

Beeke, Joel, and Ray Lanning. "Reading and Hearing the Word in a Puritan Way." *Reformation and Revival* 5.2 (1996) 67–76.

Beiser, Frederick C. *The German Historicist Tradition*. Oxford: Oxford University Press, 2011.

Boström, Gustav. *Proverbiastudien: Die Weisheit und das fremde Weib in Spr. 1–9*. Lunds Universitets Årsskrift, N.F. I.30.3; Lund: Gleerup, 1935.

Boström, Lennart. *The God of the Sages: The Portrayal of God in the Book of Proverbs*. Coniectanea Biblica Old Testament Series 29. Stockholm: Almqvist & Wiksell International, 1990.

Bourdieu, Pierre. *The Logic of Practice*. Translated by Richard Nice. Stanford: Stanford University Press, 1992. Translation of *Le Sense Pratique*. Paris: Editions de Minuit, 1980.

Brown, Raymond. *The Gospel According to John*. 2 vols. Anchor Bible 29 and 29a. Garden City, NY: Doubleday, 1966, 1970.

Bibliography

Buber, Martin. *I and Thou*. Translated by Walter Kauffman. New York: Touchstone, 1970.

Bultmann, Rudolf. *The Gospel of John: A Commentary*. Translated by G. R. Beasley-Murray, R. W. N. Hoare, and J. K. Riches. Philadelphia: Westminster, 1971.

———. "Is Exegesis without Presuppositions Possible?" *Encounter* 21.2 (1960) 194–200.

Burney, C. F. "Christ as the APXH of Creation." *Journal of Theological Studies* 27 (1926) 160–77.

Camp, Claudia V. *Wisdom and the Feminine in the Book of Proverbs*. Sheffield, UK: Almond, 1985.

Childs, Brevard S. *Biblical Theology of the Old and New Testaments: Theological Reflection on the Christian Bible*. Minneapolis: Fortress, 1992.

Collett, Donald C. *Figural Reading and the Old Testament: Theology and Practice*. Grand Rapids: Baker Academic, 2020.

———. "A Place to Stand: Proverbs 8 and the Construction of Ecclesial Space." *Scottish Journal of Theology* 70.2 (2017) 166–83.

Crenshaw, James L. "Rad, Gerhard von (1901–1971)." In *Dictionary of Major Biblical Interpreters*, edited by Donald K. McKim, 843–48. Downer's Grove, IL: InterVarsity, 2007.

Culpepper, R. Alan. *Anatomy of the Fourth Gospel: A Study in Literary Design*. Philadelphia: Fortress, 1983.

Delitzsch, Franz. *Proverbs, Ecclesiastes, Song of Solomon*. Commentary on the Old Testament 6. Grand Rapids: Eerdmans, 1972. Reprint of *Proverbs, Ecclesiastes, Song of Solomon*. Translated by James Martin. Edinburgh: T&T Clark, 1880. Translation of *Salomonisches Spruchbuch*. Basel: Brunnen Verlag, 1873.

Dell, Katharine J. *The Book of Proverbs in Social and Theological Context*. Cambridge: Cambridge University Press, 2006.

Dowling, Maurice. "Proverbs 8:22–31 in the Christology of the Early Fathers." *Irish Biblical Studies* 24 (2002) 99–117.

Dreyfus, Hubert L. *Being-in-the-World: A Commentary on Heidegger's* Being and Time, *Division I*. Cambridge: MIT Press, 1991.

Elliot, Robert. "Givenness and Hermeneutics: The Saturated Phenomena and the Historically-Effected Conscious." *Heythrop Journal* 58 (2017) 662–77.

Ernest, James D. *The Bible in Athanasius of Alexandria*. Atlanta: SBL, 2004.

Estes, Douglas. "Dualism or Paradox? A New 'Light' on the Gospel of John." *Journal of Theological Study* 71.1 (2020) 90–118.

Fontaine, Carole. *Smooth Words: Women, Proverbs and Performance in Biblical Wisdom*. Journal for the Study of the Old Testament Supplement 356. London: Sheffield Academic, 2002.

Ford, David. *Christian Wisdom: Desiring God and Learning in Love*. Cambridge: Cambridge University Press, 2007.

———. *The Gospel of John: A Theological Commentary*. Grand Rapids: Baker, 2021.

Fowl, Stephen. "Effective History and the Cultivation of Wise Interpreters." *Journal of Theological Interpretation* 7.2 (2013) 153–61.

Fox, Michael V. "The Epistemology of the Book of Proverbs." *Journal of Biblical Literature* 126.4 (2007) 669–84.

———. *Proverbs 1–9: A New Translation with Introduction and Commentary*. Anchor Yale Bible 18a. New Haven, CT: Yale University Press, 2000.

Gadamer, Hans-Georg. *Truth and Method*. London: Bloomsbury, 1975.

Bibliography

Genesis Rabbah: The Judaic Commentary to the Book of Genesis, A New American Translation Translated by Jacob Neusner. 2 vols. Atlanta: Scholars, 1985.

Giles, Kevin. *The Eternal Generation of the Son: Maintaining Orthodoxy in Trinitarian Theology*. Downers Grove, IL: IVP Academic, 2012.

Gilks, Mark. "Aesthetic Experience and the Unfathomable: A Pragmatist Critique of Hermeneutic Aesthetics." *British Journal of Aesthetics* 61 (2021) 185–98.

Haenchen, Ernst. *John 1: A Commentary on the Gospel of John Chapters 1–6*. Translated by Robert W. Funk. Hermeneia. Philadelphia: Fortress, 1984.

Harman, Allan M. "The Legacy of Matthew Henry." *Reformed Theological Review* 73.3 (2014) 181–97.

Heidegger, Martin. *Being and Time: A Translation of* Sein und Zeit. Translated by Joan Stambaugh. Albany, NY: State University of New York Press, 1996.

Henry, Matthew. *Commentary on the Holy Bible: Wherein each chapter is summed up in its contents; the sacred text inserted at large in distinct paragraphs; each paragraph educed to its proper heads, the sense given, and largely illustrated; with practical remarks and observations*. 6 vols. London: Griffin, 1860.

Hill, R. Charles. *Wisdom's Many Faces*. Collegeville, MN: Liturgical, 1996.

Jowett, Benjamin. "On the Interpretation of Scripture." In *Essays and Reviews*, 477–536. London, 1860. Reprinted by Charlottesville: University Press of Virginia, 2000.

Joyce, Paul. "Proverbs 8 in Interpretation (1): Historical Criticism and Beyond." In *Reading Text, Seeking Wisdom: Scripture and Theology*, edited by David F. Ford and Graham Stanton, 89–101. Grand Rapids: Eerdmans, 2004.

Klink, Edward, and Darian Lockett. *Understanding Biblical Theology: A Comparison of Theory and Practice*. Grand Rapids: Zondervan, 2012.

Köstenberger, Andreas J. *John*. Baker Exegetical Commentaries on the New Testament. Grand Rapids: Eerdmans, 2004.

Kugel, James. *How to Read the Bible: A Guide to Scripture, Then and Now*. New York: Free, 2007.

Kynes, Will. *An Obituary for "Wisdom Literature": The Birth, Death, and Intertextual Reintegration of a Biblical Corpus*. Oxford: Oxford University Press, 2019.

Lash, Nicholas. "Creation, Courtesy and Contemplation." In *The Beginning and the End of 'Religion,'* 164–82. Cambridge: Cambridge University Press, 1996.

———. *Easter in Ordinary: Reflections on Human Experience and the Knowledge of God*. Notre Dame, IN: University of Notre Dame Press, 1988.

———. "Interpretation and Imagination." In *Incarnation and Myth: The Debate Continued*, edited by M. Goulder, 19–26. London: SCM, 1979.

———. "On What Kinds of Things There Are." In *The Beginning and the End of 'Religion,'* 93–111. Cambridge: Cambridge University Press, 1996.

———. "What Might Martyrdom Mean?" In *Theology on the Way to Emmaus*, 75–92. London: SCM, 1986.

Lea, Thomas D. "The Hermeneutics of the Puritans." *Journal of the Evangelical Theological Society* 39:2 (1996) 271–84.

Lenzi, Alan. "Proverbs 8:22–31: Three Perspectives on Its Composition." *Journal of Biblical Literature* 125.4 (2006) 687–714.

Levenson, Jon. *The Hebrew Bible, the Old Testament, and Historical Criticism*. Louisville, KY: Westminster John Knox, 1993.

Lightfoot, R. H. *St. John's Gospel: A Commentary*. Edited by C. F. Evans. Oxford: Clarendon, 1956.

Bibliography

Lindbeck, George. *The Nature of Doctrine: Religion and Theology in a Post-Liberal Age*. Louisville, KY: Westminster John Knox, 1984.

Loader, James A. "Lebensgestaltung als weisheitliche Lebensverantwortung." *Old Testament Essays* 15.3 (2002) 715–38.

———. *Proverbs 1–9*. Historical Commentary on the Old Testament. Leuven: Peeters, 2014.

Longman III, Tremper. *Fictional Akkadian Biography*. Winona Lake, IN: Eisenbrauns, 1991.

———. *Proverbs*. Baker Commentaries on the Old Testament Wisdom and Proverbs. Grand Rapids: Baker, 2006.

MacIntyre, Alasdair. "Review of Charles Taylor, *Philosophical Arguments*." *The Philosophical Quarterly* 47 (1997) 94–96.

———. *Three Rival Versions of Moral Enquiry*. Notre Dame, IN: University of Notre Dame Press, 1990.

Maier, Christl. *Die 'fremde Frau' in Proverbien 1–9: Eine exegetische und sozialgeschichtliche Studie*. Orbis Biblicus et Orientalis 144. Freibourg: Universitätsverlag Freiburg & Göttingen: Vandenhoeck & Ruprecht, 1995.

McKane, William. *Proverbs: A New Approach*. Philadelphia: Westminster, 1970.

Meinhold, Arndt. *Die Sprüche, Teil 1: Sprüche Kapitel 1–15*. Zürcher Bibelkommentare 16.1. Zurich: Theologischer Verlag, 1991.

Moberly, R. W. L. *The Bible in a Disenchanted Age: The Enduring Possibility of Christian Faith*. Grand Rapids: Baker Academic, 2018.

———. *The God of the Old Testament: Encountering the Divine in Christian Scripture*. Grand Rapids: Baker, 2020.

Moody, Dale. "God's Only Son: The Translation of John 3:16 in the Revised Standard Version." *Journal of Biblical Literature* 72 (1953) 213–19.

Morgan, Donn. *Wisdom in the Old Testament Traditions*. Atlanta: John Knox, 1981.

Muller, Richard. *Post-Reformation Reformed Dogmatics, Volume 2, Holy Scripture: The Cognitive Foundation of Theology*. 4 vols. Grand Rapids: Baker, 1993.

Murphy, Roland. *Proverbs*. Word Biblical Commentary 22. Grand Rapids: Thomas Nelson, 1998.

———. "Wisdom—Theses and Hypotheses." In *Israelite Wisdom: Theological and Literary Essays in Honor of Samuel Terrien*, edited by John G. Gammie, Walter A. Brueggemann, W. Lee Humphreys, and James M. Ward, 35–42. Missoula, MT: Scholars, 1978.

O'Dowd, Ryan. *Proverbs*. Story of God Bible Commentary Series. Grand Rapids: Zondervan, 2017.

O'Keefe, John, and R. R. Reno. *Sanctified Vision: An Introduction to Early Christian Interpretation of the Bible*. Baltimore: Johns Hopkins University Press, 2005.

Old, Hughes Oliphant. "Matthew Henry (1662–1714)." In *Dictionary of Major Biblical Interpreters*, edited by Donald K. McKim, 520–24. Downer's Grove, IL: InterVarsity, 2007.

Owen, John. *Vindiciae Evangelicae; or, The Mystery of the Gospel Vindicated and Socinianism Examined*. Volume 12 of *The Works of John Owen, D.D.*. Edited by William Goold. Edinburgh: T&T Clark, 1862.

Pelikan, Jaroslav. *The Christian Tradition: A History of the Development of Doctrine*. 5 vols. Chicago: University of Chicago Press, 1971.

Perdue, Leo G. *Proverbs*. Interpretation. Louisville, KY: John Knox, 2000.

Bibliography

Plöger, Otto. *Sprüche Salomos: Proverbia*. Biblischer Kommentar Altes Testament XVII. Neukirchen-Vluyn: Neukirchener Verlag, 1984.

Reno, R. R. "Series Preface." *Proverbs and Ecclesiastes*. Brazos Theological Commentaries. Grand Rapids: Brazos, 2011.

Ricoeur, Paul. "Appropriation." In *Hermeneutics and the Human Sciences*, edited and translated by John B. Thompson, 144–56. Cambridge: Cambridge University Press, 1981.

———. "The Hermeneutical Function of Distanciation." In *Hermeneutics and the Human Sciences*, edited and translated by John B. Thompson, 93–106. Cambridge: Cambridge University Press, 1981.

———. "Metaphor and the Central Problem of Hermeneutics." In *Hermeneutics and the Human Sciences*, edited and translated by John B. Thompson, 127–43. Cambridge: Cambridge University Press, 1981.

———. *The Symbolism of Evil*. Boston: Beacon, 1969.

———. "What Is a Text? Explanation and Understanding." In *Hermeneutics and the Human Sciences*, edited and translated by John B. Thompson, 107–26. Cambridge: Cambridge University Press, 1981.

Rogerson, John W. "Keil, Carl Friedrich (1807–1888) and Franz Delitzsch (1813–1890)." In *Dictionary of Major Biblical Interpreters*, edited by Donald K. McKim, 606–8. Downer's Grove, IL: InterVarsity, 2007.

Schipper, Bernd. *Proverbs 1–15*. Translated by Stephen Germany. Hermeneia. Minneapolis: Fortress, 2019. Translation of *Sprüche (Proverbia): 1–15*. Biblischer Kommentar Altes Testament XVII 1. Vandenhoeck & Ruprecht Verlage: Göttingen, 2018.

Schneiders, Sandra. *The Revelatory Text: Interpreting the New Testament as Sacred Scripture*. 2nd ed. Collegeville, MN: Liturgical, 1999.

Wigoder, Geoffrey, Fred Skolnik, and Shmuel Himelstein, eds. *The New Encyclopedia of Judaism*. New York: New York University Press, 2002.

Seitz, Christopher R. *The Character of Christian Scripture: The Significance of a Two-Testament Bible*. Grand Rapids: Baker, 2011.

———. *The Elder Testament: Canon, Theology, Trinity*. Waco, TX: Baylor University Press, 2018.

———. "Trinity in the Old Testament." In *The Oxford Handbook on the Trinity*, edited by Gilles Emery and Matthew Levering, 28–40. Oxford: Oxford University Press, 2011.

———. *Word without End: The Old Testament as Abiding Theological Witness*. Grand Rapids: Eerdmans, 1998.

Smith, James K. A. *Desiring the Kingdom: Worship, Worldview, and Cultural Formation*. Grand Rapids: Baker Academic, 2009.

Stanglin, Keith D. *The Letter and Spirit of Biblical Interpretation: From the Early Church to Modern Practice*. Grand Rapids: Baker, 2018.

Steinmetz, David. "The Superiority of Pre-Critical Exegesis." *Theology Today* 37 (1980) 27–38.

Stendahl, Krister. "Biblical Theology, Contemporary." In *The Interpreter's Dictionary of the Bible*, Vol. 1, edited by G. A. Buttrick, 418–32. 4 vols. Nashville, TN: Abingdon, 1962.

———. "Dethroning Biblical Imperialism in Theology." In *Reading the Bible in the Global Village*, edited by Heikki Raisanen, 61–66. Atlanta: Society of Biblical Literature, 2000.

Taylor, Charles. *The Language Animal: The Full Shape of the Human Linguistic Capacity*. Cambridge: Belknap, 2016.

Bibliography

———. "Explanation and Practical Reason." In *Philosophical Arguments*, 34–60. Cambridge: Harvard University Press, 1995.

———. "Lichtung or Lebensform." In *Philosophical Arguments*, 61–78. Cambridge: Harvard University Press, 1995.

———. "To Follow a Rule." In *Philosophical Arguments*, 169–71. Cambridge: Harvard University Press, 1995.

———. "What Is Human Agency?" In *Philosophical Papers 1: Human Agency and Language*, 15–44. Cambridge: Cambridge University Press, 1985.

———. "Theories of Meaning." In *Philosophical Papers 1: Human Agency and Language*, 248–92. Cambridge: Cambridge University Press, 1985.

———. *A Secular Age*. Cambridge, MA: Belknap, 2007.

Trier, Daniel J. *Proverbs and Ecclesiastes*. Brazos Theological Commentaries. Grand Rapids: Brazos, 2011.

Van Leeuwen, Raymond C. "Liminality and Worldview in Proverbs 1–9." *Semeia* 50 (1990) 111–44.

Varela, Francisco. *Ethical Know-How: Action, Wisdom, and Cognition*. Stanford, CA: Stanford University Press, 1999.

Von Rad, Gerhard. *Weisheit in Israel*. Neukirchen-Vluyn: Neukirchener Verlag, 1985.

———. *Wisdom in Israel*. Nashville, TN: Abingdon, 1972. Translation of *Weisheit in Israel*. Neukirchen-Vluyn: Neukirchener Verlag, 1970.

Wagner, Siegfried. *Franz Delitzsch: Leben und Werk*. Beiträge zur evangelischen Theologie 80. Munich: Kaiser Verlag, 1978.

Wallace, David Foster. "This Is Water." Commencement address at Kenyon College, Gambier, Ohio, May 21, 2005. https://web.ics.purdue.edu/~drkelly/DFWKenyonAddress2005.pdf.

Waltke, Bruce. *The Book of Proverbs: Chapters 1–15*. New International Commentary on the Old Testament. Grand Rapids: Eerdmans, 2004.

Weeks, Stuart. "The Context and Meaning of Proverbs 8:30a." *Journal of Biblical Literature* 125 (2006) 433–42.

———. *Instruction and Imagery in Proverbs 1–9*. Oxford: Oxford University Press, 2007.

Weinandy, Thomas, and Daniel Keating. *Athanasius and His Legacy*. Minneapolis: Fortress, 2017.

Whitacre, Rodney A. *John*. InterVarsity Press New Testament Commentary Series. Downer's Grove, IL: InterVarsity, 1999.

Whybray, Norman. *Proverbs*. NCBC. Grand Rapids: Eerdmans, 1994.

———. *Wisdom in Proverbs: The Concept of Wisdom in Proverbs 1–9*. Studies in Biblical Theology 45. London: SCM, 1965.

Williams, Rowan. *Arius: Heresy and Tradition*. 2nd ed. Grand Rapids: Eerdmans, 2001.

———. "Trinity and Revelation." *Modern Theology* 2 (1986) 197–212.

Winston, David. *The Wisdom of Solomon: A New Translation with Introduction and Commentary*. Anchor Bible 43. Garden City, NY: Doubleday, 1979.

Wittgenstein, Ludwig. *Philosophical Investigations*. 3rd ed. Translated by G. E. M. Anscombe. New York: MacMillan, 1958. Translation of *Die Philosophische Untersuchungen*. New York: Macmillan, 1953.

Wolterstorff, Nicholas. *The God We Worship: An Exploration of Liturgical Theology*. Grand Rapids: Eerdmans, 2015.

Yaego, David S. "The New Testament and Nicene Dogma: A Contribution to the Recovery of Theological Exegesis." *Pro Ecclesia* 3 (1994) 152–64.

Young, Frances. *Biblical Exegesis and the Formation of Christian Culture*. Cambridge: Cambridge University Press, 1997.

———. "Proverbs 8 in Interpretation (2): Wisdom Personified." In *Reading Texts, Seeking Wisdom: Scripture and Theology*, edited by David F. Ford and Graham Stanton, 102-15. Grand Rapids: Eerdmans, 2004.

Scripture Index

OLD TESTAMENT

Genesis
1	39, 66, 81, 104, 105, 107, 123–24
18:19	23

Exodus
3:14	108
12	108

Deuteronomy
6	108
6:5	37
7:8	37
10:15	37
30:14	30
30:15–20	105
32:4–5	33
32:6	107

2 Samuel
15:34	107

Job
12:13–25	90
15:7–9	39
28	118
29:2	107

Psalms
1	108
1:2	207
5:9–10	190
9:9	23
19	105
51:12	66
51:18	70
58:2	23
74:2	107
90:9	23
93:2	107
102:18 (LXX)	66
110:10	107
119	103, 105
139:13	107

Proverbs
1–9	20, 26, 33, 79, 100, 165, 169, 186–95, 192, 194, 209–10
1	195
1:1–7	23–25, 26, 174, 192, 225
1:3	32, 37
1:4	35, 193
1:7	25, 107, 168, 188
1:8	193
1:10	192, 193
1:11–14	192–93
1:12	79
1:15–19	193
1:20, 29	206

Scripture Index

Proverbs (*continued*)

Reference	Pages
1:20–33	105, 171
1:21	192
1:22	32, 193
1:22–27	193
1:22–33	193
1:26–27	210
1:28	193
1:28–33	168
1:32	32
1:24–31	121
2	103, 174
2:1–5	167, 186
2:1–15	187
2:5	188
2:6	187, 198
2:16	190
2:17	190
2:18–19	192
2:20–22	187
3	165, 174
3:1–2	186
3:1–10	174
3:10	187
3:11–20	174
3:13–20	105
3:14–15	33, 34
3:19	197, 202
3:19–20	26
3:21–35	174
3:35	187
4:1 LXX	223n206
4:3–4	187
4:6	98
4:8	191
4:20–27	103, 179n9
4:24	167
5:3	190, 191
5:5	79
5:5–6	192
5:12	167
5:20	191
6:24	190
6:32	192
7	28, 29, 30, 100, 195
7:4	98
7:5	190
7:11	192
7:12	192
7:18	192
7:21	190
7:22–23	192
7:25–27	39
7:26–27	192
7:27	79
8	26, 28, 88, 169–75, 177, 186–95
8:1	29, 88, 170, 210
8:1–3	29, 97, 105–6, 177, 186, 224
8:1–11	77
8:2–3	170, 188
8:4	97, 106, 171, 180, 206, 223n206
8:4–5	187, 225
8:4–11	31, 33, 89, 93, 94, 97, 106, 178, 179
8:5, 35, 97, 171, 178
8:6, 106
8:6–8	178
8:6–9	170
8:7	33, 106
8:7–9	33
8:8	33
8:10	179n8
8:10–11	171
8:11	94
8:12	78, 94, 97–98, 179n8
8:12–21	34–35, 78, 89–90, 93, 94, 97–98, 106–7, 179, 225
8:12–16, 90, 94
8:13	104, 105, 107, 121, 168n56, 170, 172, 188, 196, 207
8:14, 180
8:14–15, 107
8:14–16, 36, 170, 172
8:15, 78, 172
8:15–16	36–37, 180
8:16	187
8:17	94, 179, 206, 207
8:17–21	37–38, 79, 94

Scripture Index

8:18	90, 171, 179	9:13–18	194
8:19	33, 104, 171	9:14	194
8:20	172	9:16	191, 195
8:21	171	9:18	79
8:22	62–67, 99, 113–15, 119, 124, 128, 180, 196, 202	10–31	169, 171, 174, 187, 194, 207, 210
8:22–25	39	10:3	209
8:22–26	95, 181	10:22	209
8:22–29	81, 95	14:21	209
8:22–31	26, 38–39, 80, 90, 91, 93, 94–95, 99–100, 104, 107, 113, 119, 125, 129–30, 172–73, 180–82, 187, 196, 202, 206	15:25	209
		15:33	168
		16:1	209
		16:33	209
		19:21	209
		22:2	209
		26:28	190
8:23	68, 115	28:23	190
8:23–25	196	28:27	209
8:24	107, 115	29:3	98
8:24–25	66	29:5	190
8:24–29	99, 123–24, 198	29:13	209
8:25–29	42	30	103
8:26–29	40–42		
8:27	107, 115, 196	**Ecclesiastes**	
8:27–29	172, 181, 197	10:15	77
8:27–30a	95		
8:30	62, 95, 116, 124–25, 128–29, 197, 198, 201, 207	**Isaiah**	
		6:8–10	97
8:30–31	42–44, 95, 99–100, 181, 197	11	105
		11:2	90, 180
	8:31, 81, 180, 206, 223n206	11:4	23
8:32–36	44–45, 92, 100, 108, 173–74, 182	16:13	107
		33:15	23
	8:33, 197	45:19	23
8:34	98, 108, 191, 207	45:21	107
8:35	181, 187, 207, 224		
8:35–36	207	**Jeremiah**	
	9, 195	30:20	107
9:1	65, 195, 202	31:22	66
9:1–6	194	52:15	128
9:3	125, 194		
9:4	191, 195, 206	**Lamentations**	
9:7–12	194	5:21	107
9:10	107, 168, 188		
9:11	194		
9:13	189, 192		

Ezekiel

2:3–5	97
3:7	97

Hosea

2:4ff	37
3:1	37

Habakkuk

1:12	107

APROCYPHAL/ DEUTEROCANONICAL BOOKS

Sirach

24	197–98

Wisdom of Solomon

7:22	198
8:3–4	198
9	198–99

NEW TESTAMENT

Matthew

11	130

Luke

24:44	4n5

John

1	130, 199, 213–15, 217
1:1–4	224, 225
1:1–18	224
1:3	63
1:4	214, 223, 224
1:5	214
1:6–8	215
1:7	219
1:9	213, 224
1:9–11	213
1:14	221
1:17	221
2:1–11	223
2:13–25	223
3	215, 217, 218, 219
3:16	214, 216
3:16–21	216, 224, 225
3:19	223
3:19–21	213, 216
3:21	221
4	223
5	217
5:1–18	223
5:17	62
5:35–36	215
6:1–15	223
6:16–21	223
7:37	77
8	217, 218
8:12	217
8:48–59	9
9	217–18, 223
9:1–2	218
9:4–5	218
10:10	223
12	219, 221
12:24	219
12:25–26	219
12:35–36	219, 220
12:36–43	220
12:37	220
12:42–43	221
12:43	220
12:44	219, 220
12:44–50	224
12:46	220
13	220–21
13:30	215n165, 221
14:9–10	62

Scripture Index

17:3	218
18:3	221
18:38	221
18:39–40	221
19:1–16	221
19:12–13	221
19:39	217n179
20:1	221
20:8	221
20:14	221
20:18	222
20:19	221
20:20	222
20:25	222
20:29	219
20:30–31	4n3, 224
20:31	215, 219
21	222, 223
21:1	222
21:4	222
21:5–6	223
21:24	215

Ephesians

2:25	66
4:22	66

Philippians

2	200
2:5–11	9

Colossians

1	130
1:13	81

Revelation

3:15	129

Name/Subject Index

Act-consequence nexus, 209
Adulteress, 38, 189–90, 193
Adulteress, see also Strange Woman
Albright, W.F., 21, 184, 185
Aletti, J.N., 170n60, 172n63, 190n64, 191, 192
Ancient Near East, cosmology, 107, 115, 123–24, 126
Ancient Near East, instructional material, 20–21, 106, 165
Appropriation, of meaning for present context, 51–52, 53, 57–58, 82, 109, 133–34, 139, 142–44, 152–53
Arius/Arian, 59n1, 61–64, 113, 116–17, 125–26, 130, 199
Astarte, 22
Athanasius, 75n58, 77, 80, 81, 113, 116–17, 124, 126–27, 130, 131, 199
Athanasius, assumptions of reading, 72
Athanasius, background, 59–60
Athanasius, on appropriate speech of the Son and the Father, 61–63
Athanasius, on Proverbs 8:22, 65–67
Athanasius, on the difference between offspring and work, 67–68
Athanasius, on the Son's uniqueness vis-à-vis creation, 63–64
Athanasius, on the unity of the Son and the Father, 64
Augustine, 205n133
Ayres, Lewis, 59n1

Baehr, Peter, 151–52
Bartholomew, Craig, 64n24, 76n60, 86, 132
Bauer-Kayatz, Christa, 22, 37, 90, 184
Baumann, Gerlinde, 207
Beasley-Murray, George, 214n161, 215n166
Beeke, Joel and Lanning, 82
Being-in-the-world, 17, 133, 144, 154, 175, 177, 195
Bereshit Raba, 39
Bible, as Scripture, 5–6, 153–54
Bible, as symbol, 4–8
Bible, as witness, 13–14, 212
Bible, as Word of God, 4–5
Boström, Gustav, 22, 189
Boström, Lennart, 32n59, 183, 195n93, 205n135
Bourdieu, Pierre, 156–64
Brown, Raymond, 216
Buber, Martin, 153–54, 173–74
Bultmann, Rudolf, 71, 216, 219, 220n191, 221n198
Burney, C.F., 40

Camp, Claudia, 183
Canon, 8
Canonical Approach, 8, 212
Cartesian dualism, 134
Childs, Brevard, 8, 212
Collett, Don, 8n22, 181n15, 185n44, 200, 201–2, 211
Cornelius à Lapide, 73
Creation, order and limits, 25–26, 42
Cultural-linguistic approach, 203

Name/Subject Index

Dame Folly, 28, 183, 189–95
Dame Folly, contrasted with Personified Wisdom, 190–92
Dame Folly, role of speech, 190, 192
Dame Folly, see also Strange Woman
Delitzsch, Franz, 112–17, 131
Dell, Katharine, 190
Demiurge, 63
Distanciation, 140, 142, 147n31
Dowling, Maurice, 59

Earnest, James, 64n25
Elliot, Robert, 50n7
Estes, Douglas, 214n164
Ethics, 23–24
Ethics, Two Ways, 108
Explanation, as phase in interpretation, 135–36, 140, 142, 143, 148

Father/teacher, 186–189
Fear of the Lord, 25, 35, 168–69, 178, 188
Fontaine, Carole, 208n144
Ford, David, 29n29, 159n20, 160n24, 182n22, 214n160, 220n193, 225
Formation, 25, 179, 192, 194, 211
Formation, and desires, 37, 41n105, 82, 100, 162, 168, 178–80, 182, 186–87, 188, 192, 194, 206
Fowl, Stephen, 58n37
Fox, Michael, 21, 24, 25, 30, 31n55, 31n56, 32n60, 34n71, 34n72, 36, 43, 96–101, 133–34, 158n16, 167, 168n55, 170n60, 179n11, 182n27, 183, 186n44, 187n49, 191n72, 193n85, 194n88, 202
Fusion of Horizons, 56–57

Gadamer, Hans-Georg, 5n10, 9n23, 49, 52, 53–58, 71, 210
Genesis Rabbah, 199n104
Gilks, Mark, 54n25
Greco-Roman literary culture, 60–61

Habitus, 158–64, 168–69, 170–75
Habitus, and formulation, 162–64
Heidegger, Martin, 158
Henry, Matthew, 73–85, 131
Henry, Matthew, background, 73–74
Henry, Matthew, on Proverbs 8, 76–82
Henry, Matthew, on the distinctiveness of the poetical books of the Old Testament, 74–76
Henry, Matthew, sense of historical distance, 75–76
Hill, R. Charles, 166n47
Hirsch, E.D., 143n17
Historically effected consciousness (*wirkungsgeschichtliches Bewußtsein*), 55–56, 210

Immanent frame, 149–50

Jesus Christ, forms of faith in, 12–14
Jowett, Benjamin, 127, 132
Joyce, Paul, 69–70, 69n41, 71
Justin Martyr, 299

Köstenberger, Andreas, 216
Kugel, James, 61n11, 70n43
Kynes, Will, 37n85

Lady Wisdom, see Personified Wisdom
Language, 14, 146–48, 203, 212
Lash, Nicholas, 7n17, 65n26, 145n28, 154n45, 173–74, 203–6, 207, 210
Lea, Thomas, 73n53
Lenzi, Alan, 197n97, 208n142
Levenson, Jon, 8n19, 11, 19n1
Light, comparison of metaphor in John with voice of Wisdom, 224–25
Light, metaphor in the Gospel of John, 213–24
Lightfoot, R.H., 216, 222n201
Lindbeck, George, 203n124, 206

Name/Subject Index

Loader, James, 27n40, 29, 29n43, 33, 35–36, 37, 44n118, 209
Longman, Tremper, 123–27, 131, 202
Love, reciprocal between Wisdom and student, 37, 44–45, 98, 121–22
Love, the Lord God as object of human love, 37

Maat, 22
MacIntyre, Alistair, 103
Maier, Christl, 189
Marcellus of Ancyra, 60
McKane, William, 180
Meinhold, Arndt, 29n42, 30, 32n61, 34n71, 93–95, 174
Melanchthon, Phillip, 73
Metaphor, 33–34, 142–43, 183–84, 201, 213–14
Metaphor, in Proverbs 1–9, 26–28
Moberly, Walter, 6n12, 13n31, 27n37, 39n94, 43, 153, 213, 214n164, 216, 224
Mode of being, 18, 133, 137, 139, 144, 148, 154, 175, 177, 181, 183, 188, 195, 201n116, 205, 206, 211, 212
Morgan, Donn, 166n47
Muller, Richard, 75n55, 80n64
Murphy, Roland, 166n47, 187n49, 189n55

Nicene Christology, 63, 64, 129
Nicene Creed, 64, 109, 126–27, 200, 203–6, 211
Nicene Trinitarian theology, 72, 80, 203–6, 207, 210

O'Dowd, Ryan, 197n98
O'Keefe, John, and R.R. Reno, 62n16, 75n55, 75n56
Old Testament, and history, 13
Old Testament, as Christian Scripture, 6–8, 10, 13, 14
Old Testament, distinct hermeneutical issues, 4, 6–7
Old Testament, relationship to New Testament, 212–13, 224–25

Only-begotten, 67–68, 67n33
Owen, John, 73, 80n65, 83n72

Pelikan, Jaroslav, 59n2
Personified Wisdom, 29, 30, 178
Personified Wisdom, accessibility, 29–31, 171–72, 191
Personified Wisdom, and Jesus/the Son of God, 125–26, 129–30, 199, 206
Personified Wisdom, and Torah, 103, 104, 105, 107, 125n18, 198
Personified Wisdom, audience, 31–32, 97, 106, 171–72, 177–78, 193
Personified Wisdom, background, 21–22, 27–28, 37, 90, 94, 105, 118–19, 184–85
Personified Wisdom, benefits, 35–38, 89, 170–71, 179–80
Personified Wisdom, comparison to theme of light in John's Gospel, 224–25
Personified Wisdom, impact of personification, 33–34, 36, 90–91, 92–93, 101, 120–21, 125, 174, 183–86, 195, 206
Personified Wisdom, relationship to Lord God of Israel, 30–31, 39–42, 91–92, 94, 100–101, 118, 125, 129–30, 182, 194, 195–211
Personified Wisdom, relationship with father/teacher, 88, 89, 186–89
Personified Wisdom, role in creation, 26, 39–44, 39n94, 63, 81, 84, 91, 114, 119–20
Personified Wisdom, role of speech, 192
Personified Wisdom, value, 32–33, 170–71, 178
Philo of Alexandria, 199n104
Plain sense of Scripture, 69–72
Plöger, Otto, 33, 88–93, 94, 185, 197n99, 202
Postmodernism, 127–28

Name/Subject Index

Preconceptions/prejudice/
preunderstanding, 15, 50–51,
53–55, 119–20, 169, 202, 210
Preconceptions/prejudice/
preunderstanding, see also
tradition
Proverbs, and the afterlife, 79
Proverbs, chapter 9 as triptych, 194
Proverbs, comparing the three voices,
192–94
Proverbs, formation of the book,
27–28, 33, 102–3, 104, 105,
184–85
Proverbs, historical context, 20–22,
102, 121–22, 125
Proverbs, pedagogy, 166–68, 187

Quintillian, 60–61

Reference, and texts, 141
Ricoeur, Paul, 14n32, 16–17, 139–45,
164n39, 178n4, 201n116
Rule of Faith, 8, 18, 62, 72, 75

Schipper, Bernd, 42–43, 101–9, 167,
186n46, 188n51, 194n87,
194n88
Schneiders, Sandra, 3–18, 8n21,
20n2, 216
Secularity, 148–52
Seitz, Christopher, 6, 59n1, 69
Speech-act theory, 162
Stanglin, Keith, 76n60
Stendahl, Krister, 49–53, 65n26
Strange Woman, 29, 189
Strange Woman, as adulteress, 30,
189–90

Taylor, Charles, 41n105, 72n48,
78n62, 84n77, 127, 146–53,
156–64, 184, 185
Tradition, and reading, 54–55, 137,
206–7
Tradition, and Scripture, 9–11
Tradition, Christian, 10, 65
Transformation, as goal of reading
Scripture, 16–17, 87, 109,
153–54, 169

Treier, Daniel, 127–30, 131–32, 200–
201, 202, 211
Trinity, Doctrine of God, 203–11

Van Leeuwen, Raymond, 24, 26–27,
37n87, 41, 192n80
Varela, Francisco, 156n4, 157–64
Von Rad, Gerhard, 87, 117–22, 131,
208

Wallace, David Foster, 150n35
Waltke, Bruce, 23n21, 25n28, 25n30,
29n47, 128, 194n87
Weeks, Stuart, 20n5, 21–22, 95n9,
128, 155n1, 165–66, 174, 190,
192
Whitacre, Rod, 222n203
Whybray, R.N., 20, 33, 34n72, 185,
191
Williams, Rowan, 59n1, 62n23,
68n38, 207
Wisdom, 24, 98–99, 103, 156
Wisdom, and embodiment, 157–58
Wisdom, as know-how, 25, 103,
156–64, 165–66, 169–75
Wisdom, as know-how, see also
Habitus
Wisdom, as mental power, 133–34,
156, 179n11
Wisdom, gaining wisdom, 99, 161–
62, 165–66, 186–87
Wisdom, in Christian frame, 164–65
Wisdom, see also Personified
Wisdom
Wittgenstein, Ludwig, 157
World behind the text, 12–13, 87, 97,
102, 109, 132, 216
World in front of the text, 12, 15–18,
109, 133–34, 139, 142–45,
177–80, 183, 206, 207
World of the text, 12, 13–15, 16, 18,
26, 35, 87–88, 90, 92, 93, 97,
102, 109, 132, 141, 143, 145,
206, 211, 216

Young, Frances, 39, 60–62, 64n24, 72

www.ingramcontent.com/pod-product-compliance
Lightning Source LLC
Chambersburg PA
CBHW050348230426
43663CB00010B/2042